Value in a Changing Built Environment

Value in a Changing Built Environment

Edited by
David Lorenz
Karlsruhe Institute of Technology
Karlsruhe, Germany

Peter Dent
Oxford Brookes University
United Kingdom

Tom Kauko
University of Portsmouth
United Kingdom

This edition first published 2018 © 2018 John Wiley & Sons Ltd.

Registered Offices
John Wiley & Sons, Inc., 111 River Street, Hoboken, NJ 07030, USA
John Wiley & Sons Ltd, The Atrium, Southern Gate, Chichester, West Sussex, PO19 8SQ, UK

Editorial Office
9600 Garsington Road, Oxford, OX4 2DQ, UK

For details of our global editorial offices, customer services, and more information about Wiley products visit us at www.wiley.com.

Wiley also publishes its books in a variety of electronic formats and by print-on-demand. Some content that appears in standard print versions of this book may not be available in other formats.

Library of Congress Cataloging-in-Publication Data

Names: Lorenz, David, 1977- editor. | Dent, Peter, 1951- editor. | Kauko, Tom, editor.
Title: Value in a changing built environment / edited by David Lorenz, Karlsruhe Institute of Technology, Karlsruhe, Germany, Peter Dent , Oxford Brookes University, United Kingdom, Tom Kauko, University of Portsmouth, United Kingdom.
Description: Hoboken : Wiley, 2017. | Includes index. |
Identifiers: LCCN 2017042801 (print) | LCCN 2017045467 (ebook) | ISBN 9781119073659 (Pdf) | ISBN 9781119332596 (epub) | ISBN 9781444334760 (paperback)
Subjects: LCSH: Value. | Real property. | BISAC: BUSINESS & ECONOMICS / Real Estate.
Classification: LCC HC433 (ebook) | LCC HC433 .V35 2017 (print) | DDC 333.33/2—dc23
LC record available at https://lccn.loc.gov/2017042801

Cover Design by Wiley
Cover Image: © teekid/Getty Images

Set in 10/12pt WarnockPro by SPi Global, Chennai, India
Printed and bound in Malaysia by Vivar Printing Sdn Bhd

10 9 8 7 6 5 4 3 2 1

Contents

About the Editors

David Lorenz is co-chair of the Centre for Real Estate at the Karlsruhe Institute of Technology (KIT) where he is Professor for Property Valuation and Sustainability. David is also the director and founder of a real estate management, valuation and consulting firm located in the southern part of Germany. He has more than 15 years of experience in valuation, asset management and property development. He has published extensively on the role of sustainability in real estate management and valuation. David is a Fellow and Spokesperson of the Royal Institution of Chartered Surveyors (RICS). During the past years he was actively engaged with several research projects administered by RICS and UN.

Peter Dent is affiliated to Oxford Brookes University where he currently participates in International programmes in real estate valuation and finance. For eight years he was the Head of the Department of Real Estate and Construction before taking up the post of Comerford Climate Change Fellow in 2008. Latterly he was Director of International Programmes helping to develop and manage professional and academic programmes. Throughout his career in practice and in academia he has had close associations with the RICS and for the last ten years he has worked with the Institution to promote value systems and code of conduct across Asia. During his career he has published widely including two books (Property Markets and Sustainable Behaviour (2012) and Towers, Turbines and Transmission Lines: Impacts on Property Value (2013).

Dr. Tom Kauko is an academic labourer with wide remit within real estate economy and urban affairs. He received a M.Sc. degree in Real Estate in 1994 (Helsinki University of Tech, Finland), and a Ph.D. in Geography in 2002 (Utrecht University, The Netherlands). He has worked for Oxford Brookes University, UK, the Norwegian University of Science and Technology and OTB Research Institute, Delft University of Technology, The Netherlands. He has carried out research on urban real estate, housing and land-use studies. He is currently based in the historic seaside town of Portsmouth (UK), where he works with lecturing and research for the School of Civil Engineering and Surveying at the University of Portsmouth . His interest is in strategic issues such as valuation, sustainability, urban renewal, resilience, and innovations, and related spatial development and town planning issues. He has over 70 publications and c. 100 conference presentations.

Note on Contributors

Andrzej Bilozor graduated with an MSc in the Faculty of Geodesy and Space Management at the University of Warmia and Mazury in Olsztyn in 1999. In 2004, he obtained a PhD in technical sciences in the discipline of Geodesy and Cartography. In 2005, he was employed as assistant professor in the Department of Planning and Spatial Engineering at the University of Warmia and Mazury in Olsztyn. His major fields of research interest include Spatial Planning, Spatial Management, Geoinformation, Decision-Making Systems, Real-Estate Valuation, application of the fuzzy set theory. He is the author of more than 65 scientific publications.

Maurizio d'Amato is Associate Professor at DICATECh, Technical University Politecnico di Bari, Italy, where he teaches real-estate investment and valuation. He completed his undergraduate work in economics at the University of Bari and worked for several banks in real-estate finance sector before attaining his doctoral degree in Planning, specializing in Valuation methods, at the Politecnico di Bari. He has served as a contract professor in Real-Estate Valuation for several years and a faculty-appointed researcher at the Politecnico di Bari. He has been Scientific Director of the Real Estate Center of Italian Association of Real Estate Counselor (AICI). He has also been professor of Real Estate Finance at University of Rome III, Real Estate Appraisal at SAA School of Business Administration University of Turin and Real Estate Appraisal at online University UNINETTUNO. He is Fellow Member of Royal Institution Chartered Surveyors (since 2004) and Recognised European Valuer (since 2012).

Stephen Hill is a land economist and director of C_2O Future Planners in London, an urban change consultancy. He has worked throughout England on the practice and policy of new housing growth and regeneration since 1970, in private, local authority, and housing association settings, in consultancy, and for English Partnerships. As its Head of Millennium Communities and National Standards, he coordinated the UK Government's executive agencies, Commission for Architecture and the Built Environment (CABE), the Housing Corporation in mapping and harmonizing their approaches and standards for sustainable buildings and places; the work was later absorbed (partly) into the Code for Sustainable Homes.

Thomas Lützkendorf, Prof. Dr.-Ing. habil, is director of the Centre for Real Estate at Karlsruhe Institute of Technology (KIT). He holds a PhD (1985) and Habilitation (2000) in the area of implementing sustainable development principles within the construction sector. Within the scope of teaching and research activities he is concerned with questions relating to the integration of sustainability issues into decision making processes along the life cycle of buildings. Prof. Lützkendorf is a founding member of iiSBE and involved in standardisation activities at European (CEN TC 350) and international (ISO TC 59 SC 17) level.

Malgorzata Renigier-Bilozor graduated with an MSc in the faculty of Geodesy and Space Management at the University of Warmia and Mazury in Olsztyn 2000. In 2004, she obtained a PhD in technical sciences in discipline of Geodesy and Cartography. In 2005, she was employed as assistant professor in the Department of Real Estate Management and Regional Development at the University in Olsztyn. Her major fields of research interest include Systems of Real-Estate Management, Value Forecasting, Decision-Making Systems, Real-Estate Valuation, Data Mining (especially application of the rough set theory). She is an author and coauthor of more than 70 scientific publications.

Radoslaw Wisniewski graduated with an MSc in the faculty of Geodesy and Land Management at the University of Warmia and Mazury in Olsztyn in 1997. In 1999, he obtained a PhD in technical sciences in discipline of Geodesy and Cartography. In 2000, he was employed as assistant professor in the Department of Real Estate Management and Regional Development at the University in Olsztyn. His major fields of research interest include Real-Estate Management, Application of Artificial Intelligence in the Real-Estate Market (especially application of artificial neural networks), Systems of Real-Estate Management, Value Forecasting, and Systems Theory. From 2005 to 2012, he was Vice Dean of The Faculty of Geodesy and Land Management at the University of Warmia and Mazury in Olsztyn. From 2012, he has been Dean of The Faculty of Geodesy and Land Management at the University of Warmia and Mazury in Olsztyn.

Introduction

At the time of the collapse of Lehman Brothers in 2008, the value of their real-estate holdings amounted to 23bn USD. Most of this was valued using the discounted cash flow (DCF) method and, almost exclusively, included office buildings and larger shopping malls. Since then, some of this portfolio has been sold, whereas others have been foreclosed. In 2011, the corresponding value diminished to an estimated 13.2bn USD, with received returns of 3bn USD during the 3-year period (2008–2011).

The fact that few have openly criticised this is bewildering – until one realises that apparently too much is at stake to get this mistake acknowledged. Two questions, however, arise about Lehman Brothers: (1) Why did the investors place 80% of their portfolio in the same 'basket'? (2) Did they even see what was written in the appraisal reports? Perhaps, no one dares to ask these kinds of questions, because as in Shakespeare's comedy: 'The more pity, that fools may not speak wisely what wise men do foolishly'.

As urgent as the financial crisis problem is, the range of problems affecting and being affected by property valuation issues is potentially much wider. It could also be argued that many of these problems – economic–financial, social–cultural and environmental–ecological ones – are interdependent. Therefore, this book sets out to look at valuation issues in general rather than focusing specifically on only one type of concern such as the so-called financial crisis. The logic underpinning how various kinds of real problems, misconceptions and dilemmas are interrelated, and possibly meshed with the ongoing sustainable development discourse, is a recurring topic of this book. Crucially, whilst sustainable development – or even real-estate sustainability – is not the sole focus of the book, the implications of this issue crystallise one key concern addressed within this book: the quality of valuations, that is to say, their reliability and robustness, transparency and traceability.

Apparently, the 'whys and wherefores' of valuation is an under-researched topic within real-estate economics. This is the principal justification for the selection of topics, and if the valuation process is one of the key topics of the book, another must be the basis of this valuation – that is to say, how empirical analyses of prior valuations and market evidence can help us reach such high-quality valuations. At the same time, homes, offices and other real estate that are subject to valuations need to be seen as part of a sustainable market context. However, the reinvestment of extra profits with long-term plans in mind – in other words, economic sustainability of real-estate-based assets, markets

Value in a Changing Built Environment, First Edition.
Edited by David Lorenz, Peter Dent and Tom Kauko.
© 2018 John Wiley & Sons Ltd. Published 2018 by John Wiley & Sons Ltd.

and values indeed – has also traditionally been a neglected topic (but see Bryson and Lombardi, 2009).

The aforementioned issues are the two lines we set up for our approach: one is about valuation seen as a process, and the other is about markets and other relevant context where value creation and price setting takes place. Thus, on the one hand, we are interested in how the valuer chooses to operate in a given situation; on the other hand, we are also interested in the changing environment within which the valuer eventually has to operate.

The Book's Main Theme

The way of perceiving the built environment is undergoing change. It has to, because of the new requirements attached to the sustainable development agenda (since the 1992 Rio Earth Summit, Local Agenda 21 and, more recently, the 2015 Paris Agreement hailed as an 'historic turning point') and the proposed policy solutions following the financial crisis of the late 2000s. Unfortunately, because of the complexity in the cause and effect in both our natural climate systems and our modern economic systems, there is unlikely to be a quick fix. However, beyond the complexity in the systems themselves, contributory factors may be intransigence, lack of understanding, lack of commitment or simply that the hegemony of money markets and their short termism makes it difficult to enable a broader-based interpretation of value where the currency of exchange is based on the environmental and social as well as the financial assets of a building.

This book explores the professional foundations on which the valuation exercise and the valuation profession rest. It aims to address this potentially limited understanding of the concept of property value by explaining the intrinsic linkages between economic, environmental, social and cultural measures and components of property value. In this way, it may be possible to pave the way towards a more holistic approach to property value.

Our conceptualisation of value goes beyond price. This is because we examine why a particular price is paid for a property asset, and we investigate in detail how professionals arrive at their estimate of value which will then influence their client's willingness to deal at a given price. Although, of course, price is based on estimates of value, this book attempts to unwrap many of the traditional assumptions that have underpinned market participants' decision-making over the past few decades.

When exploring the price–value association (or discrepancy), the book aims to incorporate social, environmental and economic concepts of value into a broader concept of property value. In doing so, the book puts forward the argument that a blindfold application of valuation theories and approaches adopted from finance is unlikely to be able to cope with the nature of property as an economic and public good. This claim is especially important at this moment in time, in a situation where the sustainability requirements being imposed are changing the decision-making environment concerning investment in the built environment.

Real-estate valuation plays a pivotal role in this decision-making, and we must ask ourselves the following question: how can this new body of knowledge improve the practice in both business and social domains, given the nature of specific professions – in our case, those pertaining to the real-estate industry? Hill and colleagues (2011) see this role 'embedded in some ideals, professional values, autonomy of practice and independence of opinion' (p. 315), and to be a professional requires not only a body of knowledge but also 'a role definition and sense of identity; public interest; and ethical conduct' (Hughes *et al.*, 2013). Professional identity, independence, public interest and ethics therefore play a crucial role in a professional's assessment of real-estate valuation. As a process, such valuations therefore need to be sustainable in a broad sense. Here, we are concerned with financial sustainability, that is, how robust are the valuations performed to support investment decisions in the direct and indirect markets; environmental sustainability, that is, the impact of real-estate location, use and efficiency on the environment and social sustainability, that is, addressing the growing gap between those who have access and those deprived of access – both wealth creation and poverty creation and the impact on extremism at both ends.

The Book's Key Messages

The role of the valuation professional is to provide professional advice. This is not just about financial value, but it ought to, somewhere, cover the aspects of guardianship through appropriate management of landed and built assets. Too often, the advice is just about the price derived from limited criteria. This is more the role of an agent or a realtor and not of a professional adviser.

The role of the valuation profession is important in the struggle to implement sustainable development principles within the property sector in particular and within society in general. There are two main reasons for this: (1) 'the building sector contributes up to 30% of global annual green house gas emissions and consumes up to 40% of all energy' (UNEP SBCI, 2009, p. 3), and it therefore has the potential to provide the most cost-effective opportunities to cut down energy and resource use and to contribute to human health at the same time; (2) mainstream financial professionals and property market participants are less willing to include sustainability issues in property-related decision-making processes unless and until sustainable building features and related performance are integrated into property valuations. Deloitte (2014) believes that there is 'substantial room for deepening sustainability implementation in certified buildings, where in-use performance can remain stubbornly below design expectations.' (p. 2)

There are, however, some barriers to implementation. These are as follows:

- A gap exists between the current situation (in which the challenges imposed by sustainable development create new pressures and realities) and state-of-the-art valuation theory, standards and practices.
- Whilst it can be argued that in a growing number of cases, valuations reflect sustainable credentials of buildings, sustainable development thinking needs to be integrated at a deeper level into valuation theory, standards and everyday practice; that is to say, a new protocol or model for valuation and professionalism is needed.
- Financial valuation methods and approaches do not really work for property assets because property is not traded in a perfect market.

We need to better understand what we are doing when assigning value to a particular building or groups of buildings; that is to say, while considerable attention has been paid to focusing on improving the performance of our value prediction models, much less time has been spent on advancing our understanding of the fundamental behavioural underpinnings that drive value and provide explanation as to how the property market works. Valuation methods have to reflect market sentiment as demonstrated through the prices paid. However, the valuer (as professional advisor) has a responsibility to make the investor become aware of all the implications of the value figure derived. How far therefore can a valuer influence value practice and eventual price?

The valuation exercise is not only a positive science; that is to say, valuers are not only here to 'reflect the market'. Instead, valuers have a normative professional responsibility towards society at large, which adds a moral dimension to the property professional's valuation and consulting work. This is something that is challenged by scientists, scholars and academics trained in neoclassical economics (including more practical minded people such as valuers and business economists). The normative aspect may, for instance, concern the particular developments in terms of 'value stability' and 'economic sustainability' and the setting of enlightened (adaptable) recommendations for private investment as well as policy and planning.

To expand on the last point, it is not uncommon that policymakers (including policymakers in national governments, multilateral organisations and global corporations) use and look to economic theory and evidence in order to guide policy. Since policies – outlining and guiding humankind's, governments' and corporations' overall strategy and actions – are so vital for sustainable development, the economic discipline plays a crucial role. The increasing extent to which policymaking bears on economics raises the methodological question about the relationship between a positive science concerning 'facts' and a normative investigation into what ought to be or what is estimable. 'Most economists and methodologists believe that there is a reasonably clear distinction between facts and values, between what is and what ought to be, and they believe that most of economics should be regarded as a positive science that helps policy makers choose means to accomplish their ends, though it does not bear on the choice of ends itself.' (Hausman, 2003, Chapter 2)

This view is questionable, mainly because the discipline of economics is guided by values or by individual's views of what is right and wrong. Consequently, economics is greatly influenced by economic scientists' beliefs as to how people in fact behave (Hausman, 2003, Chapter 2). There is evidence that studying theories that are based on the assumption or principle that individuals are 'self-interested' (masters of nature) leads to people – and thus, to societies – who regard self-interested behaviour more favourable and to become even more self-interested (Marwell and Ames, 1981; Frank *et al.*, 1993).

One argument put forward in this book is that 'taking' to achieve individual self-interest in itself is not sustainable. There has to be at least an equal level of 'giving' to sustain species self-interest. In the restricted area of real estate, this might be through lower profit margins or financial returns to provide higher efficiencies in resource consumption or through the positive embrace of green leases and green education. However, an overriding question in this whole debate is as follows: What is sustainability?

Put simply, sustainability embraces the financial, social and environmental decision-making in the field of real estate. The problem of virtual money becoming confused with real wealth has created a crisis in real-estate investment markets and consumer markets across the world. The impact on political life has been seen through a general lack of confidence and revolt against austerity measures which, in themselves, are attempts to redress the balance and achieve sufficiency against the excesses of the past decade. These measures have spread out into the social arena with protests, unemployment and poverty. Each of these are links in a chain which impinge on real-estate markets, whether residential, retail or commercial.

This evidence suggests that many societies have been living unsustainably (i.e. beyond both sufficiency and beyond affordability). As a whole, in all its dimensions, sustainability seems to be something outside the boundaries of our social systems (whether financial, social, political or physical): something that has a meaning but only in context within its own system. It is not a balance sheet or an air-conditioning system or a green space. Sustainability in the Hmong community in Vietnam is very different to sustainability in the Jewish community in New York City. Its meaning is parochial, but its actuality is universal. It is both inside and outside the system, and as such, it may be difficult to fully understand it. For example, often, we can only describe what is not sustainable, but even that can only be a partial judgement.

The concept, on the one hand, steeped in technical jargon, scientific formulae and inconceivable consequences creates a remoteness which is outside most people's sphere of experience/knowledge. In stark contrast, on the other hand, is the immediacy of a financial crisis, a parenting decision or a space heating solution – all of which have an impact on the levels of sustainability. There is therefore an ambivalence about the concept which allows arguments for 'business as usual' to abound. Nevertheless, we should strive to incorporate our own meanings to the concept in our lives (professional, social and private) in order to avoid potential destruction of the conditions of our reproduction (i.e. resources to sustain future generations). Specifically for the valuer, as a professional adviser, the ethics of sustainable solutions should form an important part of any appraisal and judgement when advising a client.

The Book's Methodology and Starting Points

This book necessarily addresses different areas within the property valuation context. We aim at a protocol partly at the higher level and partly at the detailed level of analysis. The book is a comprehensive whole of five parts, but with each part either meant as an essay (Parts 1 and 5) or as a collection of independent (or at least 'semi-independent') essays (Parts 2–4). The insights and conclusion from these contributions will eventually be used to strengthen and support the main argumentative chain and the book's key messages (Fig. 1).

The book's starting points are a brief description of the current state of affairs, developments and changes and analysis of likely consequences for valuers, valuation theory and practice as well as an explanation for proposing an alternative protocol to valuation and decision-making processes in the property industry. This is further dealt with in the following:

Brief Description of the Current State of Affairs, Developments and Changes

When describing the current state of affairs, it is difficult not to mention the issues of climate change, economic cycles of boom and bust, worldwide inequality (particularly in an urban context) and the need to tutor the emerging economies. These are just some of the arguments on a macro level where there is an ever-increasing awareness – even

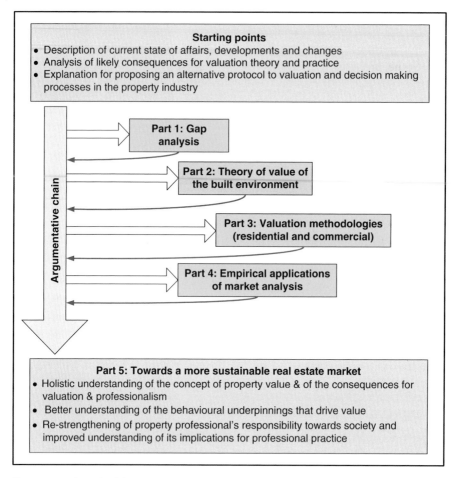

Figure 1 Book methodology.

worldview – about the set of disturbing problems facing the owners and occupiers alike. Climate change is getting more and more accepted as an overall paradigm – not only in natural sciences but also in social sciences and general economics. Even a relatively 'hands-on' discipline such as (spatial) planning has been reconceptualised to the core (see e.g. Bulkeley, 2006).

Ostensibly, climate change is causing glaciers and icebergs to melt as well as increased precipitation and storm floods and, subsequently, water level rise. This leads to flooding and other hazards, mainly in river and coastal zones, which become increasingly risky locations to live in. The inhabitants of these areas move away if they can. As such, the same areas have been economically prosperous for centuries due to the logistic possibilities associated with such locations. How many of the large cities of the world are located by the coast or are situated by the course of a main river? When these areas suddenly become unattractive for people and business alike, they also become prone to multiply increased financial risk (cf. Hill and Lorenz, 2011).

Further changes include the 'investment climate', in a situation where private and public investors are increasingly looking for new (i.e. more sustainable) approaches to investment (examples for this can be found in the publications of the United Nations Environment Program Finance Initiative). In these circles, there is a tendency to move away from a fixation on financial metrics and measures of performance alone. However, at the same time, property assets are also increasingly seen as a medium for short-term trading. This potentially can be a significant contributory factor in many of the problems that we are facing.

While there is also a strong focus on sustainability within the current political discourse as well as a tendency to increase the stringency of environmental legislation, these efforts are both neither fully translated into practice (lack of tools and mechanisms, etc.) nor sufficiently powerful to change behaviour (see the Copenhagen Climate Conference).

There is a considerable amount of literature on sustainability-related issues, regarding both the general economy and the property and construction industry in particular. However, whilst the majority of publications identify the problem, there is a lack of guidance on what to do next (i.e. practical courses of actions for individuals and professionals). In general, in professional life, there is more interest in defining and thinking about what professional ethics mean, rather than focusing on what consequences result from them, for professional practice.

Political and social value systems are strong and shape decision-making to a certain extent. An individual's behaviour is usually embedded in a social context. 'Social and interpersonal factors continually shape and constrain individual preference.' (Jackson, 2005, p. vii).

It is evident that in some parts of the world, value systems (of individuals and corporate) are changing. Certain businesses and investors start realising/understanding the benefits of taking responsibility towards the environment and society. Corporate Social Responsibility is becoming a factor of success. In some parts of the world, this takes place more rapidly than in other parts. This can happen for a number of reasons, for example, changes in material wealth and education and environmental change.

In general, it can therefore be argued that due to the changes/developments described earlier, there is a conflict/gap between current professional practice and the current business, societal and political reality (see Part 1 – Gap Analysis).

Analysis of Likely Consequences for Valuers, Valuation Theory and Practice

In such circumstances, the role of the professional valuer needs to be more multidimensional and pluralistic than it has tended to be in the past. The body of knowledge that underpins the profession needs to be broadened; stated differently, good (i.e. ethically and politically correct) professionals must update their understanding according to the requirements stemming from the arguments described earlier. To some extent, this is already happening: for example, the RICS has, over the years, produced a range of research publications addressing 'green' issues and sustainability, some in the context of valuation. In addition, the RICS has published several Information Papers and Guidance Notes on how to address sustainability considerations within valuation reports. They are intended to help to achieve this broadening of thought processes. For example, VPGA8 of the RICS Valuation – Professional Standards July 2017 ('The Red Book') advises that 'while valuers should reflect markets, not lead them, they should be aware of sustainability features and the implications these could have on property values in the short, medium and longer term' (p. 138). However, The Standards as a whole tend to emphasis the short term, as encapsulated in the mandatory bases of value set out therein.

At a more general level, we could argue that the knowledge required for professionalism always forms a part of a normative context. This, however, raises issues about professional ethics both at the micro and at the macro level. For example, do valuers have any obligation towards society at large or only towards their clients? In other words, do professionals have any social responsibilities? If so, how does a professional reconcile any conflict between these and the personal responsibilities to clients?

One of the key issues is the role that valuers perform in getting the message across. In the past, this tended to be at a fairly basic level when it comes to market value determination. However, it is a truism that the most direct route is often not the most efficacious. This is especially true where there is a need to assess the value of assets that have historically displayed non-linear performance. Such assessment often relies on a simple model using 'bandwagon, network and lemming effects' to arrive at a value. The contagious impact of these effects as they become 'market data' leads to 'mistakes' and increases their deficiency as comparable evidence when dealing with complex problems (Weil, 2010, p. 1447). At the moment, in many quarters, it seems that, despite all the sophisticated software and hype about sustainability, most valuers just want to 'do the deal' (often at any cost). So, is it just about money? Can all aspects of a property (its costs and benefits) be expressed in monetary terms to arrive at a 'value'?

Jacobs (1994) sees the neoclassical approach turning the environment into a commodity. He goes on to say that 'while allocating resources "optimally" in an economist's terms … is certainly one way of conceiving the "most benefit" to society, it is not the only way … it is concerned only with individual preferences, and it measures only totals for all individuals not distributions between them'. This approach is therefore too simplistic. It gives meaning to things, and it ascribes value to those meanings. But meanings are derived from neoclassical logic, and in a way, this simply classifies 'environment' as a concept with clear boundaries and may therefore fail to acknowledge its total, global perspective and impact. In a way, we are seeking ontological meaning, not one-dimensional financial meaning. Money 'translates the many-sided diversity of things … [as] homogenous' … [and] … empties out 'the core of things, their singularity, their specific value, their comparability' (Lash, 1999, quoting Simmel).

In a way therefore, evaluating things in monetary terms deprives them of their primary significance. The sustainable environment exists for itself, it has existential meaning; to then ascribe a market value to it creates a distance between the subject (the environment) and the object (money). Once this becomes culturally accepted then, symbolically, the sustainable environment can be bought and sold as part of any privity of contract real-estate transaction. However, this privatisation fails to deal adequately with the social consequences of degradation to that environment.

Such meanings have to be translated into terms of transaction. This takes place in markets. In developed economies, these markets are sophisticated and exist within mature institutional frameworks. For example, Harvey (2000) identifies the following as the functions of the real-estate market.

- To allocate existing real property resources and interests. In this way, an equilibrium market price is achieved. In this way, the market reflects preferences.
- To indicate changes in demand for land resources and interests. These occur mainly due to expectations of future yields, taxation, income or tastes, institutional factors.

- To induce supply to adjust to changes in demand. This can change by developing real property, changing existing interests.
- To indicate changes in the conditions upon which land resources can be supplied, for example, improved construction techniques.
- To induce demand to respond to changes in the conditions of supply.
- To 'reward' the owners of land resources. This is a by-product of the market. There are two kinds of reward: Return on capital invested and Return for risk.

As such, the market and its agents are not only indicators of activity, they are also motivators. There is a positive role to play here. Valuations have often been accused of backward looking (i.e. a valuer will gather information from the past and then project forward to indicate income stream variability and/or capital value change over time). This tends to assume a static, passive market. However, property markets are dynamic, and valuers have an active role to play in generating that activity. The role of the valuer could be seen as not only indicating opportunities but also inducing change. This implies being at the cutting edge of knowledge on technological change and market movements but also the impact on value. In fact, the valuer is the arbiter of value and can, in some way, induce value, through information exchange. In the case of green buildings, how will the valuer value? The simple answer today is, in the same way that he/she has always valued externalities, through the market mechanism. If someone is willing to pay more, then, it is worth more; if not, then, it is not worth more. The valuers will 'induce' the highest price, but they cannot prescribe it (cf. Goering, 2005).

In fact, the problem is not so much with the process; after all, price is determined by supply and demand, and the valuer can only have marginal influence on its level in any particular market at any point in time. Sophisticated financial models can be used to demonstrate net benefits over the life of the building, and whilst this should not be eschewed, such future real benefits may have only limited impact on the drivers of value particularly if they relate to unborn generations.

In a way, this is again looking at the symptom and not at the cause. To find the cause, we might need to trace back through the valuer, his profession, the institutional framework, the economic and corporate cultures and politics (see Kauko, 2004b). This will involve examination of the institutional and environmental economics, social theory, behavioural studies as well as, more specifically, valuation methodology (i.e. dealt with more fully within Parts 2, 3 and 5).

Explanation for Proposing Alternative Protocol to Valuation and Decision-Making Processes in the Property Industry

We suggest a change to another model because cycles will eventually occur, but they need smoothing, in the face of financial losses for investors – and indirectly also the tenants. Ethical considerations must play a part as well; otherwise, these losses will spread beyond those directly involved to include, potentially, the globalised society at large.

While cycles of boom and bust occur, the property profession can do a lot to make them less damaging. Therefore, we suggest a different role for value analysis, because the relevant actors within the property industry need to add the smoothing and also ethical aspect to their mindset and business or administrative management strategy. While there are several professional practitioner groups with a direct stake (e.g. facility managers), intermediaries are also important in dealing with values. Among all professional groups, valuers have a very important mediating role; in order to be credible, their behaviour cannot afford to be detached from the behaviour of the owner and user groups.

But why is this a problem? Why should we care about the self-inflicted suffering of individual valuers? Is it not true that, in the long term, society regulates itself after each round of prosperity and crises? We need a final missing link in our argument here. It is because valuers represent authority to many actors, and when the same valuers make bad decisions, these actors bear the consequences. Therefore, the valuers' role is to take responsibility for their decisions/advice. Thus, they need to make solid decisions based on updated knowledge. In sum, while not necessarily the principal authority, the valuer is authority nonetheless. It is this authoritarian role that they must deserve, because they owe that much to those actors who inevitably will be affected by their decisions/advice negatively in the short term – be it merely financial losses or more dysfunctional circumstances such as social problems or environmental hazards. One of the main issues here is a perceived complacency among valuers. This potentially can create anachronistic market behaviours and is often born of a lack of imagination and willingness to challenge the current practice.

Our end argument is therefore that there can be an alternative protocol – at least one that recognises a social dimension to value. Moreover, we argue that the valuers must take a wider interest in the impact of their advice. While it may or may not be true that the more altruistic aspects are only considered by elites, a failure to adapt is likely to lead to missed business opportunities for a wide array of property professionals due to the threat of worsened reputation.

The overarching objective of this line of argument is to provide an alternative framework to consider for decision-making rather than to give advice to (and certainly not to) reform valuation practice. From an analysis of values (Part 2), we proceed to an analysis of valuation (Parts 3 and 4) and propose an alternative as food for thought. Finally, we try to locate the debate within the broad discussion of new value drivers (Part 5). We do not, however, advocate that traditional valuation frameworks or models are obsolete, simply that there is something beyond that, and as professionals, valuers should equip themselves to have a broader and deeper look.

We have inevitably different scenarios for different kinds of circumstances. Of course, we are encouraging socially and environmentally responsible investment policy. But within this setting, we believe in different elements for different professional or cultural groups. In doing so, indirectly, we accept that there are different characters of a place – and indeed different values – or at least different loadings for one value – attached to one and the same place. An example of this way of working is IGLOO Regeneration, a successful real-estate organisation that seeks not only to harness the history of community and place but also to create history through imagination, impact and identity.

The fact is that value systems change, and as a consequence, the basis for price premiums (and discounts) will change as well (e.g in relation to energy and social issues). English Partnerships, for instance, requires the client to meet a certain quality threshold before the price estimate is announced, thereby incorporating the normative element of valuation to their business model. Thus, in a changed value system, the role of the valuer should also change. This is our condensed message.

What follows is organised in five substantial parts. Part 1 explores the literature and identifies some more or less well-known 'gaps' which also are framed as research problems for us. In more specific terms, this part shows a discrepancy (hence gap) between existing and desirable state of affairs regarding how value and market definitions are treated in real-estate analyses. Part 2 deals with value from a theoretical point of view. After that, Part 3 discusses various methodological aspects of the treatment of our main themes: valuation, value, price, market and sustainability. Part 4 then switches to empirical and practical applicability issues within the framework identified by earlier parts. In doing so, it turns into somewhat different directions, namely the dynamic and localised context underlying valuation formation. Finally, Part 5 returns to the issue of valuation and addresses this in the context of professionalism. It also attempts to tie together all the aforementioned aspects and suggests some future courses of action.

Part 1

Gap Analysis: Anomalies and Paradoxes, Questions, Dilemmas and Motivations

Tom Kauko, Peter Dent, Stephen Hill, Maurizio d'Amato and David Lorenz

Background

One of the overarching issues of this book concerns the possible connection between the two meta-discourses of financial crisis (reasons, faults, repercussions, coping strategies and prospects), on the one hand, and sustainable development in its ecological–environmental (i.e. green), social, cultural and economic dimensions, on the other. Intuitively, one would, at least, see some overlap between the former discourse and the economic sustainability dimension; but, does a more profound look reveal, in addition, more subtle issues to take notice of within the broader spectre of the situation?

At first sight, one would doubt the existence of any such linkage; is it not true that, while the global property market downturn may be a temporary phenomenon, the sustainable development agendas and discourses require a longer time frame? To paraphrase Indy Johar, Zero Zero Architects, UK (discussion at EU Sustainable Energy Week, Brussels, 12 April 2011), (urban) sustainability requires a time span of at least two generations ahead. Furthermore, many (perhaps most) real-estate managers seem to be optimists and consider the crisis a temporary phenomenon as there is a belief in recovery such that, as soon as we are over bad times, the markets will pick up again, and at that time, being in a new market situation, we will also be able to command premiums for any sustainable features (e.g. Thiet, 2011).

However, there is a genuine concern that, whilst the global financial and property market downturn (with the most dramatic stage unfolding during 2007–2008) may superficially appear to be a temporary phenomenon, there may be more serious structural weaknesses in both markets. These relate to both the framework and the way in which the underlying value is assessed. Regarding the former, Shiller (2008) suggests that 'we are running bullet trains on ancient track' (p. 11), referring to the need for institutional reform to meet the nature of sophisticated global finance and real-estate instruments. Ailon (2015) makes the point, concerning the latter, that 'financial market cultures should complement the technique-based focus with a focus on the hidden or yet uncovered "spirit" behind finance capitalism's calculative ethos'. (p. 593). This spirit perhaps lies outside of a technical or institutional expression and sits more closely in

Value in a Changing Built Environment, First Edition.
Edited by David Lorenz, Peter Dent and Tom Kauko.
© 2018 John Wiley & Sons Ltd. Published 2018 by John Wiley & Sons Ltd.

the area of restraint and guardianship. In this sense, it relates more to Appadurai's embodied moral sensibility, 'which precedes action or organization and amounts to a collective psycho-moral disposition' (Appadurai, p. 519). If therefore the individual is moulded by the social, then there is an important role to be played by social and professional institutions in creating a sustainable environment in its widest sense (i.e. to include the environmental, the financial, the social and cultural).

Unfortunately, what, in part, seems to have happened to create and sustain the recent financial crisis is a gradual decline in collective responsibility which, in turn, encourages 'a breakdown in moral codes releasing greed, hatred and delusive behaviour'. This then has the potential 'to work against physical and biological laws and leads to a deterioration in society and nature' (Daniels, 2003, p. 20). This creates a downward spiral of moral degradation, irresponsible actions and extremism. These, in themselves, tend to narrow individual's perspective of their power to succeed and the certainties of their rights and their particular points of view.

So, perhaps, the worst excesses of the financial crisis were caused by agents treating markets, mistakenly, as sources of too much certainty with the intention that this would disguise or mitigate layers of risk. This was achieved by applying such 'magical practices' as formatting, framing, likenesses, manipulations and charts as means to forecasting (Appadurai, p. 528). However, these tend to limit exposure to the range of uncertainties across a market and create potentially misleading data sets. This, in itself, then reduces enquiry and examination of situations. Much critical information remains unexamined, and decisions are made based on limited perspective.

What we seem therefore to have is a market with an inadequate institutional infrastructure to control activity and a methodology which has been pared to comply with a formula which provides short-term solutions. To address this in the context of both financial and environmental sustainability, there is a need for a combination of a robust process, a holistic method of evaluation, a risk mitigation strategy and an attitude of sufficiency (i.e. a combination of right method and right mindset).

In these circumstances, it would be helpful to encourage greater understanding through education which explores the interlinking of financial, economic, social, cultural, environmental and ecological matters in general – and real-estate matters in particular. Indeed, 'black boxes' in our knowledge regarding issues such as saving resources and combating poverty can and should be filled by the fruits of education, apt governance and technological progress. We need both more sustainably legitimate and financially sound behavioural models on all levels, ranging from the individual consumer and citizen to the small firms, via local community and governance interests, to corporate strategies and government agendas. Underlying this, 'the mindset that caused environmental problems is not going to solve environmental problems' (Dent *et al.*, 2012, p. 11). This equally applies to the financial dimension.

Thus 'yes', the discoveries related to the financial crisis and sustainable development must be seen as belonging to the same overall paradigm shift. This relates to long-term administrative behaviour (via an institutional approach), long-term market behaviour (heterodox economics approach) and human behaviour in general (behavioural approach). These should be 'long-term' perspectives, and the valuer's behaviour ought to be fitted into this bigger picture. How this is achieved is an integral part of the narrative of this book.

Valuation is not just an information processing exercise. There are judgements and assumptions that have to be made which add a cognitive element. 'Market value, in its role as a standard, provides a benchmark that market participants can use to compare various property interests, calculate rates of return/risk and evaluate relative investment strategies.' (Ramsey, 2004, p. 350). However, the anomaly is that valuers also have a fiduciary role to help avoid conflicts of interest. The valuer is concerned not only with 'problems of knowing value' which is a cognitive role, but also with 'providing an independent opinion of value', a fiduciary role (Ramsey, 2004, p. 351).

Property Market Impacts

We do not know yet if the current global crisis is temporary or more permanent. Even if the former is true, we could argue that the damage done by the crisis has long-lasting consequences for the producers, consumers and intermediaries living off the real-estate industry. There ostensibly will be fundamental changes in the attitudes, demand and supply structures, markets, regulative measures and policy initiatives and, most certainly, directions taken by technological progress (e.g. Joss, 2011).

What is then the correct course of action? It would be rather difficult not to see any such changes as integrated onto the broader sustainable development discourse which, in one way or another, focuses on the need to improve the usage of Earth's resources – natural, material and human alike. At any rate, this has already been recognised in both 'financial-' and 'sustainability-'biased circles: it seems to have been a combination of 'infectious greed' and 'blind faith' (Partnoy, 2010) that caused the financial crisis.

Property professionals and others involved in the property markets (financiers, developers, designers) need to have a broader understanding of the concepts of value and how value is determined. Existing practices and protocols of professional property valuation are increasingly recognised as inadequate and outdated when dealing with an increasingly sophisticated set of criteria. The paradox is that a market value provides a single figure to represent a set of unique untested criteria which exist at one point in time in a fixed location, whereas, in reality, clients more often need some measure of performance which incorporates an evaluation and provides an holistic impact assessment. This is a higher level of analysis where the main target is market signalling and structures rather than simply the technical issues in relation to estimation.

This is examined in more detail in Part 3 of the book. However, what we are doing throughout this book is to address an urgent and central concern of property valuers and other professionals involved with property value to understand and account for value in the property market. In doing so, we provide theoretical and practical insight into the criteria for making professional estimates and explanations showing how value is accrued and how it is distributed.

What we search for in this chapter is an innovative way to expand the current theory of value formation: for both organic value creation and intentional price setting mechanisms and processes alike. Here, we can provide a link to the economic sustainability concept and, in that way, to the broader sustainable real-estate debate once again.

Out of the Comfort Zone

There is increasing recognition among the wider public but also specifically within parts of the property and construction industry that the maintenance of life and well-being depend – to a significant degree – on the environmental performance and wider impacts of buildings and the built environment (e.g. Lützkendorf and Lorenz, 2005). This suggests that the current understanding of property value needs major revision. In fact, it is becoming evident that a property's economic value also depends on the property's capability to create and protect environmental, social and cultural values and that an isolated analysis of mere financial variables is not adequate for capturing the concept of property value (see d'Amato and Kauko, 2012). It is therefore not a surprise that the current valuation practice falls short in rewarding investment in 'green' (i.e. environmental–ecological) and 'sustainable' property (see e.g. Warren-Myers, 2012).

Therefore, the aim of this book (particularly Part 5) is to put forward proposals for new modelling which acknowledges both private and public value. When extending the scope of valuation in this way, particular attention furthermore needs to be paid to the way the future is assessed. An auxiliary point is to be aware of the danger of letting valuation automata replace the valuer entirely. This way of viewing the world brings us closer to normative analyses, as we already indicated in the introductory chapter.

As we already asserted, our starting point is that we recognise a certain 'gap' between the difficulties of valuation and the competence or awareness of individuals to sort these difficulties (Mooya, 2011, p. 2275). The problem formulated at the end of the introductory chapter is that there is room for improvement in the way that real-estate professionals – notably valuers – undertake their work. This part of the book explores in detail why this is the case.

The identification of 'gaps' meshes sustainable development laggardness, ethical issues and other problematic circumstances. In order to explore these, we seek to achieve the following aims:

- Elevating or strengthening the appraisal profession
- Assessing future risk (utility and financial performance)
- Addressing how to deal with market cycles in general and bubbles in particular
- Complexity in the valuation exercise
- Relationship between valuation and assessment of risk
- Moral and ethical context for markets; that is to say, creating trust in the profession together with appropriate valuations is necessary for the market to function, especially as we now know that the property market underpins the whole banking system
- The difference and unknown relationship between an equity and a property
- The problematic contribution of finance to real-estate valuation
- The unsuitable assumptions set to explain the real-estate market
- What we can learn (what we have not learned and what we do not want to learn) from the sub-prime and other real-estate crises of the past.

If we look at the relatively new sustainability discourse, the uncertainty becomes especially evident. At the moment, the situation is such that, while owners and users alike are being increasingly convinced about the economic benefits of green or sustainable property stock, to engage practicing valuers will require some time (see Warren-Myers, 2011). To recognise this discrepancy more widely among researchers would already bring the empirical literature a step forward. To date, at least Warren-Myers and Reed (2010) identified at the time a huge knowledge gap for valuers in Australia and New Zealand: namely, only 35% of the surveyed valuers admitted to actually having valued 'a building promoted as having sustainable attributes' which prompted these authors to think of solving this problem through 'up-skilling and understanding of sustainability and industry rating tools'. Thus, with time, the valuers' knowledge gap would be filled. However, when Warren-Myers and Reed also surveyed the corresponding opinions of property investors, no such knowledge gaps were found. Instead, it appeared as if the investors care about knowing the performance of the building rather than its rating. They concluded that the difference in opinion between these two groups of actors was due to the tendency of valuers to be misinformed about sustainable investment strategies that focus on cost minimisation and value enhancement. Fuerst *et al.* (2011) make the point that 'the lack of adoption of sustainable features is linked with the lack of an appropriate investment return through the pricing process'. This has been explained by imperfect information, split incentives, risk aversion, high discount rates and skills shortages, inter alia. In addition, there may be other reasons that, despite its importance, sustainability may not be reflected in property prices (p. 49).

No doubt, knowledge and understanding have improved since the publication of her paper, but Warren-Myers (2012) paints a worrying picture about the inconclusiveness of how and how much sustainability – mainly green building – was addressed in valuation practice. After reviewing the literature comprising hypothetical analyses, case studies and quantitative investigations, she purported that market value and value of sustainability were not necessarily considered as the same thing. She noted, inter alia, that there were large variations between the reported effects of green certification on both rent increase (0–51%) and value increase (1–31%). In addition, she found that, in some cases, the treatment of sustainability was arbitrary and detached from market evidence. She concluded that hedonic price models were applied even though they fail to indicate this relationship conclusively and that valuers, as a result, remained ill-equipped to deal with the changing market in which sustainability factors were likely to play a role in the future. In the same vein, Warren-Myers and Reed (2010) note that hedonic studies alone are insufficient to confirm possible sustainability premiums in commercial property values. This is further highlighted by Fuerst *et al.* (2011), where, whilst they are able to demonstrate a price premium for certified properties, they express similar concerns over methodology.

Arguably, to only focus on sustainable real estate – usually only green buildings – is a misconception, however. Namely, one should not consider merely the sustainable buildings and sites, but also the less sustainable ones, as bad design or deteriorated structures might be seen as a risk factor, in which case, a negative price correction is needed in comparison not only to the sustainable cases but also to the average case (cf. Runde and Thoyre, 2010). In the present study, we are considering the existing built environment – this should be a logical choice as, in any circumstances, the role of the new built sector is only a small percentage per year. In doing so, we are nevertheless attempting to bridge the gap between new requirements, much involving the sustainability concept, and existing standards, where such issues are absent. We do this in the knowledge that it may well be that new build is easier, even if more expensive, than retrofitting existing buildings, as evidence from the US suggests (see Goering, 2009).

We also have to be aware that the emerging economies will generate new real-estate markets of massive proportions, and accordingly, the imperative must be to avoid the same mistakes made in the developed world. This is a key issue – and a real concern – which also necessitates a more normative role for valuation than has so far been acknowledged (Mooya, 2011, p. 2277). Kimmett (2008) purports that 'engaging the normative' would help to make the practice scientific or at least more relevant. One possible path to success is how the 'green' criteria together with 'the community aspect' can be integrated into the basic business culture and to all specific procedures therein (e.g. discounting the future cash flows). Obviously, all cash flows have to be sustainable in the sense that they have to reflect the market forecasts; however, the argument is more about the confidence levels of sustained uplifts in cash flows and the downside risk explained through discount rates (i.e. real estate that is future-proofed by complying with regulations and so on is more attractive and less risky compared to lower rated properties).

In such a setting, a share of the profits would be reinvested back into environmental–ecological and social–cultural elements (cf. Bryson and Lombardi, 2009). Furthermore, for this to continue recursively, good governance and inclusive real-time management would be needed (Kauko, 2012).

It could be argued that, in a generic sense, the establishment of institutions such as the market, the firm and the state has generated economic development through history. At present, new institutions are needed to similarly cause sustainable development. The difference then must be to move the focus from merely economic to also include environmental–ecological and social–cultural development goals. With an increase in such dimensions, the task, however, becomes more complex than before. The question then is, what are the implications of this for valuations and what is the rationality of these valuations (see Vatn, 2005)?

Vatn (2005) also argues that if only individual values are at stake, market valuation is acceptable. However, if we deal with irreversible damage to the environment, or even uncertainty of such effects, the so-called precautionary principle must be applied: that is, moral considerations are valued to be higher than cost–benefit analysis, and no scientific evidence should be required in order to apply the best measures available. This general argument aligns neatly with the normative role of valuation brought up in the introductory chapter, as it shows that it can be greater than the positive role.

To set the agenda for developing new thoughts on value, valuation and sustainability in the built environment, the argumentation is roughly as follows:

First stage: Most of the time, the mainstream economic view of value based on market equilibrium (value equals capitalised present value of rent or historically paid price of similar case) does not hold.

Second stage: Alternatives to the mainstream view have been proposed within various (until recently forgotten) literatures: classical and heterodox economics, arts and philosophy, town planning, economic geography and so forth.

Third stage: While there have always been such deviant thoughts about value setting being non-rational (in a narrow economic sense), the post-financial crisis and climate change agenda have brought us to a new reality, where the first two moments are recognised explicitly.

Fourth stage: Arguably, today, sustainability (to be precise, sustainable real-estate development/market outcomes in various dimensions) should generate a premium, which implies a normative role in the determination of value and, in this way, setting the benchmark for valuation practice.

When extending the last stage, the nature of the problem might suggest that professionals may not be doing their work professionally or responsibly enough or they may not be sufficiently well-equipped to do so. We argue that change is needed.

The 'what' of sustainability is only a side issue in this book, albeit a necessary one, considering how the sustainable development discourse continues to permeate all land-use and real-estate-related disciplines and application areas today. The issue is how to deal with new elements caused by sustainability. This is not a straightforward one. To give an example, there is a risk of including sustainability when no basis for it exists; similarly, there is the risk of neglecting sustainability considerations when there is a basis for it (see Runde and Thoyre, 2010).

The Social Mind

Sustainable development requires not only a radical rethinking of consumption economies and the addition of green accounting but also the unthinking of the foundations of modern science and politics. You cannot have it without the creative destruction or rather deconstruction of both capital and science. Otherwise, you reproduce the limitless limit (i.e. the existing conditioned mind persists). In other words, the way that we think about the world and conduct our lives through current production and consumption frameworks needs radical transformation. Perhaps, this is too much for some to cope with (particularly for those working in the real-estate profession). This goes beyond the professional, the political and the economic, but it is those institutions and the social systems that they create that will need to be strong enough to achieve such transformational development which can sustain human life on the planet.

Social science since Durkheim has been concerned about showing that the intrinsic properties of things such as money, fashion, art, real estate do not matter. They were only a surface onto which social needs and interests are projected. Individuals, maybe, cannot see this for themselves; they think they like fashion because of what it is. The ground for belief in these intrinsic properties is revealed by the social sciences to be a result of their softness, the pliability in the face of objective forces such as the market and the social. Just so with real estate, architects and developers fashion our minds to certain types of design, configuration or space aesthetic. Once again, the thinness of objects (i.e. clothes, space, facilities) is emptied in the name of the thingness of objects (i.e. markets, institutions). The real-estate agent's particulars are not available just to describe a property. They are written to entice through the use of all the same marketing jargon that we see on our television screens day in, day out. We are being sold a vision, an image, something with no substance, a narcissistic reflection of ourselves in the social pool.

This illusion is further enhanced by society through its institutions. It could be argued that society has a dual-edged power: first, as the replacement of the transcendental ego, it has no origin and is all powerful and able to shape arbitrary matter (i.e. give life structure and meaning). On the other hand, it is moulded in turn by vast economic forces. But, why does society, if it is so powerful, need objects as screens on which to project? In order that the objects do not appear to be worthless, we are manipulated to believe that they reify, reflect, materialise, embody society and maintain social order. Equally, some substantial objects or misunderstood elements are externalised.

'An "externality"… is very different from a social context: formatting market institutions in ways that entail specific modes of calculation involves framing a range of features as relevant, and by definition excluding others (these are no longer economic factors, but cultural or ethical or political). The latter are not a context within which market behaviour is conducted but are themselves a result of the very same operation through which the market is (provisionally) defined in the first place. Externality and framing describe the way in which "insides" and "outsides" emerge, and change, in relation to highly political and material processes. The very patterning of elements within the market that entail "calculativeness" appear there because of (disputable and unstable) acts of separation and division, not because "values" are imported from a pre-given outside to be applied to an equally given inside'. (Barry and Slater, 2002, pp. 182–183.) Therefore, real-estate valuations are framed within a particular context. This is usually based on the dominant cultural ethos in a professional body which, itself, is often derived from a traditional view of society treating any new externality with a degree of suspicion and scepticism.

Investment agents work together to produce 'house views' (organisational views) – restricted choices of how to proceed in the volatile markets and then 'act to restructure patterns of investment by working to market and legitimise the "house view" through a process of "presentations" to potential investors, "placing financial bets" and promoting "rumour", thereby producing "market opportunities". In this way, investment agents literally "engineer" the market place by directing flows of capital into, and out of, spaces and places'. (Pryke and Lee, 1995).

Lack of Political Awareness in the Profession about Changes in Value Systems

The most significant gap is in the lack of political awareness in the profession about the changes in value systems that have occurred particularly over the last 30 years. This is mainly due to the impact of neo-liberal political economic thinking on ethics and knowledge.

Many professional bodies claim that sustainability is at the core of their activities. For example, the Royal Institution of Chartered Surveyors, one of the largest organisations for property professionals worldwide, adopted a dedicated sustainability policy in 2005, which is strong on the 'what' but says little about 'how' or 'why'. Professionals remain unclear about how to respond to complex and inter-related environmental, social and economic challenges, when they probably mostly imagine having a simple set of one-dimensional responsibilities to their clients or shareholder value. At best, professionals are confused about how to balance their technical competences and public interest responsibilities.

Our particular/further proposition is that both the valuer and land economist roles need to be reframed within the RICS Charter. This Institution is recognised as a globally authoritative expression of ethical standards and for public interest purpose. It could be that the most all-embracing and important requirement of surveyors is 'securing the optimal use of land and its associated resources to meet social and economic needs'.

There is greater awareness that some aspects of economic value are being generated and/or are only possible by the externalisation of social and environmental costs, which create societal damage, but in economic as well as social and environmental spheres. The valuation profession has not developed its ethical position on this and, more importantly, has not changed its educational requirements for surveyors to be aware of the dilemmas. Whilst it is no longer the role of the RICS to be prescriptive about every aspect of content in education, the Institution could expect to see a seam of sustainability running through most courses of study along with other issues which are not directly related to property but influence property decision-making such as global economies, international investment and transportation. However, it could be argued that the value of being a professional, by virtue of membership, demands more of the mutual obligation to be informed about issues that are important to the political economies in which they operate. Many surveyors think this takes them out of what they think is their main function in objectively technocratic work at which they feel more comfortable. This will be revisited in Part 5 of this book.

Professional Values

In one's professional life, one way to view professional development is to apply Lawrence Kohlberg's system of moral development (Kohlberg, 1976). Therefore, if we relate this specifically to the RICS requirements for learning and the moral principles that govern conduct (i.e. ethics), level 1 (pre-conventional morality) is concerned with the vocational learning followed through university programmes and the assessment of professional competence (APC). The two stages can be highlighted as follows:

Obedience and punishment orientation. At the outset, the morality of the profession is external to the student. It is what others show by example in programmes and structured training.

Individualism and exchange. At this stage, the subject, still seeing morality externally, learns that there is no one right view.

'Norms and core values that underpin ethical behaviour derive from a combination of individual and organisational experiences, including family, education, environment and work. 'Norms' reflect a strong degree of common acceptance, whereas 'core values' are inherently aspirational and have not yet become norms'. (RICS, 2009, p. 13).

Once a graduate surveyor passes the APC, they then move on to a junior position in their consultancy or organisation. They will have learnt and understood the 'core values' of the profession. At level 2 (conventional morality), they gain a greater understanding of the conventions, rules of conduct within their profession. These two stages are the following:

Good interpersonal relationships. Here, the surveyor should live up to the expectations of the community (employer and professional body) and behave in 'good' ways.

Maintaining the social order. At this stage, the surveyor starts to become more concerned with society as a whole. The emphasis is on obeying laws, respecting authority and performing duties so that the social order (i.e. professional standards) is maintained. 'Given the economic value of the built environment…as well as its social and environmental impact, everyone in society is potentially affected by surveying ethics' (RICS, 2009, p. 16).

At level 3 (post-conventional morality), the surveyor will mature and see their role from a more objective, social perspective. Here, the surveyor should be aligning deep thinking in a professional manner over and above a short-term commercial perspective.

The final level at this stage is rarely achieved, but it should provide the vision for aspirational leadership. The two levels are as follows:

Social contract and individual rights. The surveyor (now in a senior position) begins to think about society in a very theoretical way, stepping back from their own parochial business needs and considering the rights and values that a society of professionals ought to uphold. They then evaluate in terms of these prior considerations.

Universal principles. Democratic processes alone do not always result in outcomes that we intuitively sense are just. A majority, for example, may vote for a law that hinders a minority. Thus, Kohlberg believes that there must be this higher stage which defines the principles by which we achieve justice. Few, he believes, achieve that level (Crain, 1985).

Whatever level the individual surveyors achieve will be tempered by the system within which they operate. This will determine their 'morality'. In a general sense, it is the market system which creates the dominant culture into which surveyors (and their professional bodies) commit themselves. This market itself is controlled not by property but by the way property is communicated and transacted. Money therefore becomes the medium of communication in the market place. We could conclude from this, as O'Neill does, that the market place only responds to the preferences of those who have the money for buying and selling, excluding the 'commercially inarticulate': the poor, the future generations and the non-humans (O'Neill, 2002).

'Wrong Coding' of the Market System

Modern society can be seen as distinguished into functionally specialised systems such as economy, law, politics, religion, science and education (Gren *et al.*, 2003). Each of these sub-systems can be coded and programmed to create observational possibilities. 'Programs open the system to the world and establish links between operations of different specialised subsystems. At the same time, the binary code determines the main distinction that the system operates on'. In the case of the economy and, more specifically, in this current discussion, the property market as a system, the code is 'having money/not having money', the program is supply/demand, the operation is payment and the medium is money. An interesting point here is that 'compared with the relative stability of codes, programs may change quite easily' (Gren *et al.*, 2003). So, the market is the totality of payment operations that are the communication form that dominates the determination of value. As payments on their own are meaninglessness, the market runs a program of pricing to indicate the conditions for the execution of payments. In the case of property, this is by way of either market rents or market values. What the market does not contain is the material aspects of production; only communications grounded in costs and benefits make sense to it. It cannot therefore easily incorporate environmental concerns unless these are seen as part of consumer preferences and thus reflected in the price. In other words, the market can satisfy consumers but not necessarily citizens.

What a system can notice in its environment is then completely determined by what is selected by programs and submitted to the codes of any particular system. Theoretically, therefore, the market system could be changed to code sustainable/unsustainable if it knew how to value the code beyond the pricing mechanism.

Gren *et al.* (2003) go on to suggest that society as the sum of systems is only then capable of solving problems that can be registered by the systems. So, any multifaceted problem is solved by *n*-systems, each dealing with what it registers of the problem in its own way and through its observation of other systems. As society gets more and more differentiated in this way, the systems are transformed from stratified to flat differentiation and operate via inclusion/exclusion. The picture is then of co-evolution; an evolution not driven by the status quo, but by the social (in this case, market) selecting what it will treat as a meaningful environment (in this case, the binary code: sustainability/unsustainability).

Environmental economist Vatn (2005) has a related point here: when we move from individual to common goods, social rationality and dialogue (the forum) are the only apt institutional structure to select and that the emphasis here should be on the communicative process. Vatn furthermore stresses the role of the civic society, on the one hand, and the corporate (social) responsibility, on the other. We may then ask two questions: One, who makes the decisions about setting these values? Two, based on what data are the decisions made? To provide answers, Vatn underscores the need to establish public competing information channels.

Ehrenfeld (2008) makes the point that unsustainable practices will remain until 'the beliefs and norms that drive industrialized economies' are replaced by new sustainable ones. Relying on new, ever-more sophisticated band-aid technologies (Clark, 2002) according to Ehrenfeld, attacks the symptoms only and is simply 'shifting the burden'. In this way, it is easy, in Clark's words, to suppress the psychological crises that could be the cause of the environmental one. This then becomes a decision not solely about green building technology, finance, 'mathematical or analytic rules' but one that is a holistic evaluation of a system of complexity taking account of the future as a resource (asset) as much as an uncertainty (liability).

Out of this aspect, it should be possible to develop a strong argument to say that there needs to be change in the workings of the market and those in it, as well as those living off it more indirectly such as estate agents and data providers. The problem is not so much about not having the apt knowledge but about setting credible guidelines that would enable applying this knowledge.

Here, it should be noted that we do not always have to explicitly address sustainability concerns in order to touch the relevant issues at stake. Price (1993) argues that discounting (as an accounting practice and as a theoretical framework) is misleading at best and is detrimental for the society and environment at worst. He mentions the examples of the builders of the cathedral and the developers of the eighteenth century landed estates in England, who looked at the future rather than at the contemporary practices/ideals and how we appreciate them for that. While this critical discussion is not about sustainability, but about discounting future gains, Price makes this point clear: hundreds of years ago, the builders had knowledge that we do not have. These grand projects would have been unprofitable to build using present financial models, but we appreciate them for the boldness of the decisions taken at the time. The conclusion here is that, in some cases, the old-time practices of developing the built environment were more sustainable than today's counterparts. We indeed look myopically at gains as individuals, and we tend to say one thing and do the opposite; but to encourage doing this as a general model of behaviour without learning would be rather harmful for future generations.

Lack of Linkages to Any Belief System

If a buyer and a seller agree on a price based on supply and demand criteria, sophisticated techniques will have limited impact on their own. This book therefore also covers the issues of mindset. We cannot change a mindset – all we can do is to say that, to change the price to reflect sustainable issues, the societal value systems need to change. In other words, it is about education. It is interesting here to explore the potential differences emanating from the way an individual in the West is brought up to think (based on the foundation of Abrahamic religions) and how this compares with the Eastern thought. The influence of Sharia law, for example, has come to prominence in many parts of the world, but, equally, do behaviour patterns formed through Confucianism and Daoism, for example, impact on investment behaviour. Such thinking might explain in part the paternalistic central control economy that survives in some regions despite many injustices in the Western eyes. There has, of course, been much written about the Jewish (and subsequent Christian derived from the Graeco-Roman tradition) belief system and its effect on aspects of capitalism. Here, in this book, we consider how morality fits into belief systems and influences sustainable behaviour.

There is a view that late Western capitalism has severed links with any belief system apart from the technological fix and consumerism (disregarding former UK prime minister and latter-day peace envoy Tony Blair's conversion to Catholicism). The consequence of this might be that 'lacking a sense of the sacred we were doomed to a bad result' (Mander, 1992, p. 191), or as Zohar and Marshall (2004) suggest, 'it is only when our notion of capitalism includes spiritual capital's wealth of meaning, values, purpose, and higher motivation that we can have sustainable capitalism and a sustainable society.' (p. 4).

This 'lack of the sacred' may have aggravated the problem and caused an effective solution to be less readily attainable. However, it might seem, according to Zohar and Marshall, that capitalism itself is not the problem; it is the a particular model of capitalism that has been followed in the West which has certain specific flaws which have now become apparent over the last 50 years. Mahbubani identifies three of these as follows: (1) the West regards capitalism 'as an ideological good, not a pragmatic instrument to improve human welfare'; (2) 'for capitalism to survive, all classes have to benefit from it'; finally, (3) the promotion of this ideology to the people without acknowledging how to deal with 'the critical concept of "creative destruction"'. This aspect of continuous learning and renewal was downplayed and created redundant skills and redundant resources.

In contrast, the basic concepts of Daoism (one of the main belief systems of the East) are that 'the way is ever not doing and yet nothing is left undone' (Wu Wei), (Lao zi Chapter 37) and 'reversal is the movement of the way' (Fan Zhe Dao Zhi Dong), (Lao Zi Chapter 40). That is, Daoism teaches about opposition, contradiction and change. It acknowledges that the world is constantly changing and full of contradictions. In order to achieve one's goal, a person should stay or react in the opposite.

The impact of Confucianism has also influenced the nature of capitalism in the East. The Chinese term for moderation is 'Zhong Yong'. This is the doctrine of the Golden Mean and has the same meaning as 'nothing too much' in Greek (Lin 2002). 'It is used in moral philosophy to refer to moderation in all things, neither going to excess nor falling short of the mean' (Zhang, 2002, p. 329). In other words, 'moderation' means 'not extreme but harmonious' (Lin, 2002, p. 109), and the concept of 'moderation' has been a major influence on Chinese people. 'If one understands this application of the Doctrine of the Golden Mean, one can understand the whole game of Chinese politics [and business] in the last thirty years' (Lin, 2002, p. 113).

Both Confucianism and Daoism emphasise and share concerns about harmony and holism. The concept of harmony is the basis of Chinese philosophy, which is conspicuously different from the philosophy of the Greeks. This is because 'a peculiar but important aspect of Greek philosophy is the notion that the world is fundamentally static and unchanging'. They seek independence, and it is implied that it is possible to discover the Truth. Conversely, Chinese philosophy considers that the world is constantly changing and harmony is the most important issue embodied in it. It is a common belief among Chinese people that every event is related to every other event and that the universe is composed of two forces, namely Yin (feminine, dark and passive) and Yang (masculine, light and active). Every aspect and facet of nature is imbued with these two forces, which must be in balance, and this is called harmony (Lin, 2002).

Nisbett suggests that Japanese (in this case) ask 'how' questions, thus emphasising an initial event, that is, the instigator of what is now happening. So, they look backwards for explanation. On the other hand, Americans (in this case) ask 'why' questions, thus beginning with the outcome; that is to say, this is the goal we seek to achieve, now what do we have to do to get there! In these circumstances, an Eastern investor may not be concerned at all about where they are going, just see where events take them, that is to say, 'go with the flow'. On the other hand, the natural instinct of a Western mind might be more connected to be more future-oriented and be more fragile and perhaps fearful of changes that could occur to disturb what they have, that is, a natural resistance. This could materialise as an Eastern wide-angled view of life (any property decision affects the whole environment – uncontrolled) and a Western tunnel vision (any decision is based solely on property factors – controlled).

An interesting further observation is that Confucianism teaches a man to be a good citizen, that is, someone with a relationship with his fellowman and with the State. On the other hand, the Christian Catechism teaches 'the chief end of man is to glorify God'. That is to say, man 'should be a good man', with a very personal, individual aim without necessarily any relationship or identity with anything other than himself (apart from, of course, God). In other words, he does not necessarily have to be a good citizen. Equally, we suppose that the Eastern man does not necessarily have to be a good man. On that point, what is good, what is bad?

This line of argument has relevance in the present discussion because, if it is accepted that Western values are flawed under the existent economic model, then exporting this model to the East and other emergent markets will accentuate the fundamental deleterious impact it has on the natural environment and social structure as well as long-term financial health.

When we consider decisions taken over 30 years ago, traditional property valuation textbooks suggest a well-travelled road to value determination through a standard set of processes. The excited debate in the 1980s and 1990s over conventional versus contemporary valuation methodology and the corrections recommended by Mallinson following the early 1990s crisis represented little more than a sideshow. Running parallel were the Basel Accords (I, II and III) attempting to deal with credit risk, regulation, market discipline and stress testing. The solution had not been grasped, as demonstrated by the latest financial crisis. In addition, there has been another overlay which has been rumbling on independently since Our Common Future in 1987 and the first Rio Summit, 5 years later. This relates to issues with sustainability and environmental risk. It is only in recent years that these two strands (finance and environment) have been linked in any sense of the word, and although Basel III does not address systemic environmental risks, there are positive signs that indicate that environmental risk is seen as a threat to financial performance. This has become ever more important as new economies around the world start to emerge. So, in addition to the North–South dilemma, there is a West–East one which needs to be understood at the cultural level.

Concluding Remarks

The fundamental issue at the centre of this book is property value. Both finance and environment should play an important part in the determination of value. How this is achieved is addressed elsewhere, but this part of the book has attempted to reveal a gap behind the notion of value itself by suggesting that there are anomalies and paradoxes both in the concept of a market value and in the mechanisms in place to reflect externalities. So, for example, market value should be both a cognitive and a fiduciary standard. This part, however, identifies some 'magical practices' which may create bias in the former and eschew the latter. It questions the way in which we think about capital accumulation and value assets. Equally, there is a paradoxical situation between the environmental and the financial elements of any appraisal. Far from being independent variables, they have considerable interdependence, and this needs to be explicitly acknowledged and signalled within the valuation process.

This leads on to (1) questions on the nature of value and the interpretation of information; (2) dilemmas concerning short- and long-term time frames and the nature of forecasting together with the broad institutional framework and the more limited behaviour of markets and individual market intermediaries; (3) motivations need to be understood to signal levels of objectivity and strength of client influence in the interpretation of value.

While being a side issue as far as this book is concerned, it is difficult to deny the effect of the sustainable development paradigm on the development of humankind, when looking back at the last 40 or so years (since the first Club of Rome doom-mongering of the early 1970s). How would the world look without paradigms preoccupied with pollution control, energy saving or resource saving (including financial crises)? Would we be flying cheerfully outside the balconies on James Bond type of one-person helicopters? Would we have colonies on the Moon? In such a world, we might not remember what the proverbial 'saving for a rainy day' means. We probably would not have heard of ecological footprints, social cohesion or reinvesting wisely. As for the property valuation practice being carried out in this Brave New World, it does not even bear thinking. Here comes the crux of our argument: the future is yet uncertain, and we must take into consideration the worst-case scenarios when interpolating from the current situation marred by crises after crises, caused by irreversible decisions being made on our behalf by 'hidden persuaders', who have established 'the parameters of the discussion, even the parameters of thought' (Mander, 1992, p. 23).

On the other hand, we have some ideas of best-case scenarios as well, and the issue now becomes that of finding the most effective path towards reaching such situations. We need to move away from 'the strict imperatives of rational economic man to embrace a wider conception including new, collective-based sources of utility or welfare and dynamic preferences, linked to social norms, that can be altruistic or philanthropic … [however].... economic choices can still be rational when satisfaction is derived from sources other than short-term monetary gains for the individual'. (Daniels, 2005, p. 257).

Part 2

A Theory of Value in the Built Environment

2.0

Introduction

Peter Dent

In a world where money has become disembedded, individual nations have much less control compared to global enterprise over their ability to promote well-being. As a virtual, global resource, money is used to selectively allocate the means of development, and thus, to control the welfare of nations. In times of financial crisis, this allocative process pursues 'a flight to quality' which, over time, tends to exaggerate the gap between the rich and the poor. In this way, the more vulnerable (people, regions, nations, non-human) tend to be excluded (or, at the very least, marginalised) in favour of those with the power of control. In the context of built environment, this can have a significant impact on what is built, where it is built, how it is built and for whom it is built.

The question of environmental and ecological value has been examined by many authors (see, e.g. O'Neill *et al.*, 2008). In what follows, some of these notions are taken as a starting point to consider some of the 'economic' value theories and how these incorporate wider issues of moral perspectives within a monetary exchange. The term 'value' is also compared with 'price' and 'worth' to expose similarities and differences in order to try to understand how adequate monetary measures can be used alone in arriving at a 'sustainable value'.

This part of the book takes this debate further by asking the following important question: what are the value categories and for whom do they exist? Values can be quantitative (i.e. translated into some form of relative measure), attributive (i.e. identified in qualitative terms) or axiological (i.e. understanding values as both universal and local moral codes). From this starting point, it may be possible to understand the way in which sustainability can be incorporated into the overall property valuation process. This not only relates to the valuation of individual buildings but also includes landscapes, townscapes as well as traditional direct and indirect investment property portfolios.

Value in a Changing Built Environment, First Edition.
Edited by David Lorenz, Peter Dent and Tom Kauko.
© 2018 John Wiley & Sons Ltd. Published 2018 by John Wiley & Sons Ltd.

Property Ownership

In order to understand property value, it is first important to understand something about ownership and the purposes of ownership. It is fair to say that up until the modern era, production and the ownership and valuation of land and thus profit were inextricably linked. However, land ownership is now no longer in a crucial relationship with production, 'it does not in itself imply any control over the process of production'. Former landed estates were owned as integral parts of a wider role within communities, and although for this group, land ownership is still '…both the basis and the determinant of economic activity, and it is also firmly related to a particular conception of social relationships' (Massey *et al.*, 1978), but it is now a much smaller group than before. Two other forms of land ownership now predominate, particularly in urban environments. These are industrial (or commercial) land ownership and financial land ownership. These three make up the real-estate sub-markets: owner-occupier, user, investor and/or developer markets.

Interests in land in the case of industrial land ownership are held because it is a condition of production. 'The economic relation to landownership is consequently dominated by considerations of the relevance of particular characteristics of land to the process of production'. Land and building values are principally the premise of internal accounting rather than active transaction. On the other hand, financial land ownership operates 'through the medium of electronic communications and expert systems' (Massey and Catalano, 1978) as just another sector in which to invest. It has become a set of quality-less credits and debits rationalised by the market and based on a set text, largely unexamined range of criteria. What has also happened is that investment instruments have become more complex and specific. This is especially so with property derivatives where values are derived indirectly through indices (Leyston *et al.*, 1997).

We could speculate that, in the first case (i.e. landed estates), value is more axiological. Quantitative value has to be determined under certain circumstances, but the motive of ownership has a broader perspective; it performs a community role. There is a conscious identity with its environment, both social and natural. In contrast, institutional investors (i.e. financial land ownership) are holding property specifically for financial reward (both income and capital), and accordingly, quantitative value is crucial both from an accounting and a from transaction point of view. Of course, such holdings will still have some acknowledgement of the community, but this tends to be the broader, more disparate community of shareholders, policyholders, stakeholders and so forth.

In urban markets, industrial and financial land owners have come to dominate and set the rules. However, even those landed ownerships in the urban environment tend to seek maximum economic efficiency and to concentrate much more on the financial aspects of property holdings than either the attributive or the axiological sense of value.

Cognitive Economy

These senses of value (i.e. attributive, axiological and quantitative) define a way of seeing the world. They create an order that ranks the properties of land and buildings into a specific reality according to a particular view of the world such that a building can have a range of values (both quantitative and qualitative) based on the individual perceptions of elements or qualities that any one building might exhibit. Meaning, and hence value, '… is therefore relational in the sense that what an expression means is a function of its inferential/computational role in the person's internal system of representations, his cognitive economy'. (Churchland, 1989, p. 344).

This is the first step towards understanding how a quality such as sustainability relates to value. It is this cognitive economy that underlies all our actions and decisions, individually, corporately, nationally, culturally. The representations that make up this economy are derived from a person's upbringing or a market's sentiment or a country's history. In other words, we do not approach each day-to-day activity neutrally with a blank sheet of paper. We rationalise by positioning a good within 'a space of goods, in a system of differences and similarities, of distinct yet connected categories' (Callon *et al.*, 2002, p. 199). It is the dynamics of the market and the economic agents within it that will classify 'singularities and substitutabilities' of goods (Callon *et al.*, 2002, p. 201). These goods can be qualified and requalified based on levels of overall market activity, availability of finance, competition, need, external economic factors and so on. This re-qualification can happen unconsciously through changes in technology, aspiration, sentiment and so on, or it can be a conscious process through regulation and control. It will also appear to happen almost unilaterally as modern markets have been seen to be 'embedded in enduring networks, moral frameworks and chains of transactions' (Slater, 2002, p. 239). Under these circumstances, the notion of objectivity and 'arm's length' deals may be difficult to achieve particularly in the very specialist field of real estate. The market is determined more by the nature of the networks, their moral fibre and the tension between parties in the chains (both investors and occupiers).

Behavioural Characteristics

There is already a blueprint on which new experience is overlain. Decisions are guided by both internal and external determinants. We each possess 'a unique combination of mental and emotional characteristics' (Gibler *et al.*, 2003) which will influence our value perceptions and our decision-making. Internal determinants, according to Gibler and colleagues, include motivation, attitudes, perception, personality and lifestyle. Internal characteristics reflect and are reflected in a variety of external determinants of behaviour. 'Powerful forces construct social reality – parenting, schooling, television, advertising, dress code, corporate ethos, military drill' (McIntosh, 2002, p. 104). These external determinants include culture, social class, reference groups and family.

Both internal and external determinants can apply to individuals, corporates and institutions. They create the cultural environment within which values are derived. They will also influence the more broadly based moral behaviour and the barriers that decision-makers perceive as boundaries of ethical practice.

Moral Values

There is a sense that the holding of, and the free exchange of, property rights does create opportunities for social responsibility and moral growth. In financial markets, the latter has tended to take a back seat over the past century, but such universal rules of help to others and fairness (the basic tenets of morality) should not be denied in civilised society. However, the market mechanism would appear to be based simply on the exchange of goods, services, property and so on, for monetary reward. This again, on the face of it, would seem to be readily quantifiable. However, underlying the process of exchange is a series of value negotiations both between parties and within parties. Some are conscious, some are unconscious. Markets can be seen as social systems which exhibit their own value systems consisting of the following:

- An axiological value or interconnected axiological values.
- Rules, concerning links, which are considered obligatory, between values.
- Criteria of evaluation, that is to say, practical directions as to how objects, facts, properties and so forth, are to be classified, based on an adopted value principle or set of value principles.
- Rules of reasoning and argumentation adopted within the system (Najder, 1975).

Property sub-markets can be seen in a similar way. For example, rewriting Najder's four value system points to relate to property markets might look similarly to the following:

- Institutional frameworks and cultural analysis
- Market analysis and comparability producing local value determinants
- Valuation methodology
- International valuation standards.

Where these are underpinned by social responsibility alongside private utility, then both public and private costs and benefits as externalities can be included in real-estate solutions. So, for example, free exchange could enable moral growth in the following ways (Casebeer, 2008):

- Exchange environments can themselves evolve creatures that are prone to cooperation as much as competition.
- Exchange environments afford critical opportunities for cultivation of the classic virtues.
- Exchange environments afford incentives to develop and maintain moral standards.

The classic virtues here are those set down by Aristotle in his Nicomachean Ethics: courage, temperance, generosity, pride, good temper, truthfulness, wittiness, friendliness, modesty and righteous indignation. It could be asked, how relevant are these to the role of the present-day valuer? Well, most of them clearly continue to be instilled in Western culture. But they also underpin the ethics and code of conduct expected of valuers as outlined by professional organisations such as the Royal Institution of Chartered Surveyors (RICS).

How these are implemented in our daily lives can best be observed through Kohlberg's six-stage system of moral development as identified in the chapter on Gap Analysis in this book. This can relate equally to societies, individuals and markets, although its principal intentions are in the processes of human development from childhood to mature adulthood and citizenship. This system is interesting in the context of this part of the book as it highlights some of the wider concerns that exist in addressing the evaluation of sustainable features in real estate, particularly if overlain by risk scenarios (both cultural and individual).

Sustainable Decision-Making

Sustainability is a concern both inside and outside a building's physical shell. The risks of long-term unsustainability in the construction and use of buildings are of equal concern. Both sustainability and the risks of unsustainability embrace financial, social as well as environmental considerations. Valuation, equally, is concerned not solely with the physical building but also takes account of its technical specification, its location, its impact and so forth. Evaluative decision-making (the impact of risks and returns on value) is therefore set within a broader context than just a building, just a client or just a location. Those making decisions must also be consciously aware of morality within a much wider context, whether it be individuals, markets, professions, institutions or nations. In all cases, the 'relative' moral position is a mathematicised morality. In this way, 'risks are related directly and indirectly to cultural definitions and standards of a tolerable or intolerable life' (Adam *et al.*, 2000, p. 215). Somewhere in the process, the notion of well-being should be taken into account. Here, we are concerned with professional morality and the individual member's 'buy-in' to that morality. It might be that 'technocratic expertise is no longer sufficient to generate legitimacy and that it must be shored up by loftier ideals and practices' (Fourcade *et al.*, 2007). In other words, technical mastery of models and methods of valuation, for example, need a strong ethical foundation with effective global governance, and this should come from professional bodies and institutions working closely with governments.

Finally, to summarise, the remainder of this part of the book consists of two separate chapters which examine these issues in more depth. It starts by highlighting some thoughts on economic value and how value is distinguished from price and worth (Chapter 2.1). This leads into a Chapter 2.2, which takes a wider view of the term 'value'; it concentrates on the sense and categories of value.

2.1

Economic Value: Value, Price and Worth
Peter Dent and David Lorenz

> *...the subject matter of Economics is essentially a set of relationships –*
> *relationships between ends conceived as the possible objectives of conduct on the*
> *one hand, and the technical and social environment [means] on the other. Ends*
> *as such do not form part of this subject matter. Nor does the technical and social*
> *environment. It is the relationship between these things and not the things in*
> *themselves which are important for the economist*
>
> (Robbins, 1935, p. 38).

This chapter considers, in broad terms, some of the underlying principles behind 'economic' value theory, the market mechanism and the relationship between the economics of free enterprise (private gain) and moral sentiment (social benefit). The term 'value' is also compared with 'price' and 'worth' to expose the similarities and differences in order to determine if adequate monetary measures can be used alone in arriving at a 'sustainable value'.

The Dominant Economic System

Development is a 'mechanism through which a whole rationality was to be learned' (Escobar, 2005, p. 140). The Western economy has come to suggest a 'positive unconscious' for a particular type of development where rationality essentially represents private profit achieved through maximising an individual's goals in a market environment. In its mature form, the market formed within the Western economy '... implied, on the one hand, the full commodification of labour, land and money – and, consequently, the subordination of all social aspects to the laws of the market – and, on the other, the constitution of the economy as an autonomous realm, separate in particular from morality and politics' (Escobar, 2005, p. 144). In this system, order is managed through price. One consequence of this is that, not only do social relations become 'embedded' within the economic system rather than the other way round but also the social becomes subordinate to production and consumption. Morality becomes a kind of 'bounded' morality seen as an economic good and valued accordingly. Writing in the 1820s, William Thompson considered that 'the individualistic pursuit of wealth within a competitive market, whether that market be in a capitalist or a socialist society, led inevitably to five evils' (Hunt, 2003, p. 72). These were 'the principle of selfishness inherent in competitive rivalry', 'the systematic oppression of women', 'the economic instability caused by the anarchy of the market', the fact that 'insecurities of capitalism' would not be eliminated and finally, the market 'retarded the advance and dissemination of knowledge by making the acquisition of knowledge subsidiary to greed and personal gain' (pp. 72–73).

Whilst markets are probably more regulated today, some aspects of each of these 'five evils' still persist and may be inherent elements in any free-market-based system. These also relate to the three aspects of sustainability. For example, the oppression of not only women but also classes of society, cultures and nation states is a social aspect. Economic instability has recently arisen due to 'the anarchy' (i.e. disorder due to lack of effective governance) of the market which has exposed the basic insecurity of capitalism itself, even the mature systems of the most powerful Western economies. This highlights the lack of long-term financial sustainability. Finally, the environmental aspect, amongst others, is often hampered by vested interests seeking to capitalise on market shares by withholding information or delaying development. These could all relate to 'the principle of selfishness' in which case, it is important to consider ways to rebalance the activities of the market, not just through external control but also through a greater integration of moral thinking into the decision-making process. This would, of course, require a change of mindset.

Plato identifies three elements of an individual's mind which mirror the driving force of any system such as a state or its economy. These are (1) reason (the reflective element), (2) appetite (the irrational element) and (3) spirit (the enterprising element). These should be in balance in order to create a 'healthy city'. At the global level, we do not have that balance. The economic system has created a 'luxurious city' system (the North or Western economies) and an impoverished city (the South or Third World states). The neoclassical framework as developed in Western economies is based on 'the assumption of ubiquitous substitutability of goods' (O'Neill *et al.*, 2008, p. 102), i.e. the irrationality of 'rational man'. This is epitomised by the insatiable desire for more gratification and 'the pursuit of unlimited material possessions' (Plato, 1980, p. 123). These are the 'mad desires in the hearts of fools' (p. 412).

Whilst, on the one hand, this encourages entrepreneurial creativity, on the other, it also has a tendency to create an environment of self-seeking profit. To avoid the latter, some form of control or regulation needs to be in place in such a way as not to unduly deter the former. However, the 'invisible hand' might intervene; it seems that such a market system inevitably will lead towards 'an anthropology based not on needs and use value, but on production and exchange value' (Escobar, 2005, p. 157).

Rational Knowledge

Since Descartes, we have come to see ourselves as the subject of everything, relegating everything else to the role as object. This world view was maintained through science and economics. 'Rationality and reason, as the central myth of the secular scientific world, gave rise to the myths of objectivity, dualism, linear time, progress, utilitarian morality, economics, the work ethic, development, and the autonomous authority to discern absolute truth by reason and logic alone' (Raine, 2003, p. 80). The subjective knower was isolated from the world of objects, which, in turn, lost much of its meaning. That subjective knower decided what is knowable 'and what are the standards to be used to assess the certainty of knowing' (Escobar, 2005, p. 160). The process of colonising this world view has more recently been challenged both from the social and the environmental point of view. Whilst most emerging economies have adopted the Western view to development, many incorporate a more pluralist view, admittedly some more progressive than others, but all raising questions about the dominance of the Western model. These questions have been more acute since the overheating economies and the development of new debt-backed vehicles have created a world financial crisis.

Now rational Western man seeks to solve the problems of the world through the price mechanism without realising that 'certain kinds of social relation and evaluative commitments are constituted by particular kinds of shared understanding which are such that they are incompatible with market relations' (O'Neill, 2007, p. 25). Sustainability, in all its guises, is one such arena where monetary measure is constitutively incommensurate. It is not possible within an anthropology of technical production and exchange values to address the issues underlying either an ethical professional position or a more general sustainable lifestyle in an holistic way. 'From a neoclassical perspective, the source of our environmental problems lies in the fact that environmental goods are unpriced' (O'Neill, 2007, p. 61). This could be overcome through applying tradable property rights to environmental goods through shadow pricing or contingent valuation. However, sometimes, good decisions can be arrived at without a common measure to trade off costs and benefits. For example, traditional cost–benefit analysis does not take account of assumptions about differing perspectives on valuing life, levels of uncertainty and the status of the future (Aldred, 2009, p. 146). This might be the case with sustainability. According to Robbins (1935), '… value is a relation not a measurement' (p. 56). Value, in this sense, is a relative term which is not a number which measures material welfare but is, in his view, an expression of how best to use scarce resources.

Is sustainability an issue of philosophy, psychology or simply disciplinary technique? From René Descartes' dualism to Paul Taylor's interdependencies, from Richard Thaler's ideas on Prospect Theory to Krishnamurti's freedom from the known, from the standard valuation techniques to more complex qualitative as well as quantitative analyses, where does the truth lie? This is not just an economic problem, it embraces a whole range of disciplines, none of which should be isolated to create a bounded rationality which fractures the vital link to sustainable decision-making.

In order to understand this better, the next sections in this chapter concentrate on the key concepts of value, price and worth in an effort to explore the nature of valuation and its markets and to come to some conclusions which will form the basis of any models that are subsequently developed.

Value

Most of our conscious actions result from choice, and according to Najder (1975), valuations are among the most stable conscious determinants of motivation. He cites the following three basic senses of value:

- The quantitative sense, where value is an expression of what something is worth; translatable into or expressible by some unit of measurement or comparison.
- The attributive sense, where value is a valuable thing or quality; something to which 'valuableness' is ascribed.
- The axiological sense, where value is an idea which makes us consider given objects, qualities or events as valuable.

These senses of value overlap and coexist in acts, properties and things. In essence, axiological value is created through the institutional framework and culture of a society. In that sense, it becomes the fundamental principle which determines the baseline for both attributive and quantitative value. All three act as stimuli for decision and action. As such, none are wholly independent, all influencing each other in varying degrees at different points in time, under different circumstances.

In the context of property valuation, the term 'value' is usually attributed to the quantitative sense of market value. In this sense, value is market-driven, that is, the criteria used to arrive at an end figure are based on market evidence. Most often, this requires some form of comparative analysis based on known criteria or rational assumption. In the case of owner-occupied property, this will generally be on a capital value basis. For property held for investment purposes, the variables for comparison will be income streams and yields. Provided there are sufficient comparable transactions in the market place, the process of valuation is relatively straightforward. However, when dealing with special properties (i.e. due to design, location, use or internal configuration) or properties that have unique features or represent a new generation of facility, then comparability becomes less stable. This would be the case where new premises arrive onto the market having enhanced features such as energy efficiency, alternative energy sources and climate control efficiencies. Here, the valuer, upon arriving at a valuation, will need to review the assumptions in light of rental and yield expectations. Such factors might be seen as having no direct benefits over standard designs, and therefore, there will be no impact on value. Equally, those benefits or disbenefits may be considered to have an impact on the estimate of value. It is, however, the valuer's responsibility to provide a well-reasoned argument for the final opinion and to ensure that the client is made fully aware of the implications of acquiring or occupying this building as opposed to any other.

To perform their role effectively, valuers need to have a detailed understanding of all the facilities available in newly designed sustainable accommodation. This should not just be a 'tick box' exercise but should involve a detailed examination of the performance of the building over a period of time to demonstrate medium-term costs and benefits and how this may influence yield or rental movements. In the case of investors, it is a matter of matching both the risks/return criteria and the portfolio effect. For occupiers, it is a process which examines utility, ensuring that the premises provide effective accommodation for the working practices of the organisation.

We are at a crossroads in our understanding of value as it relates to property. At the general level, nothing changes. Value is an estimate of price. Valuers, as professional advisers, determine their estimate based on the market. Although most commentators believe that there should be a value differential between 'green' and 'non-green' buildings, reasoning for this is often muddled as though a label is sufficient to justify the premium on the sustainable model or a discount on the existing standard version. There, therefore, seems to be a gap in market information. If those in the industry believe that sustainability commands a differential then how this is understood and communicated through market price needs to be made transparent. Otherwise it could be argued that the market is not working efficiently. There could be many reasons for this: education and training, client pressure, inertia, intransigence, technical and transferrable skills. There may be others, but what seems to be clear is that either through legislation and control or through pressure from outside of the property profession, valuers need to ensure that they are proactive in understanding and explaining the consequences of sustainability on client properties. This applies to all aspects of sustainability, that is, financial, social and environmental. It also applies to the way in which the market integrates new values into the mechanism for decision-making.

The real-estate market as such is not organised in the same way as stock markets. It is not centrally managed but, similarly to stock markets, it works on the flow of information. Underlying that information flow is a foundation of ethics and values (in their wider sense) which create the framework within which advice is given and decisions are taken. As far as new technology in buildings is concerned, so far, these ethical values have appeared as conscious, sometimes almost evangelical, statements portraying an indisputable moral imperative to invest in and occupy 'green' buildings. The weight of this type of pressure rarely works in itself. Over time, change may become the norm, but, in the short term, there is often a sizeable negative reaction based on scepticism and resistance to change.

However, markets are not static. They are dynamic mechanisms that are based on attitudes and aspirations. They reflect objective truths which vicariously transmit cultural values. As such, markets can be seen as cultures in themselves, and valuers have an important role to play beyond simply reflecting current practice. As professionals, they need to seek out solutions that achieve more than short-term financial goals. By seeking a greater rationality in environmental and social exigencies as well as financial reward, valuers may be able to demonstrate longer term sustainability of business objectives.

This can best be achieved by considering markets as cultures in more detail. In this way, as suggested by Abolafia (1998), there are two main benefits. First, rationality is not taken for granted. Rationality is 'a community-based, context-dependent cultural form' (Callon, 1998, p. 74). In property markets, professionals, as part of the community, come to rely on specific tools to guide their decision-making. These tools tend to encourage 'herd-like behaviour' based on intuitive judgement.

Second, market rules and roles 'reflect power, status, and historical contingency (path dependence) in the market' (Callon, 1998, p. 75). These are not immutable but are there to be challenged. It is the role of those most powerful in the market to constantly seek to interpolate assumptions and question traditional thinking. This creates a dynamic culture which is constantly aware of the need to redefine problems and their solutions in line with emerging information, societal shifts and technological development. One of the issues here is the potential conflict between professional ethics and commercial client requirements. There is evidence that it is, in fact, the client who, to a large extent, governs the valuation process through power rather than the expertise of the valuer. Levy and Schuck (2005) categorise this power under four headings, that is, expert, information, reward and coercive and procedural. The strength of the influences, and hence the final outcome, depends on factors such as valuer integrity, importance of outcome to client and client size (Amidu and Aluko, 2007), lack of transparency and business culture (Chen and Yu, 2009).

Price

If the valuer advises on value, then it is the market that determines the eventual transaction price. This may, or may not, be the same as the estimated value provided by the valuer. Price becomes the evidence that is used in future analysis. However, it has been constructed; it is then deconstructed into its constituent parts to support future valuations. Prices are therefore used as objective measures of value. One of the problems with this is that prices are determined on the basis of imperfect knowledge. The market has levels of efficiency but is not perfect. So, eventual price is determined through 'pricing scripts' (i.e. a set of standard routines that operate as a form of cognitive manual for the variety of pricing decisions that need to be made). These are very often a combination of internal processes and software and external regulation. To an extent, the eventual price is also determined using 'reference values' (i.e. numerical values as integers or percentages for certain variables in the calculation). Whilst these aid the 'complex, multifaceted decision-making process' (Velthius, 2005, p. 118), they do not (and cannot) provide a price that takes account of every aspect of a building, its impact and its performance. These represent shortcuts (heuristics) to decision-making and are part of the culture of the market. In addition, as influencers, are confirmation bias, subjective opinion, perception, randomness and so on. 'Real markets are wild' (Mandelbrot and Hudson, 2004, p. 104); they do not operate similarly to a spreadsheet calculation. They are, however, normalised by the recognised techniques adopted by particular professional communities as standard procedure. Not only this, but also 'economics can shape behavior because it works in part as a norm for the agents in the market' (Guala, 2007, p. 152). So, an economic system learnt as part of professional training or academic study becomes part of the norm of the market. This would normally develop as part of a professional's experience, but essentially, it is unlikely to change radically in the short term, regardless of any cultural shift. In the case of a concept such as sustainability, a seven-stage psychological reaction can be identified as follows:

Stage One – Little response. There is a feeling that it is big and it is new and it is something that I don't understand. It worries me, but I don't plan to do anything about it.

Stage Two – Denial. I know how to value. Sustainability has nothing to do with my professional work. It's about sandals and long hair and crop circles.

Stage Three – Depression. God I'm depressed. All anyone seems to talk about these days is sustainability. I know how to value, but it seems there is growing pressure on me to include sustainable factors in my valuation.

Stage Four – Letting Go. OK I give in. My confidence cannot get any lower. I accept that sustainability is important to me as a valuer. I will have to see how it can be included in my valuations.

Stage Five – Testing. Well things don't seem to be so bad. I can simply adjust my spreadsheet by changing a percentage here and a value there plus add a bit of blurb to make it sound as though I am a sustainability-literate professional.

Stage Six – Consolidation. Whoops that did not work particularly well. I now understand the complexities of trying to calculate the impact of social or environmental goods in monetary terms. It cannot be done simply. I need greater understanding, and I need to approach the issue from a different perspective. This is more about time and space than I had first imagined.

Stage Seven – Internalisation, reflection and learning. I need to see the whole picture. My client wants the best financial deal, but to achieve that, we need to work with the environment (both natural and social) to gain the greatest return on the investment or to improve the viability of the organisation. All three (financial, environmental and social) must work together, and my client is relying on me to provide the advice in an integrated and holistic way. Perhaps, next time, by thinking sustainably, the pricing mechanism will not overheat, and we will be able to avoid another financial crisis.

Worth

An assessment of worth seeks to determine whether the market price for a property represents an over- or underpricing of the asset from the viewpoint of a specific owner or potential investor. In everyday terms, it is a means of determining whether the investment represents good value for money. The comparison with market price can then be used to facilitate the decision-making process on whether to buy, keep, sell or improve the asset.

Calculations are based on DCF valuation techniques, employing a forecast of income and capital receipts over a predetermined holding period. That forecast is then discounted at the owner's target return to determine the owner's assessment of the capital value of his asset. 'A key advantage of the DCF approach is that it provides a more accurate profile of value across the forecast holding period, enabling more critical decisions to be made' (Mansfield, 2009, p. 97). This accuracy, however, is only ever going to be as good as the inputs into the calculation. Most of the input data requires subjective judgement, and the foundation for this must be a combination of client requirement, an appreciation of the client's business, market knowledge, an understanding of building performance and the range of external influencers that, from time to time, will affect the variables.

The key elements to take account of and incorporate into a calculation of worth are as follows:

1) Target return.
2) Net income stream, determined by the following:
   - rent review and lease renewal dates,
   - potential voids,
   - rental growth prospects,
   - non-recoverable revenue expenditure.
3) Capital expenditure on improvements that enhance the market value of the asset.
4) The performance period.
5) The exit yield used to capitalise the income stream at the end of the holding period in order to find the price for which the investment might be sold.

Overtly, these demonstrate a process leading to financial sustainability for a single building which can then be incorporated into a more detailed analysis within a portfolio of properties, if necessary. This can apply equally to owner-occupiers and investors. Less quantifiable are the environmental and social sustainability attributes of the property under scrutiny. In Section 6.4 of RICS Valuation Information Paper no. 13 (RICS, 2009, p. 16–17), a series of questions were set out to guide the valuer in determining the impact of various sustainability issues. The following underlying question remains: if a company, an investing institution or a developer employs a valuer, what do they hope to gain? Is it simply a quantifiable value (i.e. a market value or an assessment of investment worth)? Or, is it a broader professional service? Who are the market makers? In other words, to what extent do valuers or property professionals more generally frame markets rather than just interpret them? If this is the case, then enframing a market does not happen just by 'employing methods of the classification or calculation that economics may provide' (Mitchell, 2007, p. 245). There also has to be an understanding of 'changes in market participants' value systems' (Lutzkendorf and Lorenz, 2011, p. 258). The problem is that, it is not easy to incorporate sustainability factors into a valuation without incurring the dangers of 'double-counting'. Attempts such as correction factors or lump-sum adjustments seek to separately quantify sustainability intangibles. This is potentially dangerous and, according to Muldavin (2010), should be avoided in favour of a more integrated approach.

These ideas will be explored in more detail in later chapters of this book, but, for now, it would be useful to return to the more fundamental issue of where sustainability sits within the market mechanism.

It seems clear that no one 'would be willing to finance a green building if it is not expected to generate economic benefits' (Galuppo and Tu, 2010, p. 143). Any argument in favour of environmental or social aspects of a building therefore has to demonstrate a viable financial case, with or without legislative regulation or control. This, in many ways, has been the reverse of what has actually been happening in the whole sustainability debate. The environmental issues have been highlighted as an intergenerational issue raising questions about the arbitrary way in which this generation discounts the resources available to future generations often seeking ways to recapitalise natural resources to maintain a balance in the ecosystem. This naturally raised issues regarding the socio-economic imbalance between the North and the South, Western economic models and emerging economies and so forth. This approach initially seems to have alienated the business community until recently, when it became clear that there is a business case for all three pillars of sustainability. It can affect the financial bottom line through '… brand enhancement, open up niche markets, and contribute to the "psychic income" of employees, understood as the non-material benefit or self-image of working a particular job, and can result in higher productivity and a lower rate of churn' (Kimmet, 2006, p. 2). Beyond this are CSR and SRI which have moved beyond the window dressing notions that they started as, to become powerful indicators of corporate value systems. The way in which information is handled and knowledge communicated is an important economic role for valuers to perform. If this does not happen, then, either an opportunity will be lost to engender a sea change in the way we provide and use accommodation, or this will go ahead, by other agencies leaving valuation consultancies wondering why there is no work!

More positively, research funded by the RICS considers that 'the entire property profession therefore has a significant part to play in fostering these emerging markets by informing clients as to the "direction of travel" with regard to the impact of sustainability' (Sayce *et al.*, 2010, p. 43). It also talks of 'a more detailed knowledge of the most important sustainability considerations' (p. 45) and 'a better understanding of how social values and third party interests interface with and influence market value' (p. 46). 'The real solution is to see a more fundamental change in attitude which leads to a behavioural change to complement the technical advances. This can only be achieved through the way in which we handle knowledge and develop a literacy of sustainability which informs the way in which we act' (Dent and Dalton, 2010).

Concluding Remarks

This chapter has addressed some of the frictions which exist between the three pillars of sustainability from a broadly economic point of view. It suggests that, first, there needs to be an acknowledgement that, whilst the issues of sustainability go beyond the individual property, there is a wider responsibility for those who own and use property to take an inclusive stance with regard to environmental and social issues. Secondly, sustainability is not separate from profitability; one relies on the other. It is therefore in the financial interests of property owners and users to act sustainably. Thirdly, this cannot be achieved by a 'tick box' mentality. What is needed is a change in the way we perceive our property and its impact on the environment. It is no longer effective in the twenty-first century to simply rely on Cartesian dualism. We have found the world to be much more complex than that. Holism, not division, should come from global thought. The RICS is probably best placed to lead the way in devising not only appropriate tools but also the professionalism that is needed to make the tools effective instruments of changed perception.

2.2

Sense and Categories of Value

David Lorenz, Peter Dent, Tom Kauko, Thomas Lützkendorf and Stephen Hill

In classic postulations about markets in general, four factors must be present for a property to have economic value. These factors are as follows: (1) utility – the ability to satisfy human needs and wants; (2) scarcity – the present or anticipated supply relative to demand; (3) desire – the purchaser's wish to have command over an asset; and (4) effective purchasing power – the ability of an individual or group to participate in a market (Appraisal Institute, 2001, pp. 28–31). However, in considering the particular markets for land and built property, this issue becomes somewhat more complex. Following Appraisal Institute (2001) and Gaddy and Hart (2003), property value is affected by the interaction of four basic forces:

- Physical forces including man-made and environmental externalities. Examples are climate; topography and characteristics of the land; natural barriers to future development such as rivers, mountains, lakes and oceans; primary transportation systems and public service amenities; and the nature and desirability of the immediate area surrounding a property (i.e. time–distance relationships between a property or neighbourhood and all other possible origins and destinations of people going to or coming from the property or neighbourhood).
- Economic forces including the fundamental relationship between supply and demand and the economic ability of the population to satisfy its wants, needs and demands through its purchasing power. Examples are availability of employment; wage and salary levels; the economic base of the region and the community; cost and availability of mortgage credit; the existing stock of vacant properties; new developments under construction; rental and sales price patterns of existing properties; and construction costs.
- Political and governmental forces which can overshadow the market forces of supply and demand. Examples are government controls over money and credit; local zoning, building codes and regulations, health and safety codes; rent controls and fiscal policy; environmental legislation; and restrictions on forms of ownership.
- Social forces including not only population changes and characteristics but also the entire spectrum of human activity. Examples are population age and gender; birth rates and death rates; attitudes towards marriage and family size; current lifestyle, lifestyle changes and options; attitudes towards education, law and order as well as other moral attitudes.

Property value arises and disappears in relationship to our needs. Along with an evolving knowledge and awareness that the maintenance of life and well-being depend – to a significant degree – on the environmental and social performance of buildings and the built environment, the links between the economic and non-economic (or more precisely, not yet 'monetisable') components of property value become stronger. To once again make a connection to the 'sustainable real estate' discourse, Goering (2009) predicts that, while in the United States, most commercial buildings lack any adaption or original building to energy or environmental issues, the growing number of LEED certified buildings will inevitable have impacts on the attractiveness of this group of real estate for investors as well as users. This is simply a logical conclusion based on the gradual reduction of uncertainty that is bound to occur through time (cf. Lorenz *et al.*, 2006; Eichholz *et al.*, 2010; Fuerst and McAllister, 2011). From this, it is clear that sustainability can be normalised within the value process and the impact of any building efficiencies can be reflected in the market value determination. Here perhaps, a wider issue, that is, decisions can be made related to private quantification, but still there are qualitative judgements that need to be considered based on a wider set of values and ways of moral reasoning.

Sense of Value

The question is, however, how far can all impacts be incorporated into a single monetary value? This section attempts to show that there is a sense of value which is broader than economic value. It embraces, among other value definitions, those attached to one's lifestyle and identity based on group belonging or individualism (cf. Kauko, 2004a,b,c). This is spelt out because the solution cannot come from economics alone. Insofar as this is about how to use different theoretical underpinnings to the current ones which are derived from Neoclassical Economics (NCE), this book seeks to deliver conceptual reasoning that goes beyond price. The main problem is that NCE has no explicit value theory (see Klamer, 2003). The argument about defining the relevant concepts behind value, market and sustainability is becoming more and more important and should embrace a range of disciplines. It is therefore important to combine different fields and topics.

In the simplest possible terms – or to use jargon from economics, as a 'reduced form equation' – value is determined by the interaction of the market forces of supply and demand. In order to understand value, therefore, it is necessary to appreciate the environment within which it is being determined. This involves an examination of the nature of the market and the players that create the supply and the demand. Then, of course, some consideration has to be given to the thing being valued. On the face of it, this is all very straightforward. However, there are hidden complications at every step of the way, not the least in understanding the depth and the breadth of the term value. In any exchange situation, the quantitative sense of value is part of the final decision deriving from a broader set of values embracing systems at different levels, that is, microsystems, exosystems and macrosystems. Values influenced at each level are responsible for shaping much of our intrinsic motivation (Kollmuss *et al.*, 2002). In the context of real-estate values, the valuer's role, as part of the exosystem, is to bring together the micro, property-specific data and the macro, institutional environment data in a meaningful and quantifiable way. It is evident therefore that this role is pivotal in defining the ground for decision-making.

At the beginning of the twentieth century, Sydney Smith asked the question: "What is value?" Once he had determined that it was not an attribute that could be measured by weight or volume, his initial conclusion was that it '… depends upon the desire of others to possess the thing to be valued, usually for the use that can be made of it' (Smith, 1912). In other words, it is valued for the net benefit that can be derived from its use, that is to say, its utility. As a physical asset, it has no value in itself (only a cost), but, as soon as that asset can be put to 'profitable' application, then an estimate of value can be assessed. One important question here is, how should profit be measured, and at what cost?

However, this ignores some important considerations. In the discussion about the assessment of value in business, Miller (2002) identifies the need to bridge the gap between 'quantitative elements' and the 'qualitative assessment' involved in understanding all that is around the business. This can be anything from brand name to boardroom, environment to ethics; but, in essence, it is what Miller calls 'entanglements' – the factors that influence and are influenced by the asset being valued. Of course, there have to be barriers as to how far a business sees itself 'entangled' by a particular factor, and valuations are therefore framed to restrict more remote or less significant externalities to intrude. In the case of property, it is easy to see how aspects such as environment impact can be left out of the frame in the valuation for a private client, unless there is an immediate deleterious impact. Equally, the attention to detail in a valuation for securitised property stock may be treated differently from property valuations for direct occupation.

It suggests that the quantitative elements (i.e. the yields, the cash flows, the outgoings, etc.) of the valuation process can be readily assessed to provide a value; the question is more about the validity of that value and the responsibility of the valuer in undertaking that valuation. Whilst there will be many qualitative elements backing up the variables and the comparators, there is still an arbitrariness about the qualities of data, of features, of impacts which should rely on more than individual judgement. There is an important role here for the professional bodies concerning values and moral reasoning, much talk, much less action. For example, raising the question on 'the accuracy and variation of property valuation', Amidu and Aluko (2007) indicated at the time that 'there is a growing recognition that the behavioural attitudes (i.e. in terms of decision making) of valuers may increase the likelihood of biased valuation figures' (p. 448). They go on to highlight the causes for this, including not following procedures, unexamined available information, influenced by other people's valuations, inadequate adjustment and client influence. This does suggest that the foundations on which valuation determination is based may need to be critically examined by the professional bodies to set the standards.

Categories of Value

The fundamental nature of market value is rarely interrogated despite the fact that the shakiness of these foundations can be shown using logical chain of conceptual arguments (but see Mooya, 2011). Kimmett (2008) laments the misreading of human action, as the courts merely make assumptions about the markets rather than look for a theory of value; he, furthermore, considers that the paper by Ruggles (1954) is to blame for the disappearance of 'a lingering value theory'; finally, he purports transparency and objective validation in order to make the valuation process more scientific. Ruggles (1954) notes the shortcomings of value theory in relation to empirical applications. Many of the commentators on Ruggles' paper are more cautious and moderate, however. Since the mid-1950s, hedonic and other models based on NCE have been developed into empirical frameworks where price and value are assumed to be the same. This status quo prevailed until the real-estate sustainability discourse began at the turn of the Millennium.

On the other hand, it can be argued that there always were gaps in the economic literature on value theory; thus, the real-estate economic literature is none too different on this point. In particular, economic rationality is taken for granted even though the reality may point to the opposite. This might, for example, be the result of an officially recognised cultural heritage status. To give an interesting anecdote, in the market for the traditional Jæarhus farmhouses (a rural property category from a specific region) in south-western Norway, a tighter building restriction (Class A), against all common sense, in fact means higher value than the ones with lesser restrictions (Class B). Class A cannot change as much as Class B and thus should, rationally, be appraised as a lower value property, but the opposite is true. The crux here is that while both classes of property have an antiquarian value, this is much more significant with Class A than with Class B! As a consequence, Class A also commands a higher price premium compared to Class B in the local/regional housing market. Hence, we have an art-market problem similarly to those described by Klamer (2003). In other words, less product flexibility generates a premium if it offers a greater sense of uniqueness at the marketplace – some call this a 'trophy commodity' or 'trophy property'.

To continue with the aspect of the artistic dimensions of an asset, the commercial offices designed by 'signature architects' is another case in point. When the two extreme positions of general appraisal are pure use value and pure aesthetic value, architecture is believed to be somewhere in the middle. Here, the research design contains both anti-equilibrium and pro-equilibrium arguments. According to the former view, future income streams cannot be connected to the work of art due to its complex and diverse system of values; according to the latter view, however, artistic dimensions of a real-estate asset may influence the willingness to pay (WTP) and, in this way, influence its equilibrium values as well. In fact, the latter argument is often used by commissioned architects to add realisable value to an office development, for example, by creating flagship buildings. This is connected to the conception of the use of a brand; indeed, the way the media comments on projects with signature architecture justifies this argument.

In a set of juxtapositions that follow, our general theoretical part poses two questions: What are the value categories? For whom do they exist?

Value categories (Fig. 2.1):

- Physical value: embodied energy (i.e. the amount of energy it takes to produce a green commodity; traditional green argument).
- Economic value: worth or market value.
- Value in use, functional value or serviceability.
- Existent value, social and cultural value and emotional value (Klamer, 2003: moral value) – these comprise non-monetary subcategories that do not amount to equilibria. For instance, Fusco Girard (2008, pp. 265–268) notes that ecobudgets 'promote a

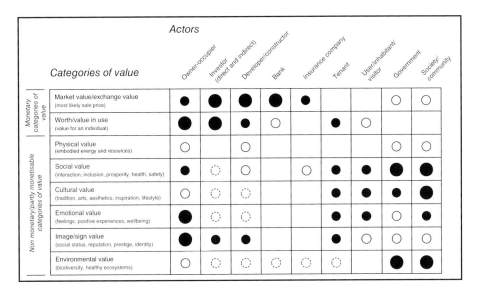

Figure 2.1 Value categories of buildings.

way of reasoning going "beyond" the economic or financial dimension, and capturing the whole set of values of the territory' such as use value and intrinsic value; that this tool is apt for assessing climate stability, air quality and beauty of landscape; that this would open a multidimensional way of thinking based on fluxes of material and energy; and also that social and symbolic values should be incorporated into this kind of valuation system.

- Antiquarian value (for being old), image or sign value (branding) – these comprise (at least partly) monetary subcategories that do not amount to equilibria (see the aforementioned point about signature architects). However, a heritage site has multiple values because different individuals or groups tend to see a certain place, or aspects of that place, differently; it might be that differently perceived values reinforce each other or lead to conflicts; furthermore, a typology for categorising 'a range of values that may contribute to the significance of a place' is seen as useful by Worthing and Bond (2008, pp. 76–79). The important point here is, however, that our changing social perceptions constantly impact these values, which necessitates a frequent reappraisal of these values as the values are a time-varying social construct (Worthing and Bond, 2008, p. 80; cf. Klamer, 2003).
- Environmental value or extended (expected) benefits of environmental or ecological quality (modern-time 'green' argument). Worthing and Bond (2008, pp. 81–92) then offer interesting cases of how heritage features are appraised based on their inherent qualities as well as some widely accepted ones.

Value for whom:

- society/government (on all levels)
- investor (direct and indirect)
- developer (may include the constructor)
- bank/insurance

- broker/agent
- owner-occupier (most important for residential property)
- tenant (most important for commercial property)
- user/inhabitant (clearly distinct from the tenant).

Figure 2.2 expands on this issue by showing the components of value creation and development together with an explanation of the economic, environmental, social and cultural categories of value and its measures. From this, it is possible to observe that, ideally, the 'enlightened' developers, government and investors should maximise the use

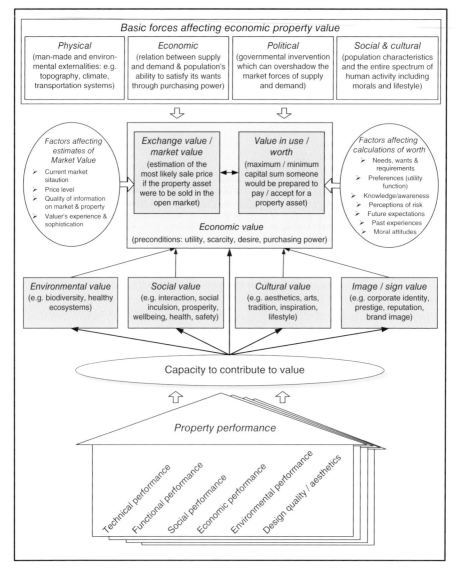

Figure 2.2 Value map.

value. However, currently, the same actors tend to minimise this value, apart from a few notable 'enlightened' – or rather, 'adaptable' or 'successful' – exceptions. In the United Kingdom, at least Urban Splash, IGLOO and ISIS are such corporations, (see Bryson and Lombardi, 2009). Others worth mentioning are Sweden's Sweco sustainable city, Shanghai's Dongtan Island 'eco-city' and projects by the US-based developers Durst and Time Equities Inc. – although the United States otherwise is seen as a laggard country in this respect (see Goering, 2009).

Depending on both the position within the value chain and the individual and institutional motives and goals, different market actors develop different value systems and measures and focus on different aspects of a property's value. These range from a focus on economic value and functional value (value in use) over cultural value to notions of emotional and sign value (see Fig. 2.1 which gives a brief overview on different value categories of buildings and indicates different degrees of relative importance for various groups of actors within property and construction markets). Finally, these different value systems and measures influence the market participants' WTP and, thus, the economic value of property assets in the market place.

To sum up, this is about extending the value and market framework towards long-term and non-economic factors. In doing so, we inevitably connect with the sustainability debate. Whilst, as is implicitly argued through the text so far, ideally, this debate is transdisciplinary, it may, in the first instance, be possible to restrict it to traditional cross-disciplinary thinking in both a given market and non-market setting. It is, at the end of the day, about our particular belief systems and the gaps that exist between short term value assessments and long term sustainable environments. We have now sketched a picture of our proposition, and further thoughts on this will be made in Part 5 after the research methodological–technical part (3) and the empirical–practical application part (4).

Part 3

Valuation Methodology

3.0

Introduction

David Lorenz, Tom Kauko and Maurizio d'Amato

Valuation is an activity with a well-known and approved methodological framework. As all human sciences, it operates in a dynamic environment. This raises several problems and challenges in the application of valuation and consultancy. Following the International Valuation Standards (IVS), the main valuation approaches accepted at international level are based on (1) market, (2) income and (3) cost. Although the differences in methodology prevail, appraisal remains a professional activity based on comparison. The final output will be an opinion of value that should be considered different from the output of an AVM/mass appraisal activity normally defined as *estimated* value.

The first of the aforementioned approaches is normally applied when it is possible to find a sufficient amount of comparable transactions. The most important method is based on sales comparison and can be developed having three to five comparables. It consists in adjusting transaction prices of comparable properties using a set of characteristics (elements of comparison) to determine the price of a property (subject).

The second method usually works with a lack of comparable transactions. It approximates the market value by assuming a direct relationship between market value and rent. Normally, if the rent is infinite, this type of method is called *direct* capitalisation. In the event of limited rent, this method is usually defined as *yield* capitalisation. Finally, there is discounted cash-flow analysis and real option modelling.

The third approach is the cost approach. Normally, it is applied when neither real-estate market transactions nor income information is available. Here, the value is computed as the sum of the value of the land and the reproduction/replacement cost of the improvements minus time-variable depreciation of these structures.

Value in a Changing Built Environment, First Edition.
Edited by David Lorenz, Peter Dent and Tom Kauko.
© 2018 John Wiley & Sons Ltd. Published 2018 by John Wiley & Sons Ltd.

As already made clear in the introduction of this book, the need for adjusting, rethinking and modifying the described practices stems from the following problems:

- Boom–bust periods resulting from market cycles
- Difficulty in gathering data for the valuation exercises
- Difficulty in organising such data when available
- Difficulty in integrating sustainability thinking into the valuation procedures.

All these problems make the valuation context particularly difficult. Is it at all possible, therefore, to explore alternative paths to deal with the challenges described? Intuitively, the more number of tests we perform, the likelier is the progress in methodology, and more reliable will be the appraiser's final opinion of value. Furthermore, better valuations equal a more stable economic system; this is especially true after the mortgage crisis. This part of the book therefore shows the various improvements that can be achieved by following alternative approaches to the same problem.

The remainder of this part of the book comprises three chapters, each of them covering a specific property category. First, Kauko presents an alternative framework for residential valuation. This chapter shows the richness and variety of value analysis approaches and methods. Then, d'Amato moves the discussion onto commercial valuation and presents an alternative approach to risk premium determination and a new approach to AVM based on DCF. Finally, Renigier-Bilozor and Bilozor evaluate the significance of land attributes for land use and developable land. Their proposition for methodological improvement here concerns the use of Boolean logic to address the problem in determining the different land-use types.

3.1

Aspects of Residential Value Analysis Methodology

Tom Kauko

One of the overarching themes of this volume is that we are living in an increasingly real-estate-dependent world (bank crises, environmental and energy issues and so forth) where market value is a key concept. However, this concept can only be approximated, and therefore, appraisal (valuation) is very important. This issue is partly technical and partly sociopolitical. Valuation by definition is about accuracy and cost efficiency. It is, on the other hand, just as much – if not more – about ethical considerations and value systems in a broader context than real-estate economic arenas.

In Part 1 of this volume, we discussed the normative role of valuation. By that, we refer to ideas on how to encourage 'twitching' of value towards a sustainable track and about 'the will to overcome inertia' in the valuation profession: the need for new tools and models that would incorporate trend smoothing and ethical considerations. In Part 2, we moved to set an outline of value types and for whom these simple monetary or multidimensional values are meant. This chapter is based on mass appraisal issues, based on the two aforementioned background discussions. The questions to ask include the following argumentation: What is the ideal definition of sustainable development in a valuation context? Is it about the diversity of value systems (let us call this Argument 1a)? Or, is it about long-term thinking in terms of reinvesting the profits harvested (Argument 1b)? What is the role of generating data on these factors (Argument 2)?

The chapter starts with three claims about sustainable residential valuation, in a mass appraisal setting: firstly, value/valuation impacts the market and vice versa, market always impacts the valuation through an ongoing feedback process; secondly, the importance to address the ethical side of the valuation and thirdly, issues concerning the need to smooth the peaks and lows of the market cycle. From this, it follows that a differentiation of preferences and sometimes also of supply-side processes and a long-term view are crucial when estimating value. While a variety of methods and data sets already exist for this, the requirement for improvement of methods and data sets remains.

Introduction

The current global economic downturn has revealed the need for new tools of property value analysis. Or, to use the old ones more responsibly than hitherto by incorporating issues that are likely to be important in the years to come. Indeed, while we have seen the advent of an econometric equilibrium modelling tradition of verifying premiums for green or sustainable price or rent premiums (see e.g. Fuerst and McAllister, 2011; Eichholz *et al.*, 2010), it could be argued that the aim here ought to go beyond merely factoring in new things in old models. Accepting this argument, the issue becomes that of how to validate and calibrate the models, that is to say, how to adjust the parameters of the operational model. However, the present contribution proposes another research strategy, namely to look at a higher level of analysis where market signals and structures are the main target of the analysis rather than technical issues in relation to estimation. This would furthermore enable us to shift towards a normative analysis, as suggested elsewhere in this volume. The normative element could, and perhaps should, focus on two important criteria of any valuation exercise: first, the ability to smooth the high peaks and lows of the price trend; and after that, to add some ethical considerations about the outcome, as to whether the result of the valuation is likely to stand against critical examination in terms of its broader economic, social and environmental consequences.

When we can aptly manage the smoothing procedures, we may convincingly argue for a normative role for valuation. Following the precautionary principle, benefit–cost analysis is never enough; in the case of uncertainty and with irreversibility, ethics is required as well [see Vatn (2005), Mooya (2011) and our contribution in Part 1 in this volume]. Three issues stand out here:

First, any 'valuer' does indeed impact the market and the sales price throughout 'hands-on' attempts – even the simplest ones – to arrive at the value. Here is a personal example: I recently bought a flat, and to be able to give an offer price, I looked at the sales statistics of similar flats in the area. I calculated an average price, then adjusted it for the particular circumstances so as to form an opinion and, finally, was able to propose a feasible price offer, which subsequently was accepted as the true one by the agent but more importantly by the seller as well.

Second, ethical aspects are important; it can be argued that by paying more attention to the ethical aspect of valuations (during the years leading up to the market peak in 2007), the financial crisis could in principle have been avoided. As we need to steer the investments on the right track, the valuers (as other professionals) do have a social responsibility as well (see Mooya, 2011). The fact that such connections are lacking traditionally is not an excuse (see Parts 1, 2 and 5 of this volume).

Third, despite the conventional wisdom, the reality is that market peaks and bottoms need smoothing. To give an example[1]: a valuer gives a value of 200,000for a property which also is sold for this price. Subsequently, the credit market conditions change and the value falls to 150,000. Mainstream/NCE theory argues that the current value is still correct. However, we argue that the value should have been set lower than 200,000 in recognition of the fact that this value – as any value plausibly – is the peak value. The valuer has a responsibility to hold back some of the bubble building by increasingly underestimating the value when the price trend is increasing; the opposite is necessary when the same trend is declining. This is the value stability argument that also connects with the sustainability agenda (see Kauko, 2010).

---

1 This example is originally given by a referee after unsuccessfully submitting an earlier draft of this paper to a journal.

This chapter is mainly about residential property and addresses the following two themes:

1) Explanation of different valuation methodologies: monetary and non-monetary approaches; methods for valuing individual properties and methods for data analysis and mass appraisal; traditional and alternative; direct and indirect; and so forth.
2) The broadening scope of property market analysis; that is to say, how examining the price development (i.e. value stability) helps us tease out the economic sustainability element, when related to an element of market environment – physical, social or other aspect thereof. In this context, the ideal definition of sustainable development is related to the diversity of value systems, long-term perspectives and data issues. (See Chapter 4.2 in this volume.)

The discussion that follows draws on prior contributions by the same author: In Kauko (2001), the generation of value was abstracted and tied to the broad urban economics and planning literatures. Kauko (2004a,b) in turn addressed 'multidimensional value' and provided some evidence with the analytic hierarchy process (AHP). Lastly, Kauko (2008a,b) and d'Amato and Kauko (2008) addressed 'sustainability issues' within real-estate economics/management in cross-disciplinary, albeit rather speculative and home-grown manner. The summary of these contributions is a three-category typology of methods in relation to data (as discussed in the previous section):

1) Mainstream (hedonic regression with developments). Statistics in a parametric distributional sense, which then validates the hedonic model
2) Other statistics and those techniques which are a bit alternative but quantitative (nonlinear, pattern recognition and so forth)[2]
3) Alternatively, based on qualitative/hypothetical data, that is to say, judgemental, possibly more qualitative approaches (e.g. the multi-attribute value tree):
   • When we need different information, that is to say, new variables (e.g. to allow for the long-term view as noted earlier)
   • When we do not have information even of the standard variables (in particular, transaction prices).

Conceptualisation

The overarching question here is as follows: why the authors of residential valuation literature do tend to focus on quantitative methods, and is there other, more qualitative-method-based research at all? The answer arguably has to do with credibility and conservatism. While the hedonics have been criticised long before the crises, alternative approaches are not widely adapted among academics.

There has not really been much research on the performance and validity issues in alternative methods and techniques since the late 1990s, thanks to the paradigm gatekeepers who protect their own interests and, obviously, strive to preserve the inertia in the field. It could be argued that any kind of work in this direction falls outside mainstream valuation research in a time when valuation research in itself – even mainstream one – is relatively unfashionable. However, we can hope that the (near) global property

---

2 Some of them comprise high level mathematics (see e.g. Mu *et al.*, 2009).

market collapse of 2008 and the ongoing financial crisis might change this situation, as the public has lost faith in the conventional ways of determining the value and its likely development. In addition, the inertia of funding organisations plays its part. Nonetheless, some more qualitative research is conducted as well. Mostly, it is in relation to sustainability and heterodox economic arguments (see e.g. Canonne and Macdonald, 2003; Dent and Temple, 1998; Diaz, 1998). Unfortunately, such research undertakings are still seen as maverick activity.

The methodology might be pragmatic instead of formal, but that is not the point here; the point is to avoid an artificial separation of dimensions – even though it hitherto has been the standard approach. We furthermore encourage looking at the location more than so far when considering its value share against that of the building.[3] In doing so, a further emphasis is placed on the behavioural and institutional elements. It then is justifiable when Goering (2009, pp. 190–191) asserts that community participation might be such an issue to include in the planning and implementation; he also proposes links to be tied between rating systems and smart growth planning. In general, the location issue is usually more complex and involves more interfering factors compared to the building issue (see Kauko, 2002). In other words, methodological holism, rather than reductionism, is required.

Inspired by Renigier-Biłozor (2008a) and the original ideas by David Lorenz, Kauko (2008b) noted that, data and technical problems notwithstanding, the methodological underpinnings (involving value theory) pose a challenge for valuation. It may be that unidentified and spatially, unevenly distributed externalities caused by technical and political changes need to be corrected in order to guarantee the sustainability of future valuations, which prompts us to look at the value as a multidimensional concept.[4] It is a reason to believe that in the future, various social, environmental, ecological and health criteria will have an impact on what is considered to provide an added value or a penalty deduction in value for a given property subject to assessment.

In the environmental valuation/economics literature, Gregory *et al.* (1997), among others, have argued that one cannot place several value dimensions under one and the same measurement, and as a consequence, multi-criteria decision modelling (MCDM) gained credibility since its use, compared to the contingent valuation and other one-dimensional monetary valuation methods as the benchmark. However, some problems still persist with this approach, especially related to context effects. These are well described in relation to behavioural and experimental economic research, such as yes-saying and protest bids (Vatn, 2005). An account of current achievements of this strand of modelling within valuation studies is given by Diaz and Hansz (2010); these authors manage to confirm a positive bias in valuations of residential property

---

3 Which one is more important then for the investor behaviour – location or the built structures? At a more global scale a reasonable aggregate would be 50% for each, but this balance in particular is context dependent. For example in urban housing market 'hotspots' (i.e. the most appreciated quarters) the location is much more appreciated than the structures, but in derelict brownfield areas as well as for rural property it is the other way around: land being of a minuscule – sometimes even negative (cf. Jones *et al.*, 2009) – value compared to the built structures. Another issue is that traditionally, sustainability analysis is biased towards the built structures, but this is largely because data on the quantitative and qualitative characteristics of the buildings often already exists readily in registers, or in any case, is relatively simple to collect, whereas corresponding data on the location does not exist and tends to be more difficult to collect. In an attempt to correct this deficit the present study therefore looks at the location.
4 Interestingly, this resonates with Klamer's (2003) account within general economics.

when they compare two groups of 'actual, real-world appraisals' to those with 'no incentive/pressure to over-value' and the ones with 'incentive/pressure to over-value'.

To continue the enquiry a bit more philosophically, the following question is asked: which one is better: statistical patterns of the past or subjective belief in projected future trends? The paradox is that value is about the latter by definition, but we tend to arrive at it using the former approach. Why is that so? It is because 'classic scientific ortho-doxy' requires it. However, there are some real helpful rational statistical approaches: for example, the less well-known residual modelling approach, where the lack of knowledge and sudden market changes are captured from the model residuals (see Renigier-Biłozor, 2008b). Otherwise, the author's take on the situation is that the valuation methods lag in the practical arenas because valuation theory is underdeveloped. To take a liberal stance here, all kinds of methods, and especially when combined into an automated valuation model (AVM), can be justified – with critical reflection of course.

Arguably, the right direction for the development of analysis of property value is to shift the focus from designing computationally extensive modelling tools for improving the accuracy of value predictions to better cope with particular market circumstances (see Kauko, 2008a). The accuracy would then concern ascertaining of the underlying cir-cumstances rather than unrealistic precision in the value estimates (we come back to this later). We must remember that mass appraisal is not the same as individual valuation. It can, furthermore, be argued that context is an important precondition to be taken into account when selecting/designing valuation methodology in relation to specific changes in the market environment. The point of departure is that we have traditional valuation methods, on the one hand, and more alternative methods for valuers to make judge-ments, on the other hand. There is another divide in perspectives, namely we also need to examine two different groups of procedures: group (1) concerns direct comparison of known cases; group (2) concerns hedonic regression or other type of indirect valuation methods and techniques that are necessary to inform about coefficients and adjustments for group (1), by the application of a statistical or mathematical model. Table 3.1 illus-trates this partition into four methodological categories.

Moreover, as valuation analysis, today, is a relatively well-established field, the issue becomes even more important for the emerging, and yet data-poor, sustainability (or sustainable development) analysis field.[5] Value can be sustainable or unsustainable with respect to a given criterion and to a certain degree. It can, for example, be about quality, affordability or product diversity. A number of different definitions are used (cf. Jones *et al.*, 2009; Kauko, 2009b). We may, for example, select a specific definition such as property value stability. The requirement of value stability connects with the idea of

Table 3.1 Categorisation of methods.

	(1) Direct	(2) Indirect
Traditional	Comparative sales	Statistical model
Alternative	Judgemental valuation	Mathematical model

5 Based on the EXPOReal in Munich, 2008, my impression was that the ideas of sustainable real estate in general are much better accepted and developed by commercial real-estate practitioners than by academia!

a certification system [proposed, among others, see also Goering (2009), Runde and Thoyre (2010)]. However, at the detailed level, it is yet to be defined whether this issue ought to be included within or outside the certification system. In other words, within the new value model, both conceptually and in the calculations, or alternatively, to keep value stability as a separate element to take into account afterwards? Thus, we have two possibilities: one, to determine what is a 'sustainable value' based on a model where a value stability variable is also included (thus, adjustment parameters are considered within the model); or two, to decide it as an external issue only after such determination. When selecting the adjustment system, care should be exercised. In the words of Runde and Thoyre (2010, p. 240): 'Care must also be taken not to double count green features where adjustments are already being made. For example, proximity to transit (site efficiency), might already be inherent in the appraiser's generic "location" adjustment.'

Methodology

It is largely accepted that the seller-driven development is able to influence the consumer preferences and the consumption patterns, although, ideally, it should be the other way around: producers being motivated to mirror the expressions by the consumers (see e.g. Galbraith, 1999). One of the classic key problems is, therefore, how to integrate the prospects of the consumer to the prospects of the producer? On the one hand, this shift towards development strategies that truly are sensitive to the buyer preferences arguably has begun to emerge in some Western European contexts. On the other hand, when looked from a global perspective, such a paradigm shift from a seller-driven to a buyer-driven market environment does not occur everywhere. For example, early evidence from ongoing work suggests that, in Hungary, the new gated-community-like developments (residential parks) are almost completely seller-driven.

The crux here is that the nature of the market varies across different institutional and geographical circumstances. It can be argued that the minimum fulfilment of an adequate approach to valuation methodology comprises an informed view of the residential market mechanisms. This necessitates comprehending the following five main elements:

Detailed analysis (i.e. argument 1a): If aiming at a detailed analysis of market for property products and locations, it is important to incorporate a diversified process/dynamic view for the demand side: that is, diversified and changing preferences of buyers and renters as well as intermediaries need to be recognised, even if the variation momentarily is modest. Market value is indeed a fragile concept (Mooya, 2011; cf. Klamer, 2003; and Stuhr, 2003, in general economics).

The long-term situation (i.e. argument 1b): If the long-term situation is the topic of analysis, it is similarly important to incorporate a diversified process view for the supply-side analysis (sellers, investors, builders, developers, planners, etc.); for shorter terms, merely a diversified static view suffices. (i.e. dynamics then only pertains to the demand side.) Related to this argument, Mooya (2011) goes as far as to suggest that value always is emergent and contingent and therefore requires a 'Heraclitean' becoming ontology rather than the 'Parmedian' being ontology applied hitherto thanks to logical positivism and NCE.

Long-term diversification and dynamics equals sustainability: As long as the market analysis concerns the long-term situation, economic sustainability becomes a natural issue. It is to observe that, due to the context-dependent normative element, here, it is particularly important to look at diversification and dynamics of how regulations vary and change.

Data on market sustainability (argument 2): The aforementioned arguments all suggest that, analysis of the market and sustainability poses huge challenges for the production and evaluation of data sets (as was argued in Introduction and Part 1) – even more so, if non-economic dimensions are included.[6] We, nonetheless, expect market actors to generate such data and make it available for analysts.

The change towards sustainable markets is uneven: As per the previous conclusion, the analysis always needs to begin from the institutional, behavioural or geographical context, then select the methods based on the available data (rather than the other way around: screen the data based on positivism/NCE assumptions). In other words, one should proceed bottom-up and employ the richness of empirical material instead of trying to fit all circumstances into the same mean-based model or methodology. As argued earlier, sustainable valuation necessitates adding dimensions and taking the longer term perspective.

Thus, the question is as follows: what kind of scope exists for incorporating these five points of improvement? When developing the argument, the aim here is to delve into the specifics of the valuation methodology and, in doing so, to create a link between market analysis and sustainability assessment.

Mooya (2009) proposes an alternative theory of market value for valuation purposes that is based on the new institutional economics (NIE) perspective of transaction cost minimisation. According to Mooya, this is prompted by 'a lack of intellectual progress' (cf. Lützkendorf and Lorenz, 2005; Lorenz *et al.*, 2006), and amidst discovery on 'newer, esoteric approaches' having 'limited uptake', this is largely due to limitations in practical feasibility (cf. d'Amato and Kauko, 2008). Furthermore, Mooya notes the possibility that methods of inefficient market valuations might have a wider significance in the development of state-of-the-art methodology (cf. d'Amato and Siniak, 2003, on Belarus; Kryvobokov, 2006, on Ukraine). Moreover, it is probably true that viewing valuers as 'score keepers' who do not influence the prices (i.e. the conventional view) in particular is a questionable assumption. Indeed, here is a reason to take on board some propositions of social theory concerning the interaction between the influence of the observer and the social environment. As the valuers affect the values in any case, their normative role needs to be made explicit! As Mooya rightly notes, 'the market on which property valuation theory is based does not exist'. It is also agreeable that, as 'valuation accuracy' is always unrealistic to narrow down, the 'valuation variation' should be a more rewarding valuation exercise and a worthwhile scientific endeavour (cf. d'Amato and Kauko, 2008). Moving along the route from 'valuation accuracy' to 'valuation variation', it is wise to keep the following comment (made by Peter Morris, principal of the construction consultancy Davis Langdon, Business Week, 16 March, 2009) in mind:

---

6 That is to say, ecological, environmental, social, cultural and so on; see Klamer (2003).

> If you look at the etymological root of the word accuracy, it means honesty, not precision. It may be more accurate to say, "I don't know," than to give someone a number.

To see the need for a paradigm shift away from the notion of reducing 'valuation accuracy' towards that of reducing 'valuation variation' within this realm is easy to understand. However, whether the transaction cost perspective really provides the best possible theory for this paradigm shift is yet unsure. While being innovative, Mooya's (2009) analysis does not provide a completely new line of argumentation. It is also worth noting that the particular remedy suggested, NIE, is still based on the principles of 'economic man'. Nonetheless, what is interesting in Mooya's study is its practical aim rather than the often-heard criticisms of neoclassical economic value market/theory – well-founded arguments in themselves, of course.

In contrast, the methodological approach emphasised in this chapter, to a great degree, draws on two schools of thought within social sciences as it merges old institutional economics (OIE) in its realist interpretation (see Vatn, 2005) with behavioural property research (see e.g. Daly *et al.*, 2003). However, it has to be mentioned that studies concerning fundamental differences between value models are relatively rare.[7] Some examples of different methodological innovations based on residential property or land sales are listed as follows.

Mainstream Methodology: The Effect of the Size of an Apartment on Its Price: In a hedonic modelling study by Frew and Jud (2003) from Portland, Oregon, it was found, among others, that a 1% increase in square metre per dwelling unit increases the price by 0.5% or 0.3%.

Mainstream methodology: The negative externality effect of location on price – Case *et al.* (2006) applied a hybrid repeat-sales/hedonic approach for the valuation of an environmental externality, namely groundwater contamination using a panel data set of 13,600 condominium sales over a 19-year period (2 years before and 17 years after the contamination had begun) in Scottsdale, Arizona. They found that the contamination effect is real and time-variant: first, growing, and then, after a number of years after the event, declining.

Mainstream methodology: The negative effect of foreclosures on price (example of institutional effect) – Using a hedonic model (with neighbourhood controls and spatial autocorrelation) and exceptionally large data set (98,828 sales plus 23,334 foreclosures and liquidations in St. Louis County, Missouri), Rogers and Winter (2009) found that the number of foreclosures in the neighbourhood reduces the single-family home sales prices with varying magnitudes depending on the model.

Demand effects – Daly *et al.* (2003) argue about a behavioural paradigm in residential valuation, in order to combat severe problems that mar the credibility of the mortgage/lending industry. They argue that consumer preferences and qualitative elements need to be better included in the value modelling used by a professional valuer. Thus, the driving logic of the methodological advance ought to shift from the traditional

---

7 In fact, from a property valuation and market value theoretical point of view, the distinction between OIE and NIE does not have significance beyond a few concepts, notably market segmentation and sub-markets (see Watkins, 2008) and 'value creation' (see Kauko, 2009a).

supply-side criteria and loan company policy towards demand-oriented motivations and also scientifically grounded evaluation of an economically sustainable valuation process.

   Comparison of rule- and case-based methods – Gayer *et al.* (2007) carried out an interesting test on the nature of the house price formation in the rental and owner-ship market: they hypothesised that the price formation is rule-based for ownership, whereas it is case-based for renting. This would occur because of the speculative nature of the former as compared to the latter. Thus, ownership of a home would be based on some simple, linear rules, but renting one's home would be based on comparable evidence of numerous cases that cannot easily be conformed to rules. In their definitions, a rule-based model depends on a bounded number of parameters, whereas a case-based model makes use of all data when defining the parameters. They used regression analysis on rental ($n = 1240$) and home-sales data ($n = 219$) from Tel Aviv to construct the rule and a similarity model to construct the cases and found out that their hypothesis was confirmed. They also recognised the effect of sample size, as the similarity model does not perform as well as the regression model on small sets. On the other hand, the benefit of the similarity model is that it has a self-correction mechanism – something that the regression model, of course, did not have. They concluded that the similarity model usu-ally should perform better than the regression model of larger data bases. Their results have some theoretical implications: namely, that in general, compared to rule-based reasoning, case-based reasoning is more prevalent in non-speculative markets than in speculative ones. Thus, the conclusion is that for rule-based systems, regression is better, but for case-based ones, similarity is to be preferred.

   This brief sample has demonstrated the richness of the discussion on value analysis methodology. The lesson learned here is that different methods can be used for either same or different valuation or estimation problems. In all cases, documentation is cru-cial. Next, the discussion moves on to more practical issues that also deserve attention.

Practical Applications

As already argued throughout this book, sustainability – even if restricted to the eco-nomic dimension – can be understood in several ways. Clear and accepted definitions are unfortunately lacking at present (see Bramley and Power, 2009). From a practical point of view, two aspects here are noteworthy: the various definitions ought to pertain to the long-term examination, and often, only a partial applicability of them is possi-ble. Furthermore, it should be noted that in real-estate economics, normally, outcome is considered more pertinent compared to processes (but see Kauko 2004a,b; Diaz 1998; Dent and Temple, 1998). This is despite the fact that choice theory by definition requires analysis of human decision-making beyond mathematical formality that usually is based on incorrect assumptions (Mooya, 2011).

   A fruitful point of departure might be the aforementioned concept of 'value stability'. Property value stability is measured on the basis of the property value when it is related to one or more other indicators. For example, house prices related to assessed quality indicators at given locations or for a given property type. Nonetheless, property market sustainability comprises much more than the property value stability concept. Here, two different questions arise:

1) The Where question: how the price developments of different areas within one and the same city are diversified in space in relation to the quality variable. This is a qualitative aspect that lends itself to cross-sectional methodology (involving physical, social, cultural and functional considerations).
2) The When question: how different time periods show different price developments in relation to the income development. This is a quantitative aspect that lends itself to time series modelling methodology.

The main issue here is to distinguish between unsustainable, economically sustainable and non-economically sustainable cases using a value stability indicator as measured in terms of price per quality or price per income (see Kauko, 2008a,b).

Summary and Concluding Discussion

When broadening the scope of property price/value analysis, the aim is to create a link between market analysis and sustainability assessment. The starting point is that we have two different broad scientific approaches or perspectives to valuation and market analysis: one, hedonic, which has been extended in recent years; two, the alternative or non-market perspective which, to a great extent, is still in the testing stage. The approach described here falls in between those two but closer to the latter. More specifically, this approach draws on two schools of thought within social sciences as it merges OIE with behavioural studies.

Two aspects here are noteworthy: the various definitions ought to pertain to the long-term examination, and often, only partial applicability of them is possible. A fruitful point of departure might be the aforementioned concept of 'value stability'. Property value stability is measured basis of property value when it is related to one or more other indicators. For example, house prices related to assessed quality indicators at given locations or for a given property type. The suggested improvement is about smoothing the price trend, on the one hand, and about a qualitative addendum (plus or minus), on the other.

This chapter has emphasised the normative role of valuation. The way we understand and explain property value is apparently undergoing a paradigm change. In the old paradigm, the separation of the various dimensions (economic, physical, social, cultural, etc.) was acceptable, because using the hedonic model, which would not have been possible without this manoeuvre, was considered the higher level goal. In the new paradigm, the higher level goal is not instrumental, but to increase the realism of the analysis.

It is to note that the sustainability aspect is being brought to the fore even more than hitherto due to the financial crisis. Undoubtedly, the crisis has strengthened the defence/credibility of this position even more. We cannot pretend to ignore the fact that the research climate towards deviant lines of thoughts within real-estate valuation at present is more favourable than it was before 2008. While facing problems at a practical and a policy level, this opportunity for theoretical contribution is too good to be missed!

The analysis continues in a later contribution in this volume (Chapter 4.2). And consistent with this shift in topic, the discussion will shift from technical and moral/ethical issues that the valuers eventually must face towards the production of market (and other) knowledge that informs (but does not force) the valuers.

3.2

Aspects of Commercial Property Valuation and Regressed DCF

Maurizio d'Amato

Real-Estate Appraisal is an important professional activity with consequences for economic and financial stability of the economic system. The increasing importance of sustainability in building construction and management has practical and professional consequence in valuation activity (Lorenz and Lutzkendorf, 2008). Assumptions and inputs that influence real-estate valuation may be greatly conditioned by sustainability. Nonagency mortgage crisis demonstrated the importance of real-estate valuation activity. According to Basel II agreement and EU Directive 2006/48/CE, banks should provide periodic automatic valuation to appraise the property units that guarantee the mortgage-lending process. In the valuation activity for mortgage-lending purposes, statistical and mathematical modeling is used in combination with valuation.[8] The Appraisal of Real Estate created a difference between the estimate of value as the final output of an automated valuation model and the opinion of value considered as the final output of an "in person" valuation.[9] The International Assessing Officers Association has provided a Standard on Automated Valuation Models (IAAO, 2003). This Standard follows the traditional methods of valuation: market, income, and cost. In particular, the income approach relies on the traditional direct capitalization formula (IAAO, Standard on Automated Valuation Models, Income Approach, para 3.2.3, p. 10). Equations 3.1 and 3.2 illustrate the AVM model included in the IAAO standards:

$$MV = \frac{NOI}{R} \tag{3.1}$$

where MV is the market value, NOI the Net Operating Income, and R the overall capitalization rent. The second equation stipulated in the IAAO standards is the following:

$$MV = GI \cdot GIM \tag{3.2}$$

where MV is the market value, GI the Gross Income, and GIM the Gross Income Multiplier. In this chapter, a further approach is proposed in order to create AVM models based on Discounted Cash-Flow Analysis called Regressed DCF. This method is applied for different bases of value. It can be used to determine both market value and

---

8 In some cases, automated valuation modeling in the financial sector replaced the valuation "in person" (Mcqueen, 2010).
9 The difference between single-point estimate and opinion of value emerged from 1999 onwards.

investment value. In both cases, the proposed methodology can be used for discount rate and risk premium calculation. Risk premium calculation is often based on subjective determination or financial modeling such as Capital Asset Price Method (CAPM) (Sharpe, 1964) or Arbitrage Price Theory (APT) (Ross, 1976). In this context, property characteristics are often neglected, reducing the valuation of property such as a financial asset. Methods such as single- and multifactor models coming from the realm of finance present some difficulties in adapting to the real-estate markets.

The need of an increasing attention to real-estate valuation methodologies and their capability to assist the analysis of real-estate markets has been highlighted in prior work (Lorenz *et al.*, 2007). There are several reasons for the lack of an application of such financial techniques to the real-estate markets. Among the others, real estate cannot be compared to a financial asset. Real estate comes in many different forms such as office, retail, residential, and so forth. The same property can be used in many different ways; in real-estate markets, information is asymmetric. Therefore, each model requiring perfect competition may be applied in a unique way. When we look at this from the perspective of financial assets, it is very difficult to transform a real-estate market into an asset class. And even when this transformation is successful, huge variances in prices or risk profiles of assets are likely to be incurred even in relatively small market areas. (compare for example the city of Baden-Baden and suburb of Baden-Baden). Methods that fit the particularities of the real-estate market and the characteristics of buildings as financial assets, are needed for computing risk premiums. This is what is proposed here. In this work, a set of methodologies are proposed to calculate the risk premium linked to property characteristics.

The proposed methodologies were tested on a small sample of commercial properties in Bucharest (Rumania) using only financial variables. In a further application, all the models presented may also include technical variables and sustainability enhancing characteristics. This chapter also offers a method to develop a risk premium map. In this way, the quantification of a risk premium is integrated with spatial analysis. A possible use as valuation method cannot be excluded. It can be considered as an alternative way to explore the relationship between inputs and outputs in the valuation process in order to serve the "normative" role of the appraiser whose professional activity highlights the different perspectives in the opinion of value.

The first application of these models was on a sample of 350 randomly generated cases of income producing real estate (d'Amato and Kauko, 2012). In the present study the methods were applied to a small sample of 20 observations of commercial properties in Bucharest (Romania). This small sample has been used only to demonstrate the routine of application of regressed DCF. Appraisers may appreciate the sustainability of technical solution, the robustness of cash flows, or the confidence in "green" building materials. The contribution is organized as follows: in the first paragraph, there is a brief introduction to DCF and Regressed DCF; in the second paragraph, there is a discussion on application of the three models of Regressed DCF to real estate. The third paragraph discusses about how to build a "risk premium map." Conclusions and further direction of research are indicated in the final fourth paragraph.

Regressed DCF

Discounted Cash-Flow Analysis "… results in a value indication of the asset or business based upon the present value of the expected future cash flows that will accrue to the owner ..." (IVSC, Technical Information Paper n.1). It can be considered as a method-ology to perform the valuation of a property and a real-estate investment project assessment (Baum *et al.*, 1996). While the valuation process is the estimating activity of the market value, assessment of worth estimates the investment value. The method consists in discounting several cash flows related to an interval of time called holding period. After this period, a direct capitalization is summed up to the previous value.

Several works have analyzed this methodology. Pioneering contributions analyzed DCF methodology (Downs, 1996; Ratcliff, 1972; Dilmore, 1971). Uncertainty (French and Cooper, 2000); Reliability of cash-flow analysis (Willison, 1999); and influence of vacancy and market analysis (Rabianski, 2002) are other important aspects analyzed. In particular, other contributions have highlighted the sensitivity of the output to the inputs. (Taylor and Rubin, 2002; Wheaton *et al.*, 2001; Hendershott and Hendershott, 2002). Regressed DCF is a model exploring these mathematical relationships between inputs and outputs of DCF, allowing the valuer-specific analysis. In this model, the prices of comparable properties are used as dependent variables, while the financial characteristics such as net operating income, going-in cap rate or the cap rate used for direct capitalization, the discount rate, the going-out cap rate used for reversion calculation, and the constant term as location variables. All these characteristics may be extracted from previous valuations or real transaction data. This approach has been proposed by d'Amato and Kauko (2012) as a way to calculate the discount rate and risk premium having comparables.

The chapter emphasizes the application of regressed DCF as an automated valuation method and as a method to determine the discount rate and the risk premium. The methodology is a group of three models defined as A, B, and C, analyzing the mathemat-ical relationship between the DCF inputs and outputs. In its first application, the method was applied to a sample of 350 randomly generated observations (d'Amato and Kauko, 2012). In a second application (d'Amato and Anghel, 2012), the Regressed DCF model A was applied to a small sample of DCF referred to as commercial properties in Bucharest. In this contribution, all the Regressed models A, B, and C were applied to the same sam-ple of DCF in Bucharest, in order to determine the market value, the risk premium, and the discount rate. By combining the risk premium determination with geographic infor-mation, it is possible to determine the risk premium map of the real-estate market. A comparison of the final outputs is performed. This application is based on a small sam-ple of valuations because of the difficulties in collecting data. The method can be applied not only to market value determination but also to assessment of worth. In this case, the methodologies may have the potential to determine the "market risk premium."

Discount Rate, Risk Premium Determination, and Regressed DCF

DCF is an important methodology to appraise commercial properties because the price of those properties is based on their income-producing potential. In fact, they are typ-ically purchased for investment instead of owner occupancy. DCF assumptions influ-ence the final value estimates; therefore, the quality of assumptions is a crucial issue in the assumption of DCF computations. The determination of discount rate plays a strategic role for the application of discounted cash-flow analysis. International Valua-tion Standards 2017 suggest (IVSC, IVS 105 Valuation Approached and Methods 50.30)

"Valuers may use any reasonable method for developing a discount rate. While there are many methods for developing or determining the reasonableness of a discount rate, a non-exhaustive list of common methods includes: … (f) built up method (generally used only in the absence of market inputs)".

The determination of discount rate is normally performed in several ways. The International Valuation Standards 2011 highlights these methodologies: "… C.20 The appropriate discount rate should be determined from analysis of the rates implicit in transactions in the market. Where this is not possible an appropriate discount rate may be built up from a typical risk-free return adjusted for the additional risks and opportunities specific to the particular real property interest …". In a similar way, the Technical Information Paper n. 1 of IVSC states: "… The discount rate will reflect the risk associated with the cash flows. Where the objective of the DCF model is to estimate market value, the discount rate should reflect market participants' view of risk, which may be determined from the discount rates, or return, implied by recent transactions involving similar assets. If there have been no recent transactions then it may be necessary to estimate an appropriate discount rate by considering the risk premium that would be required by an investor; that is to say, the additional return required over that obtainable from a 'risk free' asset such as a AAA rated bond.

Calculating the risk premium requires consideration of matters such as the certainty and security of the income, the strength of any counterparty and the prospects for future income growth" (IVSC,TIP, The DCF Method Overview, p. 11). One can distinguish between two different approaches to determine the discount rate for real-estate valuation purposes. The former is the selection of internal rate of return related to "trade in the market between participants" or "transactions in the market." The latter is the sum of the risk-free return and the additional risk premium (Hoesli and MacGregor, 2000). The risk-free term can be calculated as the gross redemption yield on conventional gilts. The risk premium is allowed to vary, depending on the characteristic of the property investment. In the assessment of individual worth of an investment, this term may vary across different investors.

An Application of Regressed Models A, B, and C to Bucharest Commercial Real-Estate Market

The observations are from the city of Bucharest and represent a small sample in order to demonstrate how the methods work. It represents the major part of real-estate investment in Romania. Office stock is around $1,430,000\text{m}^2$ with an average vacancy rate around 18% (lower in the central area) and prime Headline Rent 19 euro/sqm/month (d'Amato and Anghel, 2012). In the list of samples of 20 observations, some of them are real transactions, while others are offers. The complete list is provided in Table 3.2.[10]

The prices in euro are indicated with the acronym PRICE. The contractual rent is provided in Table 3.2 as NOI. The going-in cap rate that can be used in a direct capitalization, at the moment of valuation, is indicated with the acronym GICR. The GOCR indicates the going-out cap rate or the capitalization rate used to calculate the

---

10 Exactly as it was received from Prof. Angel, who provided it anonymously.

Table 3.2 A sample of 20DCF inputs in Bucharest.

	Price (DCF)	Net operating income	Going in cap rate	Going out cap rate	Discount rate
Nr	PRZ	NOI/year	GICR	GOCR	DR
1	€2,736,842.00	€168,174.00	0.061	0.076	0.100
2	€46,000,000.00	€3,902,046.00	0.085	0.092	0.105
3	€72.445,667.96	€6,766,326.80	0.093	0.095	0.105
4	€3,000,000.00	€188,350.00	0.063	0.078	0.100
5	€102,860,000.00	€8,618,400.00	0.084		1.000
6	€101,200,000.00	€7,082,449.92	0.070		1.000
7	€10,000,000.00	€856,800.00	0.086		1.000
8	€6,000,000.00	€410,400.00	0.068		1.000
9	€1,485,000.00	€138,000.00	0.093	0.101	0.108
10	€1,200,000.00	€78,000.00	0.065		1.000
11	€1,200,000.00	€120,000.00	0.100		1.000
12	€1,200,000.00	€108,000.00	0.090		1.000
13	€1,250,000.00	€84,000.00	0.067		1.000
14	€990,000.00	€88,800.00	0.090		1.000
15	€340,000.00	€30,000.00	0.088	0.124	0.105
16	€530,000.00	€49,200.00	0.093	0.093	0.108
17	€200,000.00	€24,000.00	0.120		0.135
18	€228,000.00	€19,200.00	0.084		0.100
19	€850,000.00	€54,000.00	0.064		0.090
20	€480,000.00	€42,000.00	0.088		0.090

reversion. The discount rate is indicated as DR and allows calculating the present value of the income streams associated with a property. The small sample has the descriptive statistics given in Table 3.3.

Unfortunately, not all the observations belong to the same market segment. A further selection of observations will be based on geographic characteristics of the samples. In fact, all the chosen 11 observations are situated close to the center of the city. Three models denoted as A, B, and C will be applied, having the location term (LOC)

Table 3.3 Descriptive statistics of DCF.

	Mean	St. Dev	Minimum	Maximum
Price	€17,709,775.50	€34,086,786.26	€200,000.00	€102,860,000.00
NOI/year	€1,441,407.34	€2,761,915.11	€19,200.00	€8,618,400.00
GICR	€0.08	€0.02	€0.06	€0.12
GOCR	€0.09	€0.02	€0.08	€0.12
DR	€0.51	€0.46	€0.09	€1.00

calculated as the constant term of a normal multiple linearized regression analysis. They represent three different alternatives to model the functional relationship between the price and a number of financial characteristics of commercial properties. For further information, the reader can refer to the previous works (d'Amato and Kauko, 2012; d'Amato and Anghel, 2012).

Model A

The first application is model A. The relationship between inputs and outputs in model A is given in the following equation:

$$PRICE = LOC \cdot NOI^{a_1} \cdot \frac{1}{(GICR \cdot DR)^{a_2}} \tag{3.3}$$

In equation 3.3, PRICE means the price of the property or its valuation. Therefore, the dependent variable of the method can be both a valuation and a price. The second acronym LOC means location and is automatically calculated during the regression as the constant term. The third term in the equation is the net operating income. GICR is the going-in cap rate, while DR is the discount rate. In this model there are both going-in and going-out cap rates. It means that model A can be used when the sample is composed of both direct capitalization and Discounted Cash-Flow Analysis. In log terms, equation 3.4 is

$$\ln(PRICE) = \ln(LOC) + a_1 \ln(NOI) - a_2 \ln(GICR \cdot DR) \tag{3.4}$$

The observations selected for the application of model A are provided in Table 3.4.

Starting from equation 3.3, the observations selected considered both going-in cap rate and discount rate. Therefore, observations with going-out cap rate were not considered in order to preserve the methodological homogeneity of the sample. In Table 3.5, the data for the application of the model indicated in equation 3.3 are summarized.

Table 3.4 Sample of observations selected to apply model A.

	Price (DCF)	Net operating income	Going in cap rate	Discount rate
Nr	Price	NOI	GICR	DR
1	€2,736,842.00	€168,174.00	0.061	0.100
2	€46,000,000.00	€3,902,046.00	0.085	0.105
3	€72,445,667.96	€6,766,326.80	0.093	0.105
4	€3,000,000.00	€188,350.00	0.063	0.100
9	€1,485,000.00	€138,000.00	0.093	0.108
15	€340,000.00	€30,000.00	0.088	0.105
16	€530,000.00	€49,200.00	0.093	0.108
17	€200,000.00	€24,000.00	0.120	0.135
18	€228,000.00	€19,200.00	0.084	0.100
19	€850,000.00	€54,000.00	0.064	0.090
20	€480,000.00	€42,000.00	0.088	0.090

Table 3.5 Sample of observations selected to apply model A.

Nr	Price	NOI	1/(GICR.DR)
1	€2,736,842.00	€168,174.00	162.73871110
2	€46,000,000.00	€3,902,046.00	112.27321208
3	€72,445,667.96	€6,766,326.80	101.96946776
4	€3,000,000.00	€188,350.00	159.27794001
9	€1,485,000.00	€138,000.00	99.63768116
15	€340,000.00	€30,000.00	107.93650794
16	€530,000.00	€49,200.00	99.92910690
17	€200,000.00	€24,000.00	61.72839506
18	€228,000.00	€19,200.00	118.75000000
19	€850,000.00	€54,000.00	174.89711934
20	€480,000.00	€42,000.00	126.98412698

In the original work of d'Amato and Kauko (2012), a log–log regression model was applied to a sample of observations. In Table 3.5, the logarithms of the data have been calculated in order to linearize the model. Using logarithm, a nonlinear relation is transformed in a linear one. Linearization of the model is indicated in Table 3.6, where the logarithm is calculated for each figure in Table 3.5.

Using equation 3.5, it is possible to standardize the data provided in Table 3.6.

$$z = \frac{x - \mu}{\sigma} \tag{3.5}$$

Standardization is a statistical technique (Gelman, 2007) to give equal weight to all the variables of the model. The new standardized variables are listed in Table 3.7.

Table 3.6 Calculation of logarithm.

Nr	PRZ	NOI/year	1/(GICR DR)
1	14.8223	12.0328	5.092145915
2	17.6442	15.1770	4.720935294
3	18.0983	15.7275	4.624673433
4	14.9141	12.1461	5.070650727
9	14.2109	11.8350	4.601540418
15	12.7367	10.3090	4.681543165
16	13.1806	10.8036	4.604461004
17	12.2061	10.0858	4.122744037
18	12.3371	9.8627	4.777020443
19	13.6530	10.8967	5.164197912
20	13.0815	10.6454	4.844062094

Table 3.7 Sample of observations selected to apply model A: standardization.

Nr	PRZ	NOI	1/GICR*DR
1	0.280	0.131	1.151
2	1.689	1.722	−0.116
3	1.916	2.000	−0.444
4	0.326	0.188	1.078
9	−0.026	0.031	−0.523
15	−0.762	−0.742	−0.250
16	−0.540	−0.491	−0.513
17	−1.027	−0.855	−2.157
18	−0.961	−0.968	0.075
19	−0.304	−0.444	1.397
20	−0.590	−0.571	0.304

Table 3.8 Regression output.

	LOC	NOI	1/(GICR*DR)
Coefficients	−0.0042911831041890	0.988	0.094
Adj R^2	0.99932089		
F	6622.818817		
t-Student	−0.492329199	113.9505819	9.993922899

Multiple regression analysis was applied to the sample provided in Table 3.7 to explore a mathematical relationship between small samples of 11 observations. The result of the multiple regression analysis is provided in Table 3.8.

An application of the model to in-sample observations can be considered useful for testing its efficiency. One of the measures that can be used is the mean absolute percentage error as indicated in the following equation:

$$\text{MAPE} = \sum_{i=1}^{n} \frac{\left| \frac{PS_i - AS_i}{AS_i} \right| \cdot 100}{n} \tag{3.6}$$

In equation 3.6, MAPE is the mean absolute percentage error, PS means the predicted selling, while the AS means the actual selling. In Table 3.9, the first column represents the actual prices observed (estimated with DCF). The second column indicates the application of the model. The log–log model was subjected to a process of standardization of variables. In the third column, the data have been destandardized. Therefore, in the fourth column, the predicted prices were calculated and finally, the percentage error was calculated. In the last column, the mean absolute percentage error is highlighted.

Table 3.9 Regressed DCF as valuation method of MAPE.

Nr	Actual prices	Application of the model	Destandardization	Predicted prices	Percentage error	Mean absolute percentage error
1	€2,736,842.00	0.232505811	14.7278023	€2,490,022.44	0.0902	0.0368
2	€46,000,000.00	1.685718012	17.6375192	€45,695,904.89	0.0066	
3	€72,445,667.96	1.9301325	18.1269020	€74,544,140.04	0.0290	
4	€3,000,000.00	0.282277256	14.8274579	€2,750,952.96	0.0830	
9	€1,485,000.00	−0.023152187	14.2159070	€1,492,416.30	0.0050	
15	€340,000.00	−0.760477808	12.7395852	€340,982.09	0.0029	
16	€530,000.00	−0.537808989	13.1854274	€532,547.50	0.0048	
17	€200,000.00	−1.050628008	12.1586274	€190,732.54	0.0463	
18	€228,000.00	−0.953067007	12.3539705	€231,878.89	0.0170	
19	€850,000.00	−0.312374308	13.6368075	€836,354.21	0.0161	
20	€480,000.00	−0.540328288	13.1803831	€529,867.93	0.1039	

The final result of the model is an interesting mean absolute percentage error of 0.0368, although the model is proposed for discount rate estimation. In fact, few easy mathematical passages permit to have a methodology for discount date and risk premium estimation. Starting from the following mathematical relation,

$$PRICE = LOC \cdot NOI^{a_1} \cdot \frac{1}{GICR^{a_2}} \cdot \frac{1}{DR^{a_2}} \tag{3.7}$$

it is possible to write the following equation:

$$\ln(DR) = \frac{\ln(LOC) + 0.9879310 \ln(NOI) - \ln(PRICE) - 0.0936552 \ln(GICR)}{0.0936552}$$

$$\tag{3.8}$$

In equation 3.7, DR means Discount Rate, LOC means Location Variable, NOI indicates Net Operating Income, PRICE means the price of the property (but could also be used as the value), and GICR is the going-in cap rate. The in-sample application for discount rate determination gave the results as shown in Table 3.10.

In Table 3.10, the first column indicates the coefficient of instrumental variable 1/(GICR · DR) and the second column indicates the coefficient of variable NOI. The third and fourth columns indicate the logarithm of standardized variables: NOI, PRICE, and GICR. The sixth column indicates the value of location variable of the regressed DCF. Therefore, the mean absolute percentage error between the actual discount rate and the predicted discount rate is indicated in Table 3.11.

The MAPE applied to discount rate determination based on equation 3.7 gave a mean absolute percentage error of 0.062. Both the Technical Information Paper and the International Valuation Standards indirectly define the risk premium as the difference between the discount rate determined through the regressed DCF and the risk-free

Table 3.10 Regressed DCF as valuation method of DR: model A.

	a_2	a_1				
Nr	1/(GICR*DR)	NOI	ln (NOI)	ln (Price)	ln (GICR)	ln (LOC)
1	0.0936552	0.9879310	0.1306	0.28	−1.470	−0.0043
2			1.7216	1.69	0.099	
3			2.0002	1.92	0.568	
4			0.1879	0.33	−1.365	
9			0.0305	−0.03	0.543	
15			−0.7417	−0.76	0.291	
16			−0.4914	−0.54	0.538	
17			−0.8546	−1.03	1.788	
18			−0.9675	−0.96	0.064	
19			−0.4443	−0.30	−1.308	
20			−0.5714	−0.59	0.250	

Table 3.11 Regressed DCF as valuation method of DR: empirical results.

Nr	DR standardized	DR destandardize	Predicted DR	Actual DR	Percentage error	Mean absolute percentage error
1	−0.185041396	−2.287	0.10153323	0.100	0.015332298	0.062104819
2	−0.018915585	−2.269	0.103376551	0.105	0.015461419	
3	0.028698113	−2.264	0.103911013	0.105	0.010371301	
4	−0.174458442	−2.286	0.101649671	0.100	0.016496711	
9	0.006456467	−2.267	0.103661009	0.108	0.040175847	
15	−0.025466628	−2.270	0.103303231	0.105	0.016159703	
16	0.000687889	−2.267	0.103596266	0.108	0.03899568	
17	0.11649503	−2.255	0.104903787	0.135	0.222934912	
18	−0.049475927	−2.273	0.103034961	0.100	0.030349614	
19	−0.175346683	−2.286	0.101639893	0.090	0.129332143	
20	−0.027641241	−2.270	0.103278904	0.090	0.147543381	

rate, which has been determined as 0.045 by assuming the rent of the Romanian gilt. In Table 3.12, a comparison between the risk premium obtained by the 11 comparables and the risk premium predicted through regressed DCF can be observed. As one can see, the mean absolute percentage error is 0.11.

As one can see, the Mean Absolute Percentage Error is higher in the risk premium calculation. This difference may be caused by the calculation of risk premium whose determination may be based on a build up method (International Valuation Standard Committee, Technical Information Paper n.1 para. 28). In the application of this method valuers normally determine the percentage of the risk premium in a subjective way.

Table 3.12 Regressed DCF model A as valuation method of risk premium.

Nr	Risk free	Predicted DR	Risk premium	Selected DR	Risk premium	Percentage error	Mean absolute percentage error
1	0.045	0.102	0.057	0.100	0.055	0.027877	0.110045775
2	0.045	0.103	0.058	0.105	0.060	0.027057	
3	0.045	0.104	0.059	0.105	0.060	0.01815	
4	0.045	0.102	0.057	0.100	0.055	0.029994	
9	0.045	0.104	0.059	0.108	0.063	0.068873	
15	0.045	0.103	0.058	0.105	0.060	0.028279	
16	0.045	0.104	0.059	0.108	0.063	0.066938	
17	0.045	0.105	0.060	0.135	0.090	0.334402	
18	0.045	0.103	0.058	0.100	0.055	0.055181	
19	0.045	0.102	0.057	0.090	0.045	0.258664	
20	0.045	0.103	0.058	0.090	0.045	0.295087	

Model B

The second application is model B. The relationship between inputs and outputs is given in the following equation:

$$\text{PRICE} = \text{LOC} \cdot \text{NOI}^{b_1} \cdot \frac{1}{\text{GOCR}^{b_2}} \cdot \frac{1}{\text{DR}^{b_2}} \tag{3.9}$$

In equation 3.9, PRICE means the price of the property or its value. The second acronym LOC means the location. It is generally mentioned as the constant term in the location blind models. The third term in the equation is the net operating income. GOCR is the going-in cap rate, while DR is the discount rate. As one can see, in this model, there is only the going-out cap rate. It means that the sample that can be used must have only Discounted Cash-Flow Analysis. As a consequence, the model is tested on the seven DCFs given in Table 3.1. In log terms, equation 3.9 becomes

$$\ln(\text{PRICE}) = \ln(\text{LOC}) + b_1 \ln(\text{NOI}) - b_2 \ln(\text{GOCR}) - b_2 \ln(\text{DR}) \tag{3.10}$$

The going-out cap rate is specified in the observations provided in Table 3.13.

In Table 3.13, the prices in euro are indicated with the acronym PRICE. The contractual rent is mentioned as NOI (as in Table 3.2). GOCR indicates the going-out cap rate or the capitalization rate used to calculate the reversion. The discount rate is mentioned as DR and allows for calculating the present value of the income streams associated with a property. The variables included in the B model indicated in equation 3.9 are calculated in Table 3.14.

Therefore, the logarithms of the variables given in Table 3.14 are calculated in Table 3.15.

The standardization of the data using equation 3.5 has been calculated for each variable given in Table 3.15. Table 3.16 shows the results of the standardization process of the variables given in Table 3.15.

Table 3.13 Application of model B: the observations.

Nr	Price	NOI	GOCR	DR
1	€2,736,842.00	€168,174.00	0.076	0.100
2	€46,000,000.00	€3,902,046.00	0.092	0.105
3	€72,445,667.96	€6,766,326.80	0.095	0.105
4	€3,000,000.00	€188,350.00	0.078	0.100
9	€1,485,000.00	€138,000.00	0.101	0.108
15	€340,000.00	€30,000.00	0.124	0.105
16	€530,000.00	€49,200.00	0.093	0.108

Table 3.14 Application of model B: the variables.

Nr	Price	NOI	1/(GOCR.DR)	GOCR	DR
1	€2,736,842.00	€168,174.00	130.78105214	0.076	0.100
2	€46,000,000.00	€3,902,046.00	103.04634221	0.092	0.105
3	€72,445,667.96	€6,766,326.80	100.13825164	0.095	0.105
4	€3,000,000.00	€188,350.00	128.20512821	0.078	0.100
9	€1,485,000.00	€138,000.00	91.67583425	0.101	0.108
15	€340,000.00	€30,000.00	77.11586659	0.124	0.105
16	€530,000.00	€49,200.00	99.92910690	0.093	0.108

Table 3.15 Application of model B: calculation of logarithm.

Nr	Price	NOI	1/(GOCR DR)	GOCR	DR
1	14.8223	12.0328	4.873524567	−2.570939474	−2.302585093
2	17.6442	15.1770	4.635178811	−2.381383883	−2.253794929
3	18.0983	15.7275	4.606551748	−2.352756819	−2.253794929
4	14.9141	12.1461	4.853631545	−2.551046452	−2.302585093
9	14.2109	11.8350	4.518258814	−2.292634762	−2.225624052
15	12.7367	10.3090	4.345309052	−2.091514123	−2.253794929
16	13.1806	10.8036	4.604461004	−2.376983383	−2.227477621

A multiple regression analysis was applied in order to define a mathematical relationship between the dependent variable and the independent variable in a small sample of seven observations. The result of the multiple regression analysis is given in Table 3.17.

An application of the model to in-sample observations can be considered useful for testing its efficiency. One of the measures that can be used is the mean absolute percentage error by applying equation 3.6. Table 3.18 provides the mean absolute percentage error obtained by regressed DCF as a valuation method.

Table 3.16 Application of model B: standardization of the variables.

Nr	Price	NOI	1/GOCR*DR	GOCR	DR
1	−0.1279	−0.2609	1.2999	−1.218	−1.350
2	1.2373	1.2494	0.0072	−0.046	0.195
3	1.4571	1.5138	−0.1480	0.131	0.195
4	−0.0835	−0.2064	1.1920	−1.095	−1.350
9	−0.4237	−0.3558	−0.6269	0.502	1.087
15	−1.1370	−1.0888	−1.5649	1.745	0.195
16	−0.9222	−0.8512	−0.1594	−0.019	1.028

Table 3.17 Application of model B: regression output.

	LOC	NOI	1/(GOCR*DR)
Coefficients	0.0000000000000002	0.979	0.081
Adj R^2	0.997298341		
F	1108.428969		
t-student	0.0000000000000095	45.10551355	3.71099089

Table 3.18 Model B MAPE as valuation method.

Nr	Actual prices	Application of the model	Destandardization	Predicted prices	Percentage error	Mean absolute percentage error
1	€2,736,842.00	−0.150682728	14.7752938	€2,611,130.54	0.0459	0.0681
2	€46,000,000.00	1.223796799	17.6162267	€44,733,206.61	0.0275	
3	€72,445,667.96	1.470146282	18.1254102	€74,433,017.64	0.0274	
4	€3,000,000.00	−0.106092044	14.8674590	€2,863,224.55	0.0456	
9	€1,485,000.00	−0.398877237	14.2622968	€1,563,280.11	0.0527	
15	€340,000.00	−1.192069747	12.6228350	€303,408.40	0.1076	
16	€530,000.00	−0.846221324	13.3376745	€620,123.82	0.1700	

It can be observed that the mean absolute percentage error is 0.0681. It is higher than that obtained by the application of model A. The application of regressed DCF can be explored as a method to calculate the discount rate. Recalling equation 3.9, it is possible to write

$$\ln(\text{DR}) = \frac{\ln(\text{LOC}) + 0.979\ln(\text{NOI}) - \ln(\text{PRICE}) - 0.081\ln(\text{GOCR})}{0.081} \quad (3.11)$$

In Table 3.19, the first column represents the coefficient of instrumental variable $1/(\text{GOCR} \cdot \text{DR})$, and the second column indicates the coefficient of variable NOI.

Table 3.19 Regressed DCF as valuation method of DR: model B.

Nr	1/(GOCR*DR)	NOI	ln (NOI)	ln (PRICE)	ln (GOCR)	ln (LOC)
1	0.0805493	0.9790429	−0.2609	−0.13	−1.218	0.0000
2			1.2494	1.24	−0.046	
3			1.5138	1.46	0.131	
4			−0.2064	−0.08	−1.095	
9			−0.3558	−0.42	0.502	
15			−1.0888	−1.14	1.745	
16			−0.8512	−0.92	−0.019	

Table 3.20 Regressed DCF as valuation method of DR: model B.

Nr	DR standardized	DR destandardize	Predicted DR	Actual DR	Percentage error	Mean absolute percentage error
1	−0.364474135	−2.271	0.103162	0.100	0.031615349	0.018533
2	−0.1286726	−2.264	0.103932	0.105	0.010166822	
3	0.179934472	−2.254	0.10495	0.105	0.000474477	
4	−0.377387649	−2.272	0.103119	0.100	0.031194799	
9	0.433210588	−2.246	0.105793	0.108	0.020436558	
15	−0.864331837	−2.287	0.101546	0.105	0.032894121	
16	1.121721161	−2.225	0.108118	0.108	0.002949356	

The third and fourth columns indicate the logarithm of standardized variables: NOI, PRICE, and GOCR. The sixth column indicates the value of location variable of the regressed DCF.

Therefore, the mean absolute percentage error between the actual discount rate and the predicted discount rate is provided in Table 3.20.

The B model shows a lower MAPE compared to A model. Table 3.21 shows a comparison between the risk premium obtained by the seven comparables and the risk premium

Table 3.21 Regressed DCF as valuation method of risk premium: model B.

Nr	Risk free	Predicted DR	Risk premium	Selected DR	Risk premium	Percentage error	Mean absolute percentage error
1	0.045	0.103	0.058	0.100	0.055	0.057	0.0329263
2	0.045	0.104	0.059	0.105	0.060	0.018	
3	0.045	0.105	0.060	0.105	0.060	8E−04	
4	0.045	0.103	0.058	0.100	0.055	0.057	
9	0.045	0.106	0.061	0.108	0.063	0.035	
15	0.045	0.102	0.057	0.105	0.060	0.058	
16	0.045	0.108	0.063	0.108	0.063	0.005	

predicted through regressed DCF model B. As one can see, the mean absolute percentage error is 0.018. Therefore, although model A is superior to model B as a predictor for property value, model A is superior to model B as a predictor of discount rate and for risk premium determination.

Model C

The third application is model C. The relationship between inputs and outputs in model C is given in the following equation:

$$\text{PRICE} = \text{LOC} \cdot \text{NOI}^{c_1} \cdot \frac{1}{\text{GOCR}^{c_2} \, \text{DR}^{c_2}} \cdot \frac{1}{\text{GICR}^{c_3} \, \text{DR}^{c_3}} \tag{3.12}$$

In equation 3.12, PRICE means the price of the property or its valuation. Therefore, the dependent variable of the method can be both a valuation and a price according to the nature of the sample considered. The second acronym LOC means location. It is generally indicated as the constant term in mass appraisal modeling with a constant value for location. The third term in the equation is the net operating income. GOCR is the going-out cap rate, and DR is the discount rate; finally, GICR is the going-in cap rate. The sample of this model is the one used for model B. In fact, in both the models, the going-out cap rate is a valuation input of DCF only. In logarithmic terms, equation 3.12 becomes

$$\ln(\text{PRICE}) = \ln(\text{LOC}) + c_1 \ln(\text{NOI}) - c_2 \ln(\text{DR}) - c_3 \ln(\text{GICR}) - c_3 \ln(\text{DR}) \tag{3.13}$$

The observations are listed in Table 3.22.
The variables are calculated to apply the model (Table 3.23).
As usual, the calculation of logarithm is provided in Table 3.24.
Table 3.25 shows the calculation of standardized variables, recalling equation 3.5.
A multiple regression analysis was applied to define a mathematical relationship between the small sample of seven observations and the dependent variable price. The result of the multiple regression analysis is provided in Table 3.26.
The application of regressed DCF as a valuation methodology showed the following mean absolute percentage error as provided in Table 3.27.

Table 3.22 Model C: observations.

Nr	Price	NOI	GICR	GOCR	DR
1	€2,736,842.00	€168,174.00	0.0614	0.076	0.100
2	€46,000,000.00	€3,902,046.00	0.0848	0.092	0.105
3	€72,445,667.96	€6,766,326.80	0.0934	0.095	0.105
4	€3,000,000.00	€188,350.00	0.0628	0.078	0.100
9	€1,485,000.00	€138,000.00	0.0929	0.101	0.108
15	€340,000.00	€30,000.00	0.0882	0.124	0.105
16	€530,000.00	€49,200.00	0.0928	0.093	0.108

Table 3.23 Model C: variables calculation.

Nr	Price	NOI	1/(GICR.DR)	1/(GOCR.DR)
1	€2,736,842.00	€168,174.00	162.74	130.78105214
2	€46,000,000.00	€3,902,046.00	112.27	103.04634221
3	€72,445,667.96	€6,766,326.80	101.97	100.13825164
4	€3,000,000.00	€188,350.00	159.28	128.20512821
9	€1,485,000.00	€138,000.00	99.64	91.67583425
15	€340,000.00	€30,000.00	107.94	77.11586659
16	€530,000.00	€49,200.00	99.93	99.92910690

Table 3.24 Model C: logarithm calculation.

Nr	Price	NOI/year	1/(GICR.DR)	1/(GOCR DR)
1	14.8223	12.0328	5.0921	4.8735
2	17.6442	15.1770	4.7209	4.6352
3	18.0983	15.7275	4.6247	4.6066
4	14.9141	12.1461	5.0707	4.8536
9	14.2109	11.8350	4.6015	4.5183
15	12.7367	10.3090	4.6815	4.3453
16	13.1806	10.8036	4.6045	4.6045

Table 3.25 Model C: standardized variables.

Nr	Price	NOI	1/(GICR.DR)	1/(GOCR*DR)
1	−0.1279	−0.2609	1.4839	1.2999
2	1.2373	1.2494	−0.2305	0.0072
3	1.4571	1.5138	−0.6751	−0.1480
4	−0.0835	−0.2064	1.3846	1.1920
9	−0.4237	−0.3558	−0.7819	−0.6269
15	−1.1370	−1.0888	−0.4125	−1.5649
16	−0.9222	−0.8512	−0.7685	−0.1594

Table 3.26 Model C: multiple regression output.

	LOC	NOI	1/(GICR*DR)	1/(GOCR*DR)
Coefficients	−0.000000000000000019	1.0035	0.0856	0.00301625
Adj R^2	0.999987083			
F	154832.0148			
t-Student	−0.0000000000000138	582.2056492	28.87233796	1.660951147

Table 3.27 Model C: regressed DCF as a valuation method.

Nr	Actual prices	Application of the model	Destandardization	Predicted prices	Percentage error	Mean absolute percentage error
1	€2,736,842.00	−0.128289819	14.8215781	€2,734,825.23	0.0007	0.0041
2	€46,000,000.00	1.234098897	17.6375202	€45,695,949.81	0.0066	
3	€72,445,667.96	1.460605425	18.1056900	€72,979,565.98	0.0074	
4	€3,000,000.00	−0.082711915	14.9157838	€3,004,986.88	0.0017	
9	€1,485,000.00	−0.427138777	14.2038826	€1,474,578.28	0.0070	
15	€340,000.00	−1.135795919	12.7391483	€340,833.13	0.0025	
16	€530,000.00	−0.920767892	13.1835930	€531,571.51	0.0030	

Table 3.28 Model C and its coefficients.

Nr	C_3 1/(GOCR)	C_2 1/(GICR)	C_1 NOI	ln (NOI)	ln (PRICE)	ln (GICR)	ln (GOCR)	ln (LOC)
1	0.0050098	0.0855676	1.0035140	−0.2609	−0.13	−1.495	−1.218	−0.0000
2				1.2494	1.24	0.235	−0.046	
3				1.5138	1.46	0.751	0.131	
4				−0.2064	−0.08	−1.380	−1.095	
9				−0.3558	−0.42	0.724	0.502	
15				−1.0888	−1.14	0.446	1.745	
16				−0.8512	−0.92	0.719	−0.019	

It can be observed that the mean absolute percentage error is 0.0041. It is possible to explore the application of regressed DCF as a method to calculate the discount rate. Recalling equation 3.13, it is possible to write the following equation:

$$\ln(DR) = \frac{\ln(LOC) + 1.0035\ln(NOI) - 0.005\ln(GOCR) - 0.0855676\ln(GICR) - \ln(PRICE)}{(0.005 + 0.0853676)} \quad (3.14)$$

In Table 3.28, the first column represents the coefficient of instrumental variable 1/(GOCR), and the second column shows the coefficient of instrumental variable 1/(GICR). The third column indicates the coefficient of variable NOI. The fourth to sixth columns indicate the logarithm of standardized variables: NOI, PRICE, 1/(GOCR), and 1/(GICR). The seventh column indicates the value of location variable of the regressed DCF.

Therefore, the mean absolute percentage error between the actual discount rate and the predicted discount rate is provided in Table 3.29.

The C model shows a lower MAPE compared to A model and B model as a valuation tool. As one can see, the mean absolute percentage error is 0.02. In Table 3.30,

Table 3.29 Model C: regressed DCF as a method to determine DR.

Nr	DR standardized	DR destandardize	Predicted DR	Actual DR	Percentage error	Mean absolute percentage error
1	0.002320234	−2.260	0.104363249	0.100	0.043632	0.024484
2	−0.037308957	−2.261	0.104232742	0.105	0.007307	
3	−0.031850534	−2.261	0.104250708	0.105	0.007136	
4	−0.000884775	−2.260	0.104352688	0.100	0.043527	
9	0.023710878	−2.259	0.104433761	0.108	0.033021	
15	−0.028773137	−2.261	0.104260838	0.105	0.00704	
16	0.072786291	−2.258	0.104595712	0.108	0.029724	

Table 3.30 Regressed DCF as valuation of risk premium: model C.

Risk free	Predicted DR	Risk premium	Selected DR	Risk premium	Percentage error	Mean absolute percentage error
0.045	0.104	0.059	0.100	0.055	0.079331798	0.043385351
0.045	0.104	0.059	0.105	0.060	0.012787639	
0.045	0.104	0.059	0.105	0.060	0.012488205	
0.045	0.104	0.059	0.100	0.055	0.079139782	
0.045	0.104	0.059	0.108	0.063	0.056606974	
0.045	0.104	0.059	0.105	0.060	0.012319365	
0.045	0.105	0.060	0.108	0.063	0.051023694	

Table 3.31 Comparing regressed DCF models' performances.

	In sample regressed DCF MAPE		
	Regressed DCF price	Regressed DCF discount rate	Regressed DCF risk premium
Model A	0.0368	0.0621	0.1100
Model B	0.0681	0.0185	0.0329
Model C	0.0041	0.0245	0.0434

a comparison between the risk premium obtained by the seven comparables and the risk premium predicted through regressed DCF model C can be observed.

A comparison among the three different models is provided in Table 3.31.

Probably because of the mixture of direct capitalization and DCFs models, model A is less precise than the others. It is now possible to define a geographic dimension of property risk premium. This analysis will be done in the next section.

A Real-Estate Market Risk Premium Map

In this section, a geographic dimension of risk premium estimation in real-estate valuation is addressed. It must be stressed that, although the building approach to DCF is based on the sum of a risk-free rate and a risk premium, the determination of this part of the discount rate seems not to have a spatial dimension. This is a critical issue probably originated from the origin of DCF. DCF is a financial methodology while the real-estate valuation process has a significant spatial dimension. Risk premium models, both single- and multifactor models (Sharpe, 1964; Ross, 1976), rely on unrealistic assumptions completely distant from real-estate market's reality. These models propose a risk premium as a percentage figure that appears to be applied to large geographical property market areas comprising the same "asset class." The application of IRR originated by comparable properties or based on comparables focuses the attention of the appraiser on the financial inputs and outputs. Asymmetric information divides each such market into a number of submarkets; therefore, the risk premium should be observed at a local level, starting from the empirical observation of local market and local information (Barkham and Geltner, 1995). This is the reason why bearing a risk in real-estate market is dependent on location. Therefore, an integration between spatial modeling and risk premium determination is proposed. Before using spatial modeling, it is necessary to detect the degree of spatial autocorrelation of the spatial variable x in this case, the risk premium. The most commonly used and robust indicator was proposed by the statistician Moran (Moran, 1948; Moran, 1950) and is normally denoted as Moran I test as indicated in the following equation:

$$I = \frac{N \sum_{i=1}^{n} \sum_{j=1}^{n} w_{ij}(x_i - \bar{x})(x_j - \bar{x})}{\sum_{i=1}^{n} \sum_{j=1}^{n} w_{ij}(x_i - \bar{x})^2} \tag{3.15}$$

where x is the variable (risk premium), and w_{ij} represents the set of neighbors j for observation i. In this case, the inverse squared distance between the observations has been considered according to the previous works (Des Rosiers *et al.*, 1999). The Moran I ranges from −1 to +1, and each observation is only compared with its relevant neighborhood. A positive Moran I shows positive autocorrelation; as a consequence, high values for risk premium should be located near other high values while lower value of risk premium should be located near other areas with a similar profile. In this work, the Moran I test, developed using an Excel file, showed positive autocorrelation by assuming a value of 0.33. As a consequence, there is the theoretical premise to apply spatial statistics for risk premium determination. In Table 3.32, the 11 observations used in the regressed DCF model A are listed. In this context, regressed model has been used to foresee risk premium. Using the geographic location of each observation, it is possible to draw a "risk premium map" linking the property market risk premium to local submarkets. In Table 3.32, the risk premium determination through regressed DCF and the correspondent can be observed.

Therefore, a spatial map of risk premium was run using Inverse Distance Weighting procedure offered by SURFER 8. This is geostatistical software, which can provide a map of geographically located information. IDW is the simplest methodology to interpolate a surface using point data (Fotheringham *et al.*, 2000). It estimates the value between

Table 3.32 Risk premium determination and geographical location.

N.	Address	Latitude	Longitude	Risk Premium
1	Str. Oltetului, 15, Sect.2	44.4694444	26.113056	0.055
2	Str. Dinu Vintila, 11, Sector 2	44.4536111	26.106111	0.060
3	Sos. Bucuresti – Ploiesti 172-176, S1	44.5211111	26.080833	0.060
4	Cehov, 2	44.4697222	26.089167	0.055
9	Str. Doamnei, 27-29, s1	44.4319444	26.099722	0.063
15	Bd unirii, 45	44.4266667	26.095833	0.060
16	Mihai Bravu, 90-96	44.4238889	26.137222	0.063
17	Octavian Goga, 4	44.4247222	26.119722	0.090
18	Sos. Cotroceni, 16	44.4377778	26.068889	0.055
19	Sos. Salaj, 223	44.3908333	26.061667	0.045
20	Victoriei, 68-70	44.4375	26.097778	0.045

two points i and j using a weighted average whose weight given to each point is defined using a standard distance decay function as given in the following equation:

$$f(d_{ij}) = \frac{1}{d_{ij}^{2}} \qquad (3.16)$$

The application of IDW method of interpolation gave the opportunity to draw a "risk premium map" for valuation purposes. This map is indicated in Figure 3.1.

It is evident from Figure 3.1 how the risk premium calculation follows the territory showing a closer adaptation to reality. The risk premium varies across the space, adapting the concept of risk premium to real life. It is calculated for a specific market segment.

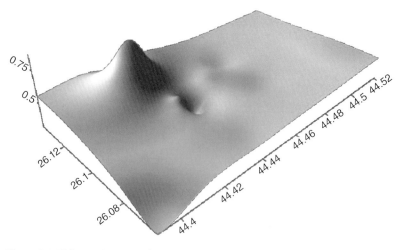

Figure 3.1 Risk premium spatial map.

It is possible to observe a peak (high-risk area) and three lower risk areas. The map proposed is a useful tool for several purposes. It can be seen as a way to address the risk premium estimation using real prices or real valuations; it also provides the spatial variation of risk premium and opens the field for further spatiotemporal models that is helpful in defining how risk premium varies with time and space. This paper offers a different approach based on real-estate market data instead of looking for solution in the financial methods. In this way, it is possible for each market segment to observe an estimated geographical distribution of the risk premium within a given specific submarket.

Investors, lenders, and valuers are supported in their daily practice in observing the risk premium and judging, within a given range of risk premiums, the most appropriate risk premium for valuing a subject property. The maps developed in different times may give an important description of risk premium variation. The use of spatiotemporal modeling may help in this. In this case, the risk premium map was created based on financial information on the assets in the sample (such as rent, going-out cap rate, and price). Therefore, with the map of risk premiums, the isolation of the effect of location on risk premium is not yet possible (map cannot be considered for the explanation of a simple linkage between location and risk premium). The use of this map must be descriptive; in fact, the risk premium is geographically distributed as indicated in the map, but it is determined by the characteristics included in the model.

It is important to stress that the map can be developed for the basis of both the market value and the investment value. In the former case, it represents the variation with time and space of the market perception of risk. In the latter case, it represents how the spatial and spatiotemporal variation of risk is perceived by the investors. The quality/reliability of the map is linked to the quality of the data and models. Further developed models – which allow the inclusion of additional variables –result in higher quality maps with more significant information. In the future – provided that further improved models and better information are available – risk premium maps that show the distribution of risk premium between individual buildings within a given area can be produced.

Conclusions and Further Directions of Research

The contribution offered the opportunity to understand how the regressed DCF works at its early stage. Three models, A, B, and C, have been applied to the same small sample determining the value, the discount rate, and the risk premium map. The small sample was located in Bucharest, consisting of valuation for commercial property. A larger sample was not available, but the value of this contribution is not in the final results but in the methodological proposal. There may be several possible future directions of research. The application of this method supporting the assessment of worth may be an interesting further direction of research. It is necessary to explain the differences among the three methods. We also need to define more complex regressed DCF models trying to also include other variables such as distance from value influence centers and the technical features (characteristics of the building, including sustainability.)

3.3

The Significance of Land Attributes in Determining the Types of Land Use

Malgorzata Reniger-Bilozor and Andrzej Bilozor

Introduction

The central principle of this book (and, indeed, its Part 3) concerns the improvement of market analysis and valuation when seen from a scientific point of view. This brings us to a related issue concerning land use (different types of property usage on a given plot of land) and its determinants. In the valuation and pricing theory, price equals a function of a set of attributes (and one of these attributes is the land use). The difference between land use and land value obviously is that, unlike the latter variable, the former is defined as a discrete measure.

In principle, determining the land-use types (and land values, for that matter) poses practical problems due to the nonhomogeneity of locations (no two plots of land can be identical), the presence of various attributes – both qualitative and quantitative – describing the locations, highly diversified access to information in various segments of the land market, and, frequently, the inability to identify dependencies between land attributes and market actors. Often, such issues are difficult to overcome using statistical modeling methods (in this case, logistic regression). This has to do with overstrict assumptions in these methods. Therefore, alternative methods that require less strict assumptions and less data consumption (i.e., require less observations) are sometimes proposed. Rough set theory (RST) is such an option. RST is based on if–then rules among conditional and decisional attributes.

In this chapter, a "flexible" version of RST is applied in order to explain the methodology. The flexibility here relates to a fuzzy modification of the crisp metrics of classical RST. This is called valued tolerance relation (VTR); see, for example, d'Amato (2007). Here, it is to note that both the classical and this flexible version of RST rely on logical relations based on De Morgan's laws. Our demonstration employs this fuzzified RST method based on geocoded land-use information from Olsztyn, Poland.

The method based on the RST accounts for the specific features of real-estate data. Developed by a Polish information technology engineer, Professor Zdzisław Pawlak, the theory is used to test imprecision, vagueness, and uncertainty in the process of data analysis. Classical RST analyses data are represented in the form of qualitative attributes. The specific features of real-estate attributes show a high level of variability in the method of encoding each attribute, and some key attributes are expressed on a ratio scale, such as the price or area, where the coding method should not be modified due to the risk of data loss. In view of the aforementioned, the authors have proposed to integrate the VTR (based on the fuzzy set theory) with the classical RST to fully deploy and analyze real-estate market data. This approach renders the RST as a more flexible tool for exploring data and analyzing observations expressed in quantitative form on a ratio scale.

Method for Determining the Effect of Real-Estate Attributes on Land-Use Function with the Use of the Rough Set Theory

No real-estate market analysis or property valuation would be complete without an evaluation of the effect that real-estate attributes have on property value. This problem is frequently addressed by analysts and professionals in the real-estate market.

The accuracy of such estimations is determined mainly by the applied analytical and computational methods. The techniques used in the analyses of distinctive properties are developed based on simple statistical relations and the principle of individual comparisons. Group appraisals generally rely on statistical analyses, mostly Pearson's linear correlation, and at least, several dozen transactions have to be taken into account. Evaluations of the effect that characteristics of a plot of land have on the type of use of that land are fraught with several problems:

- the effect real-estate attributes have on property function are fraught with several problems:
- there is a general scarcity of similar properties that differ only in one attribute;
- the existence of linear and deterministic correlations is generally assumed to facilitate the analytical process;
- the price of property has an instantaneous value;
- changes on the real-estate market are dynamic and unpredictable;
- a mutual correlation of property attributes (so multicollinearity) may disrupt the results of the analysis and its effect on property value; and
- the method of encoding property attributes is highly subjective.

In most cases, the selected subjective and objective parameters are highly obvious and easy to interpret, but they do not always represent the real phenomena or relations in the real-estate market.

Presupposing the effect and significance of property attributes, as a function of market trends, weighted or functional correlations, often leads to valuation problems when erroneous or subjective methodology is applied, from both a theoretical and a practical point of view. There are two solutions to the problem. The first involves the development of complex and advanced methods for investigating the effect of property attributes on the value of property. The second entails the use of a relatively simple analytical tool that eliminates subjective and preliminary assumptions.

The effect of the analyzed attributes on property value is often determined a priori. This is a rather worrying phenomenon because the real-estate market is a highly dynamic, changeable and – as demonstrated by recent events – unpredictable environment. The practice of anticipating trends, which seemed obvious a year ago, may produce highly misleading results because the value of real estate is a reflection on the buyers' future rather than past preferences. The most common mistakes include anticipating an increase in property prices in disregard of recent negative trends or overestimating the value of property due to its central location, which is not always a desirable attribute to the market of residential property. It is also generally assumed that commercial functions contribute more to the value of property than residential functions do and that land zoned for agricultural use deserves to be lower priced compared to industrial property. Land-use function has a considerable impact on the value of property, but it results from a number of factors, including property planning and location. Interestingly, the same function may have a different bearing on the price of property in various locations.

This study discusses a methodology for analyzing the effect of various factors on a given market phenomenon, including the influence of land-use function on its market value. This article also attempts to validate the theory of low effectiveness of real-estate markets, which is why the price is not regarded as an absolute determinant of property value.

The objective of this study was to select a method for evaluating the influence of property attributes, which most effectively determine the choice of property functions. In many spatial planning decisions, the distribution of various functions is often accidental due to the shortage of land in urban areas, an absence of compulsory purchase laws, or pressure exerted by developers on property owners. In the analyzed example, the choice of real-estate functions was determined in view of the existing resources rather than the principles of rational real-estate management or sustainable development goals. The real-estate function was not optimized in view of property prices, but it was chosen to best address the existing market situation.

The presented analysis relies on the findings by Renigier-Biłozor and Biłozor (2009a,b). This study analyzes the real-estate market in the city of Olsztyn, NE Poland. In Figure 3.2, the analyzed area was divided into units to which the predominant land-use functions were assigned.

The experimental material comprised a set of data from 121 land property transactions conducted in the Olsztyn area between January 2010 and October 2011. To investigate the effect that real-estate attributes have on land function, each property was described with a minimal set of attributes. These core attributes are usually taken into account by the local authorities to determine the manner of land use. Real-estate prices, marked successively as c_1, c_2, c_3, c_4, c_5, c_6 (Table 3.33), are conditional attributes. Real-estate function d is a decisional attribute.

The attributes were evaluated on the following scale:

c_1 – land area in m^2;

c_2 – location, encoded based on the following criteria: 1 – inconvenient, 2 – average, 3 – convenient, 4 – highly convenient;

c_3 – utilities supply, encoded based on the following criteria: 1 – none, 2 – partial supply, 3 – full supply;

c_4 – attractiveness, encoded based on the following criteria: 1 – low, 2 – average, 3 – high;

c_5 – transport accessibility: 1 – poor, 2 – average, 3 – satisfactory, 4 – highly satisfactory;

c_6 – price per m^2 of land as in October 2008;

d – function, encoded based on the following criteria: 1 – single-family housing, 2 – high-rise housing, 3 – commercial, 4 – transportation, 5 – industrial,

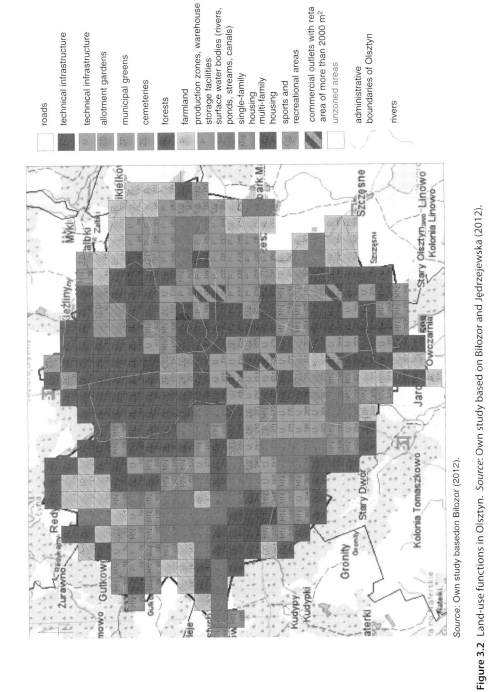

	roads
	technical infrastructure
	technical infrastructure
ZD	allotment gardens
ZP	municipal greens
ZC	cemeteries
	forests
R	farmland
P	production zones, warehouse storage facilities
	surface water bodies (rivers, ponds, streams, canals)
MN	single-family housing
	multi-family housing
US	sports and recreational areas
	commercial outlets with reta area of more than 2000 m^2
	unzoned areas
	administrative boundaries of Olsztyn
	rivers

Source: Own study based on Biłozor (2012). *Source:* Own study based on Biłozor and Jędrzejewska (2012).

Figure 3.2 Land-use functions in Olsztyn.

Table 3.33 Conditional attributes and a decisional attribute applied in the study.

	Conditional attributes					Decisional attribute
c_1	c_2	c_3	c_4	c_5	c_6	d
Area	Location	Utilities	Attractiveness	Accessibility	Price	Class of land use

Source: Own study.

6 – recreational with development options, 7 – others, 8 – warehouses and storage facilities, 9 – health-care facilities.

At the next stage, the values of each real-estate attribute were grouped according to the indiscernibility relation based on the rough set theory (Pawlak, 1982, 1991). For the purpose of analyzing this highly specific set of real-estate data and different scales (ratio scale, ordinal scale, interval scale, and nominal scale) for attribute assessment, the classical RST was expanded to include the value tolerance relation equation. The equation, developed and discussed by Stefanowski and Tsoukias (2000a, 2000b) and Stefanowski (2001), has been used in real-market analyses by d'Amato (2006, 2007, 2008), Renigier-Biłozor (2008a,b) and Renigier-Biłozor and Biłozor (2007, 2008).

The classical RST is based on the indiscernibility relation as a crisp equivalence relation; that is to say, two real-estate sites are indiscernible only if characterized by similar attributes. When the RST is expanded to include the value tolerance relation, the upper and lower approximation of the data set can be determined at different levels of the indiscernibility relation. The given relation can be expressed with the following equation:

$$R_j(x, y) = \frac{\max(0, \min(c_j(x), c_j(y)) + k - \max(c_j(x), c_j(y)))}{k} \qquad (3.17)$$

where:

$R_j(x, y)$	=	relation between sets with membership function [0,1];
$c_j(x), c_j(y)$	=	variable of the analyzed real estate;
k	=	coefficient of the standard deviation in the attribute set of a given real estate.

The equation is used to compare two data sets, that is, two sites in this case, and the obtained result within the 0–1 range marks the level of the indiscernibility relation. If coefficient k from the aforementioned equation is the standard deviation (as cited in d'Amato, 2006) of the analyzed attribute, similarity (indiscernibility) matrices for coefficient k are determined separately for each real-estate attribute. A sample matrix for the land-area attribute is presented in Table 3.34.

In the next step of the attribute validity analysis, the results generated by the aforementioned matrices are summed up, and the sum matrix is determined based on the following assumption:

$$R_j(x, p) = \max \left(\sum_{j=1}^{n} R_j(x, p) \right) \qquad (3.18)$$

where R_j is the value tolerance relation, x is the attribute of the analyzed real estate, p is the attribute relating to the conditional part of the investigated decision rule, and n is the

Table 3.34 Value tolerance relation matrix for the land-area attribute.

Area	1	2	3	4	5	6	7	8	9	10	11	12	13	14	15	...	121
1	1	0.97	0.68	0.96	0.85	0.96	0.96	0.90	0.84	0.91	0.97	0.76	0.91	0.73	0.88		0.95
2	0.97	1	0.71	0.93	0.88	0.99	0.99	0.87	0.87	0.94	1.00	0.79	0.93	0.76	0.90		0.98
3	0.68	0.71	1	0.64	0.83	0.72	0.72	0.58	0.84	0.77	0.71	0.92	0.77	0.95	0.80		0.73
4	0.96	0.93	0.64	1	0.81	0.92	0.92	0.94	0.80	0.87	0.93	0.72	0.87	0.69	0.84		0.91
5	0.85	0.88	0.83	0.81	1	0.90	0.89	0.75	0.99	0.94	0.88	0.91	0.95	0.88	0.98		0.90
6	0.96	0.99	0.72	0.92	0.90	1	1.00	0.86	0.89	0.95	0.99	0.80	0.95	0.77	0.92		0.99
7	0.96	0.99	0.72	0.92	0.89	1.00	1	0.86	0.89	0.95	0.99	0.80	0.95	0.77	0.92		0.99
8	0.90	0.87	0.58	0.94	0.75	0.86	0.86	1	0.74	0.81	0.87	0.66	0.81	0.63	0.78		0.85
9	0.84	0.87	0.84	0.80	0.99	0.89	0.89	0.74	1	0.93	0.87	0.92	0.94	0.88	0.97		0.89
10	0.91	0.94	0.77	0.87	0.94	0.95	0.95	0.81	0.93	1	0.94	0.85	1.00	0.82	0.97		0.96
11	0.97	1.00	0.71	0.93	0.88	0.99	0.99	0.87	0.87	0.94	1	0.79	0.93	0.76	0.90		0.98
12	0.76	0.79	0.92	0.72	0.91	0.80	0.80	0.66	0.92	0.85	0.79	1	0.85	0.97	0.88		0.81
13	0.91	0.93	0.77	0.87	0.95	0.95	0.95	0.81	0.94	1.00	0.93	0.85	1	0.82	0.97		0.96
14	0.73	0.76	0.95	0.69	0.88	0.77	0.77	0.63	0.88	0.82	0.76	0.97	0.82	1	0.85		0.78
15	0.88	0.90	0.80	0.84	0.98	0.92	0.92	0.78	0.97	0.97	0.90	0.88	0.97	0.85	1		0.93
...																	
121	0.95	0.98	0.73	0.91	0.90	0.99	0.99	0.85	0.89	0.96	0.98	0.81	0.96	0.78	0.93		1

Source: Own study.

number of real-estate attributes in the conditional part of the decision rule. A sample sum matrix is presented in Table 3.35.

In the next step of the discussed procedure, abstract classes were determined for each indiscernibility relation at a corresponding level of similarity between real-estate sites. A similarity level of 85% was adopted in view of the specific features of the real-estate market, the number of analyzed sites, and the diversified method of encoding various attributes. The aforementioned implies that if six conditional attributes are applied in the analysis, indiscernible (similar) sites will be sites whose sum resulting from value tolerance relation matrices (equation 3.2) is 5.1 and higher ($6 \times 85\% = 5.1$). Those sums are indicated in bold type in Table 3.35.

Abstract (indiscernibility) classes were then set for condition attributes, and in this case, they are equal to the number of sites input for analysis, that is, 121. For example, the following abstract classes are set for the first five sites:

I – 1
II – 2, 6, 7, 82
III – 3
IV – 4
V – 5, 81.

In the next step, the coverage and accuracy of approximation were determined for the sets from the family of decisional attributes. For this purpose, the entire real-estate set was divided into nine decision subgroups (corresponding to nine land-use functions, as per Table 3.33) where coverage indicators were determined. Sample calculations for

Table 3.35 Matrix of sums of real-estate values determined based on the value tolerance relation matrix of each attribute.

Sum	1	2	3	4	5	6	7	8	9	10	11	12	13	14	15	...	121
1	**6.00**	2.87	3.58	1.79	2.41	2.51	2.51	1.44	2.28	2.31	3.37	1.09	2.23	2.06	2.20		1.44
2	2.87	**6.00**	4.71	4.87	3.54	**5.64**	**5.64**	2.52	2.41	4.44	3.49	2.22	3.36	3.19	4.33		2.57
3	3.58	4.71	**6.00**	3.57	2.48	4.38	4.38	2.22	1.37	4.27	3.20	2.35	3.20	3.38	4.23		2.32
4	1.79	4.87	3.57	**6.00**	3.53	4.64	4.64	3.65	3.40	3.43	2.49	2.21	2.36	2.18	3.33		2.56
5	2.41	3.54	2.48	3.53	**6.00**	3.90	3.89	2.74	3.87	2.79	3.72	3.68	2.72	2.65	2.75		3.83
6	2.51	**5.64**	4.38	4.64	3.90	**6.00**	**6.00**	2.84	2.76	4.80	3.82	2.58	3.72	3.54	4.69		2.93
7	2.51	**5.64**	4.38	4.64	3.89	**6.00**	**6.00**	2.84	2.76	4.79	3.83	2.58	3.72	3.54	4.69		2.93
8	1.44	2.52	2.22	3.65	2.74	2.84	2.84	**6.00**	2.64	3.67	3.73	3.45	3.59	2.42	3.56		3.80
9	2.28	2.41	1.37	3.40	3.87	2.76	2.76	2.64	**6.00**	1.90	2.83	1.81	1.83	1.78	1.86		1.84
10	2.31	4.44	4.27	3.43	2.79	4.80	4.79	3.67	1.90	**6.00**	4.93	3.78	4.93	3.75	**5.90**		3.87
11	3.37	3.49	3.20	2.49	3.72	3.82	3.83	3.73	2.83	4.93	**6.00**	3.72	4.87	3.69	4.84		3.89
12	1.09	2.22	2.35	2.21	3.68	2.58	2.58	3.45	1.81	3.78	3.72	**6.00**	4.85	3.97	3.88		**5.65**
13	2.23	3.36	3.20	2.36	2.72	3.72	3.72	3.59	1.83	4.93	4.87	4.85	**6.00**	4.82	4.97		4.80
14	2.06	3.19	3.38	2.18	2.65	3.54	3.54	2.42	1.78	3.75	3.69	3.97	4.82	**6.00**	3.85		3.62
15	2.20	4.33	4.23	3.33	2.75	4.69	4.69	3.56	1.86	**5.90**	4.84	3.88	4.97	3.85	**6.00**		3.76
...																	
121	1.44	2.57	2.32	2.56	3.83	2.93	2.93	3.80	1.84	3.87	3.89	**5.65**	4.80	3.62	3.76		**6.00**

Source: own study.

decisional attribute no. 1, that is, the single-family housing function, are presented in Table 3.36.

Since the indicators of coverage and accuracy of approximation of the RST fit the classical theory assumptions, the authors of this study proposed additional coverage and accuracy indicators, which are better adapted to the value tolerance relation (as seen in the first column of Table 3.36). The coverage of the entire abstract set for a given decisional attribute was estimated by summing up the value of each indicator, as per Table 3.36. A similar procedure was applied to the eight remaining decisional attribute types.

To estimate each attribute's validity for other land functions, the entire procedure was repeated from the moment of calculating the matrix sums, by excluding every successive attribute and observing the changes induced by coverage indicators in the set of analyzed sites. A sample sum matrix without the land-area attribute is presented in Table 3.35. Since the number of investigated attributes is equal to 5 (without successive attributes), indiscernible (similar) sites will be sites whose sum resulting from value tolerance relation matrices (equation 3.2) is 4.25 and higher ($5 \times 85\% = 4.25$). Those sums are indicated in bold type in Table 3.37.

The aforementioned results indicate that the choice of function is affected by attributes that, in line with the RST, form the core of the attribute set, as illustrated in Table 3.38 (marked with a cross).

The aforementioned results merely outline the range of factors that were significant in the analyzed problem. For a more accurate description of each attribute's significance and effect on property functions, weight coefficients were calculated in reference to the

Table 3.36 Approximation of classification of sets from the family of decisional attributes for function 1 – single-family housing.

Decisional attribute no. 1	No. of sites in indisc. class of decisional attributes	No. of lower approxim. sites (classical theory)	No. of sites from upper approxim. (classical theory)	No. of positive cover sites	No. of conditional attributes from the set's boundary area	No. of conditional attributes from lower approxim.	No. of sites from lower approx. (nonre-peatable)	No. of sites from upper approxim. (nonre-peatable)
Column	1	2	3	4	5	6	7	8
Approxi-mation results	38	34	132	101	18	20	26	51
C-accuracy of approxi-mation (classical theory) column 2 divided by column 3		34/132 = 0.26						
C-cover of approxima-tion (classical theory) col. 6/col. 1	20/38 = 0.53							
C-accuracy of approxi-mation (authors) col. 7/col. 8								26/51 = 0.51
C-cover of approxima-tion (authors) col. 7/col. 1	26/38 = 0.68							
C-positive approxima-tion (authors) col. 4/col. 3			101/132 = 0.76					
sum = 0.26 + 0.53 + 0.51 + 0.68 + 0.76 = 2.74								

Source: own study.

weight of property attributes used in valuation. A general formula for calculating correlation coefficients was used, where the approximation coefficients from Table 3.36 were input in r, as follows:

$$r_i = 1 - \frac{W a_i}{W W a}$$

Table 3.37 Matrix of sums of real-estate values without the land-area attribute.

Without area	1	2	3	4	5	6	7	8	9	10	11	12	13	14	15	...	121
1	**5.00**	1.90	2.90	0.84	1.56	1.56	1.56	0.54	1.43	1.40	2.39	0.33	1.33	1.33	1.33		0.49
2	1.90	**5.00**	4.00	3.94	2.66	**4.66**	**4.66**	1.64	1.53	3.50	2.50	1.43	2.43	2.43	3.43		1.59
3	2.90	4.00	**5.00**	2.94	1.66	3.66	3.66	1.64	0.53	3.50	2.50	1.43	2.43	2.43	3.43		1.59
4	0.84	3.94	2.94	**5.00**	2.72	3.72	3.72	2.71	2.60	2.56	1.56	1.50	1.49	1.49	2.49		1.65
5	1.56	2.66	1.66	2.72	**5.00**	3.00	3.00	1.99	2.88	1.84	2.84	2.78	1.77	1.77	1.77		2.93
6	1.56	**4.66**	3.66	3.72	3.00	**5.00**	**5.00**	1.99	1.88	3.84	2.84	1.78	2.77	2.77	3.77		1.93
7	1.56	**4.66**	3.66	3.72	3.00	**5.00**	**5.00**	1.99	1.88	3.84	2.84	1.78	2.77	2.77	3.77		1.93
8	0.54	1.64	1.64	2.71	1.99	1.99	1.99	**5.00**	1.89	2.86	2.85	2.79	2.79	1.79	2.79		2.95
9	1.43	1.53	0.53	2.60	2.88	1.88	1.88	1.89	**5.00**	0.97	1.96	0.90	0.89	0.89	0.89		0.95
10	1.40	3.50	3.50	2.56	1.84	3.84	3.84	2.86	0.97	**5.00**	4.00	2.93	3.93	2.93	**4.93**		2.91
11	2.39	2.50	2.50	1.56	2.84	2.84	2.84	2.85	1.96	4.00	**5.00**	2.94	3.93	2.93	3.93		2.91
12	0.33	1.43	1.43	1.50	2.78	1.78	1.78	2.79	0.90	2.93	2.94	**5.00**	4.00	3.00	3.00		**4.84**
13	1.33	2.43	2.43	1.49	1.77	2.77	2.77	2.79	0.89	3.93	3.93	4.00	**5.00**	4.00	4.00		3.84
14	1.33	2.43	2.43	1.49	1.77	2.77	2.77	1.79	0.89	2.93	2.93	3.00	4.00	**5.00**	3.00		2.84
15	1.33	3.43	3.43	2.49	1.77	3.77	3.77	2.79	0.89	**4.93**	3.93	3.00	4.00	3.00	**5.00**		2.84
....																	
121	0.49	1.59	1.59	1.65	2.93	1.93	1.93	2.95	0.95	2.91	2.91	**4.84**	3.84	2.84	2.84		**5.00**

Source: Own study.

Table 3.38 Core of decisional attributes.

	Area	Location	Utilities	Attractiveness	Accessibility	Price
Decisional attribute no. 1	×				×	×
Decisional attribute no. 2	×	×	×	×	×	×
Decisional attribute no. 3	×	×	×		×	×
Decisional attribute no. 4	×	×	×		×	
Decisional attribute no. 5	×	×	×	×	×	×
Decisional attribute no. 6		×	×			
Decisional attribute no. 7		×	×		×	×
Decisional attribute no. 8	×	×				×
Decisional attribute no. 9*	–	–	–	–	–	–

*The results for decision attribute no. 9 were rejected – if any of the attributes are equal to zero, a given set is completely discernible; that is, it corresponds to other decisional attributes. Decision no. 9 does not show any individual dependencies in relation to conditional attributes.

$$w_i = \frac{r_i^2}{\sum_{i=1}^{k} r_i^2}$$

Source: Own study.

where:

Wa_i – approximation coefficient after removing a successive attribute;

WWa – approximation coefficient for the entire set of attributes.

The weight coefficients of attributes in each functional category are presented in Table 3.39.

In line with the RST, the following attributes affected the choice of function for a given real-estate set of objects:

- *single-family housing function* – area, location, transport accessibility, and price;
- *high-rise housing function* – area, location, utilities supply, attractiveness, transport accessibility, and price;
- *commercial function* – area, location, utilities supply, transport accessibility, and price;
- *transportation function* – area, location, utilities supply, transport accessibility;
- *industrial function* – area, location, utilities supply, attractiveness, transport accessibility, and price;
- *recreational function* – location, utilities supply;
- *other function* – location, utilities supply, transport accessibility, and price;
- *warehouses and storage facilities function* – area, location, and price.

The presented methodology for determining the effect of real-estate attributes on the selection of the appropriate land function significantly contributes to real market analysis. An analysis of real-estate transactions generated a group of attributes, which considerably affect the designation and, consequently, the value of property. The significance of each real-estate attribute was assessed with the use of the RST combined with the value tolerance relation.

In most cases, real-estate attributes are selected, and their significance is assessed based on the results of a statistical analysis. A number of conditions have to be met

Table 3.39 Weight coefficients of property attributes in the examined functional categories.

Function		Area	Location	Utilities	Attractiveness	Accessibility	Price
Single-family housing	Weight coefficient of property attribute	0.13	0.27	0.04	0.01	0.37	0.18
Multifamily housing		0.05	0.39	0.30	0.12	0.07	0.07
Commercial		0.07	0.26	0.22	0.02	0.29	0.14
Transportation		0.03	0.12	0.24	0.01	0.58	0.02
Industrial		0.05	0.21	0.21	0.07	0.18	0.28
Recreational		0.00	0.19	0.02	0.53	0.24	0.02
Other		0.00	0.47	0.03	0.01	0.27	0.22
Warehouse and storage		0.34	0.49	0.00	0.00	0.00	0.17

The aforementioned results indicate which attributes contribute most to the choice of different property functions. They are presented graphically in Figure 3.3.

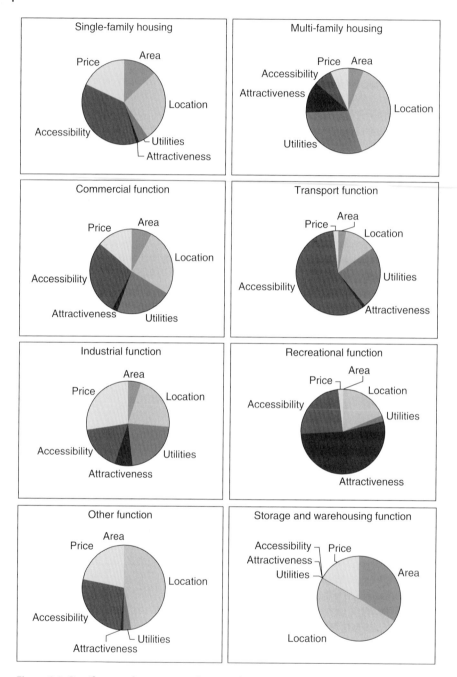

Figure 3.3 Significance of property attributes in the choice of property functions. *Source*: Own study.

for statistical analyses to produce reliable results. A sufficient set of real-estate data has to be collected (the larger the database, the more accurate the results), real-estate attributes have to be encoded on a corresponding scale (a uniform scale for all attributes is preferred), and the relations, the functional dependencies, and the distribution of all statistical model parameters have to be investigated.

The applied method for determining the effect that real-estate attributes have on the selection of the appropriate land-use function (and property valuation), based on the RST, poses an alternative to statistical analyses deployed in real-estate market surveys. The applied theory and the proposed procedure are recommended mostly for rare, imprecise data and for less effective real-estate markets.

Concluding Remarks

We have a set of attributes determining the land use for a given plot of land. This is based on actual transactions. This chapter presented an alternative method with certain benefits for assessing the determinants of land use.

What are the benefits? No specific assumptions are required for employing this kind of modeling ("the data speak for themselves"); the output of this model is unique according to a common set of conditional attributes. Therefore, there is no dependence of the final result on the shape of the function assumed (as in regression analysis). It even works with small samples and really few observations. The attractiveness for applying this method to analyzing land and real-estate prices is obvious – particularly, if one considers that having few observations is often the case in real-estate markets all over the world.

Part 4

Empirical Applications of Market Analysis

4.0

Introduction
Tom Kauko

Shift in Focus

While various principles, processes, procedures and protocols (the 4 P's, if you like) underpinning the valuation domain dominate the discussion in the other parts of the book, the focus in this part is switched towards the type of analysis carried out by social scientists and economists who do not look for a direct practical valuation application – only empirical evidence to inform practical applications. In other words, the aim of this part is to examine only supporting arguments based on empirical evidence. Thus, the focus of data issues and empirical context switches from valuation behaviour and hypothetical valuations in Parts 1–3 to actual historic market transactions and valuations in this part. However, to reassure, the former issues will be revisited in the last two parts of this volume again.

In the earlier parts of the book, the basis for our argument in favour of property market, value, valuation and/or development sustainability was mainly in some key concepts/conceptualisation supported by a selection of more or less anecdotal evidence. In this part, we move on to explore the potential valuation applicability of various empirical estimates and modelling outcomes. [Such applicability could, for example, be understood in the vein of the argument of those in the sustainability debate, who search indicators for sustainability (see e.g. Sayce *et al.*, 2007).] On the other hand, the econometrics (mainly hedonic and time-series modelling contributions) have neglected the sustainability variables and focused on more traditional market indicators [but see recent exceptions such as Eichholz *et al.* (2009, 2010), Deng *et al.* (2010), Yu and Tu (2011) and Fuerst and McAllister (2011)]. We offer here four potential cases that are

Value in a Changing Built Environment, First Edition.
Edited by David Lorenz, Peter Dent and Tom Kauko.
© 2018 John Wiley & Sons Ltd. Published 2018 by John Wiley & Sons Ltd.

based on quantitative modelling outcomes with innovative methods of data analysis. [For a presentation of some of the methodological approaches underpinning them, see Kauko and d'Amato (2008).] The key argument here is that these potential applications pertain to empirical, quantifiable evidence of price and related variables at the local and regional levels (not national or supranational levels that so often are the starting points of most empirical real-estate studies) as this is the level where sustainability problems related to property markets and land use are manifested and combated. Moreover, when more direct sustainability data is not available – which still is a reasonable assumption in most contemporary market contexts and also in our following contributions, the idea is to factor in sustainability at the level of potential applications (rather than at the level of methodology).

It is – luckily for us – already possible to find growing quantities of more qualitative real-estate applications that go beyond hedonic/NCE assumptions. In such studies, the effect of a few green/sustainability measures are not being isolated, but instead, a holistic-minded picture of the more or less green/sustainable contributions of the building/site are analysed, discussed and put in more practical clothing than what the NCE underpinnings would allow. See, for example, the following sample of studies: Lorenz *et al.* (2007) on residential property; Ellison *et al.* (2007) as well as Sayce *et al.* (2007) on commercial property; and Hemphill *et al.* (2004a,b) on urban renewal projects. Furthermore, less academic but related material has been published by Cox *et al.* (2002), Taylor Wessing (2009), RICS (2010a,b); and Sayce *et al.* (2010). See also Warren-Myers (2011, 2012) and Warren-Myers and Reed (2010).

On the basis of what we have argued (and – as it is in our nature – speculated) in the previous parts, it should be obvious that, rather than resorting to ivory-tower analysis, the new approach that we advocate should be illustrated by case studies. These would involve two different realms: on the one hand, from specific projects of investors such as Igloo who have already taken both a long-term view of their investment in mixed use regeneration schemes and their social and environmental impact and value; on the other hand, experimental new 'showcase' areas such as Vauban, Freiburg, where the whole political culture about sustainability shapes thinking about investment and its value and thus has important effects on the economy of the city, creation of new business opportunities, education and training, tourism, attracting skilled people to high-quality environment and so on. Thus, either attention should be paid to the key actors or to the place.

Finally, we must not forget that the overall purpose of this book is to advance value theory. The routes to embark on this endeavour are of two main types: one is about mass appraisal of residential property and automatic valuation methods/models (AVMs); the other is about the philosophy of value creation and price setting. While the latter point has been well covered in the three earlier parts, this part deals with the former point; it also deals with the extent to which increasing sophistication in quantification and computerisation can replace a more human-centred approach. This is an increasingly popularised problem area, partly because of education of more advanced statistical and mathematical techniques and partly because of an ongoing 'negative evolution' where problems of reliability are caused by the crisis as documented in Parts 1 and 2 in this volume. Unfortunately, the 'human valuers' are being blamed and number-crunching elevated as a solution to the problems of overinflated valuations at the time of the crisis. Here, d'Amato (2013) observes that, since the crisis begun in 2007–2008, both in practice and in academia, AVM (based on MRA/Hedonics, in particular) is more favoured compared to expert opinions, which he warns is dangerous – and I absolutely agree on this suggestion. On the other hand, in an optimistic spirit, one may argue that, to suggest that the expert valuers are to blame for the crisis only poses a challenge for expert valuers. Remember that there are no problems, only challenges!

This challenge has already been documented in d'Amato and Kauko (2008). The four chapters covered in this part are, to a great extent, following the same line of reasoning and also updating it so as to fit a post-crisis situation. The basic argument is that a statistical or mathematical approach to valuation (and other kinds of price analysis supporting the valuation) is apt – and often even necessary – to generate an estimate of market price. When such an estimate is generated, the next task is to justify how this figure was reached. This, in turn, requires analytical reasoning on three different levels:

1) The reliability and validity of the data collected
2) The accuracy of the modelling technique when the estimates are compared with actual prices
3) An evaluation of the similarity or compatibility between the market context (time, place and segment) where the valuation takes place and the data is collected.

The sad fact is that, despite the best efforts to separate the human- and AVM-based approaches – and with an increasing frequency in favour of the latter, the estimate always remains an opinion of the actual, unobservable market value (cf. d'Amato, 2013). We have witnessed this frustrating state of affairs in the standard valuation paradigm, and today, we see the same in the improved paradigm where sustainability of value (and valuation) is recognised – not the least because of the impact of the financial crisis.

Presentation of Individual Chapter Summaries

This part begins with a chapter by Malgorzata Renigier-Bilozor and Radoslaw Wisniewski. They imply that the real-estate market comprises a socio-economic subsystem, in which system complexity exists in relation to its parts such as property attributes, geographical scales, administrative procedures, actor categories, property types and market segments. Each element in the system is furthermore evaluated differently in relation to what kind of meanings an actor puts there, they point out. Finally, these authors put forward a valid critique of solely computerised appraisals. In doing so, they remind us about the importance of the delicate 'human' aspect of understanding a given market. [This much resonates with the comment by d'Amato (2013).]

In the second chapter of this part, the author of this introduction ties three analytical concepts together: AVMs, economic sustainability, and the financial crisis. Given the pivotal role of the housing bubble in the subsequent credit crunch, he raises the following question: could the global financial crisis have been moderated if prudent property valuations had been made at the time of issuing bank loans and if governments and institutions had been concerned about raising the quality of market information? Indeed, we still lack the adequate knowledge about measuring house prices and mapping the markets. As a corollary, are AVMs useful for handling mortgage-lending problems? This chapter addresses the aforementioned issues in two ways: on one hand, it presents an empirical modelling application for local housing markets; on the other hand, it examines more qualitative, rhetorical arguments for the use of AVMs in this field. After an overview of the problems involved a novel framework based on the concept of economic sustainability that is argued to connect with the financial crisis, credit crunch and housing bubble discourse is proposed – it is to note that, traditionally, housing market modelling and sustainable development paradigms are treated as incompatible. Defining a sustainable housing market depends on long-term processes and often partial criteria. An empirical module concerning the development of house prices in relation to incomes in Trondheim, Norway, in the period of 1993–2007, is added, to illustrate the power of this approach.

In the third chapter of this part, Renigier-Bilozor and Wisniewski relate socio-demographic data with a classification of market efficiency in Polish cities. The findings of this study point to enormous variations in the two applied indicators: one, turnover in relation to the population; two, household income in relation to price per square metre. The computations result in a categorisation of the cities. Using these categories for local market analysis enables construction of a decision table with different decision classes. The computation is performed with rough set theory extended with valued tolerance relation. This is a mathematical technique that has recently been introduced in a real-estate context (see d'Amato and Siniak, 2003, 2008). Renigier-Bilozor and Wisniewski suggest that this methodological approach could enhance the decision-making process in relation to real-estate management. In this way, situations where market inefficiency generates negative outcomes and further leads to misguided actions would be avoided.

In the fourth and final chapter of this part, Maurizio d'Amato deals with property market cycles. Cyclical capitalisation has been, in fact, paid relatively close attention in the recent RICS Professional global guidance note (RICS, 2013). This note recommends, among others, valuers to state their opinions on the relationship between sustainability and valuation. The prognosis of RICS is that sustainability issues are likely to gain importance over time, and therefore, [sic] valuers are encouraged to improve their awareness of any new sustainable developments that may have an impact on value, including technology, legislation, policy, fiscal measures and the wider market attitudes towards sustainability. The key issue here, as d'Amato also recognises, is how to look into the future in an income-based valuation context.

In d'Amato's analysis, real-estate market cycles have the tendency to distort the income-based capitalisation estimates. According to d'Amato, this is a fault for which the solution would be to integrate the observation of market rents with local trend analysis. In particular, he focuses on yield capitalisation for a limited number of time periods using discounted cash flow (DCF) methodology and, more particularly, on how to deal with the future in a DCF modelling exercise. The weakness about the standard DCF approach is that different assumptions generate different forecasts, and, with the myth of an ever-improving real-estate market, which, according to this author, is in itself a result of the valuation approach, resulting estimates tend to neglect the local property market cycle. The remedy offered by d'Amato is a cyclical capitalisation approach. After subsequently showing the technical theoretical underpinnings of this approach (or actually three different types of approaches), he finally demonstrates this approach with an application of London office market time-series data. While the RICS note discussed earlier arguably misses some more explicit issues of economic and social sustainability (social cohesion and sense of community, for instance), to the extent it deals with the DCF methodology, it recognises the relevant type of issues, namely that sustainability has the potential to increase the attractiveness of the investment and that valuers therefore '... should seek to collect sustainability data and use them when analysing yields' (RICS, 2013, p. 15). Against this parallel development in the practical literature, d'Amato's contribution really 'hits the nail on its head': instead of using assumptions, we should use real data despite the general convenience of continuing with the established procedure.

4.1

Directions for Exploration of New Methods of Identifying and Determining Relationships and Dependencies on the Real-Estate Market

Malgorzata Renigier-Bilozor and Radoslaw Wisniewski

Introduction

The end of the twentieth century and the beginning of the twenty-first century constitute an era of fast socioeconomic development in which creating systems for collecting, processing, and publicizing information, including geoinformation, for a variety of purposes has become essential. Such systems are indispensible in order to function properly, not only in the economic sphere but also in the social and environmental spheres. Only when these three spheres (economic, social, and environmental) are combined, can we expect the consolidated development of the whole (information) society under the conditions of autonomous development.

In reference to the introduction, the main aim of this book is to emphasize the necessity of theoretical and practical changes in the approach to determining real-estate value, preceded by an analysis of the market. All the authors of this book support the claim that the current approach to valuation, as a result of the interpretations of the influences of physical real-estate attributes under local conditions, is very simplistic. In the introduction, the authors emphasize the fact that the "… concept of property value can be explained by its components and the linkages between economic, environmental, social and cultural measures and components of property value" (see p. 2).

The real-estate market, one of the fastest developing goods markets, has become a place for large-scale investments. Nowadays, big corporations, specialized joint-stock companies, small-trade companies, and ordinary people invest in the market. All of them count on making some kind of profit. An in-depth analysis of the real-estate market (with particular attention paid to valuing real estate) under such conditions is extremely difficult and complicated, since reconstructing all the behaviors of individual real-estate market participants is (most likely) impossible. Nevertheless, such analyses should be conducted; the main reason for this is the aspiration to diagnose structures and assess the operational state of currently functioning real-estate markets. Knowledge on this subject is needed by decision-makers who take decisions based on the structure and functions assigned to the real-estate market system.

The relationships identified in the real-estate market are very complicated. Presently, the real-estate market is not only a place where one can observe the performance of a given country's economic system (e.g., Poland, France, United States, or China) or unions of countries (e.g., the European Union), it is also the competition groups for immense groups of investors, whether such groups are formed by individual investors buying flats or huge property developers realizing more advanced investments. The real-estate market has changed from a passive market to an active one. After all, it was the processes taking place in this system that turned out to be the source and cause of the financial and economic crisis of 2008, which continues to this day. Its operation in the economic system also reveals much activity in terms of financial instruments. Real estate has gained the interest of various sectors of the economy; moreover, those sectors hope to fulfill not only their personal needs (e.g., housing) but also the needs of others, especially connected with making a profit. According to Rogers (1998), a "rapid diffusion of optimal actions," including organizational efforts, may affect the total efficiency and may generate higher profits.

All these factors lead to the claim that the value of real estate and means of determining it have become important, not only from the perspective of simple buy–sell transactions but also in valuing objects of investments in scales (perspectives), which nobody used to consider a few years back. The valuation of real estate has become the foundation of a "healthily" functioning real-estate market as an economic sector in many European countries and throughout the world. Such assessment is undergoing and should undergo evolution or revolution.

Evolution is obvious – it stems from premises delivered by needs of the information society in which we live (development of procedures, processes, systems, etc.) as well as economic needs (more precisely, quickly, comprehensively, etc.). The information efficiency (of the market) signifies a state in which all publicly available information (both fundamental data and the sole history of prices) is already discounted from the current price. Changes therefore take place, only when the market receives new information (Fama, 1965, 1971, 1991). Procedures, methods, and techniques of assessing real estate will always be evolving. Such is the fate of procedures directly connected with the socioeconomic development of humans.

Revolution in such a scope is a relatively new process. Each system, including the economic and real-estate systems, is subject to a certain cycle – "product life cycle," "economic cycle," and "real-estate market cycle." This cyclical nature of events is a frequently occurring phenomenon, and the real estate is no exception. This phenomenon, however, has one very important characteristic feature – it assumes that a system will remain in a given environment. So, what happens when this environment undergoes sudden changes? The answer is simple: the real-estate market must adapt (revolution) if it is not to undergo temporal degradation; since the market must adapt, its procedures, methods, and techniques of valuating real estate must also be subjected to adaptation (revolution). The main factors of revolutionary nature can include the following: changes in the shaping of the ecological worldview (ecological footprint); an increased importance of the role of real estate, especially its value in economic and social processes (the significance of real estate as a component of wealth, investment factor); the development of modern methods for collecting and processing information (geoinformation systems, dedicated systems); increasing access to data and information along with falling costs of obtaining information (the Internet); and the development of specialized and professional methods of analyzing data and information (database systems and high processing power of computers). All these factors ought to be analyzed as a whole and separately since they permeate and complete each other. The scope of their influence cannot be directly determined by means of traditional research methods. These factors, or rather the increase in their importance, are an indication of the development of the real-estate sector as a whole. The development of the real-estate sector is not the same in different countries. In some countries, the real-estate market can be compared to a well-working "Mercedes"; in others, a "Fiat,"; and in some others, yet, a mere "Kia." In a number of countries, the real-estate market is at its initial phase of development, and there are even countries where it simply does not exist.

It should be noted that the situation we are currently observing on the real-estate markets of different countries is slowly maturing to the idea of a revolution. The valuation processes have become very important for a single investor (person), district (local government), country, or international organization. The upcoming time of changes in valuation processes necessitates finding completely new methodological solutions or revising the existing ones. This time of change is neither simple nor pleasant, especially in a situation when people and entities involved in the real-estate market (valuation, advising, etc.) posses different stores of information, knowledge, and skills. According to Peters (1997, following Pareto), a distribution has fatter tails (suggesting the inefficiency of a market where prices do not follow random walks) when information reaches the market irregularly or when the investors' response to information is delayed.

In the period of an upcoming revolution in valuating real estate, one should pay close attention to the current foundations of this process as well as identify and seek out the existing risks and problems. On the one hand, this will allow people to prepare for changes; on the other, it will enable them to be active "players" in creating these solutions as opposed to passive "observers."

This chapter presents the theoretical and practical premises for identifying the existing risks and problems in the valuation of real estate. A few different stands on valuating real estate are presented. The analysis does not have the nature of a case study. Information and knowledge by theoreticians and practitioners who deal with different aspects of how the real-estate market functions around the world are presented and applied. The notion of "valuating real estate" is used throughout the work. This notion covers not only the determination of the value of real estate by professionals (real-estate appraisers) but also the widely understood process of valuating real objects that constitute real estate for various purposes by different entities.

The Real-Estate Sector – Analysis and Challenges

Each valuation of real estate is carried out together with or partially together with processes occurring in the real-estate market system, by designated people, utilizing appropriate information resources and suitable methods of analysis and deduction. The indicated factors occur in every decision process that takes place within the real-estate market. These factors should be analyzed not only at a subjective (individual) level of importance of each of them, but also in terms of their mutual relationships and interdependence.

From the presented viewpoint, basic problems in the analyses of the real-estate market connected with the valuation of real estate can be found in the following areas:

- **The real-estate market** – effectiveness, structure, function, its environment, and so forth
- **Real-estate market participants (entities)** – preferences, motivation, information resources, skills, capabilities, and so forth
- **Real estate and its characteristic traits** – immobility, uniqueness, capital intensity, susceptibility to local influences, and so forth
- **Systems that enable the collection and analysis of information** – access to information, reliability, validity, and quality of information, costs of obtaining information, and problem with the ability to assess real-estate market information efficiency
- **Level of knowledge on the real-estate market and its participants** – complicatedness of processes, complexity of decision-making procedures, ignorance of market participants, poor "real-estate" awareness, and subjectivity
- **Research and analytical methods** – lack of appropriate methods, separation of existing methods from the research topic, impossibility of application to formal restrictions, and abuse of existing methods at variance with their purpose.

The indicated problem areas are by no means complete. They should be treated as the basic and most important, but not exclusive. On some occasions, they occur and take part in real-estate valuation processes individually, whereas in others, they participate in pairs or together. This means that their influence should be looked into both individually and collectively. In the first case, it is difficult to separate the groups of factors since only when they occur together, they allow us to understand the phenomena they describe. The analyses of problem-causing factors in groups of factors presented within this work are not to be treated separately. Some factors can be classified under various groups.

The Real-Estate Market System

The real-estate market is a system. This thesis can easily be proven and, at the same time, easily abolished. Proving it does not require much evidence. It is enough to ask the market participants about the way it functions, what structures it possesses, and what constitutes its environment, and the answers will lead to a conclusion that confirms the thesis. Abolishing the thesis is equally simple: the system cannot be touched nor seen. But the system is in fact actual and real. Transactions take place in this system, profits are made on it, and taxes are collected from real estate. Entities operate in this system along with real objects, data is registered, information is created, and phenomena and processes characteristic of this market are observed.

The real-estate market is a very complex system that often results in the low efficiency and practical verifiability of analysis results, including popularly applied statistical tools. The starting point for improving effectiveness and efficiency of valuating real estate on the real-estate market is the application of appropriate research methods and procedures that take into consideration the distinctiveness of the market. Valuation should also not be generalized to suit all markets, including the capital market. Many determinants contribute to the distinctiveness of this market that is influenced by, among others, the following factors:

- Significant differences between pieces of real estate (no two are identical).
- Inaccuracy and "fuzzy" nature of real-estate data (caused, among others, by stochastic factors, which reflect random processes that escape the commonly recognized cause-and-effect market norms).
- Absence of homogeneous functional dependencies between real-estate attributes and its decision-making element represented by the value, function, or method of managing real estate.
- Significant variation in the quantity of available information, dependent on the type of market analyzed (region).
- Complexity of data description (differences in the selection of scales for recording attributes); the same feature can be described in multiple ways and assigned a different range of appraisal scores.
- Multicriterial intended use of real estate (every piece of real estate can be utilized and managed in a number of ways).
- Lack of comprehensive information (due to the lack of homogeneous information systems for collecting real-estate data, which results in limited and incomplete knowledge about real estate and market prices).

Some of the indicated determinants could be assigned to other groups of problem-causing factors. Their significance and role are multidirectional and ambiguous.

Real-estate markets reveal little similarity. The low level of similarity can be both an advantage and a disadvantage. For investors who hope to make profits, this is an advantage. These are, of course, different for every market; however, thanks to appropriate allocative procedures, it becomes possible to make profits as a result of this diversity. Conversely, in the practice of valuating real estate, the low similarity of markets is an impediment. Uniform and homogeneous as well as standardized valuation methods cannot be applied under such conditions. The valuer is forced to choose methods in a way that is dependent on the local situation and information resources that can be found in this section of the market.

The next problem that the real-estate valuation process faces is the spatial scope (size) of the real-estate market and the various understandings of its spatial scope. "Market size," contrary to popular belief, does matter. Everyone involved in the real-estate market, especially professional valuers, always relies on a given area of the market. They do not analyze, in a spatial sense, the whole market but only its selected sections. In practice, each of them can do this differently. By choosing a different spatial scope, the valuer bases his or her findings on a different set of observations, which in turn leads to inconsistency in the valuation of real estate since the reference base can differ.

The heterogeneity of spatial scope also applies to the different understandings of spatial scope. This issue is viewed differently by the owner of a small house than by an administrative district and differently yet by a property developer investing in the real-estate market, not to mention giant international corporations for whom, for example, the localness of a market is not a part of a given district of region but rather a whole country or region of Europe or Asia. From this perspective, the Australian real-estate market can be a local market for corporations, whereas for the citizens of Australia, it will surely be a national one. The same geographical area will be described and defined differently by its various market participants. This topic will be expanded in the following sections.

Real-estate markets, as other systems of a similar nature, are not homogeneous in terms of the number of transactions realized in a given unit of time. Transactions that take place in the real-estate market are subject to changes of an often predictable nature. In Europe, on average, real-estate market participants make real-estate transactions involving approximately 5% of the total number of pieces of real estate on a yearly scale. In this context, transactions are being and will continue to be made. The transaction stream of objects is predictable. This is an important trait in the context of dynamic features of the real-estate market. It also holds great importance in the estimation of real-estate value. However, situations where transactions are not made (such as during holiday breaks) or their number is much higher/lower than the average (e.g., changes in tax law) do occur. In real-estate valuation processes, this leads to the formation of cycles on the real-estate market, trends, and "information gaps" in data series. In the context of valuation, information gaps are not only mere gaps in data series. They signify that, at a given time, information regarding the current preferences of real-estate market participants is unknown. This can lead to significant perturbations in valuation in the event when the information gap covers a period of dynamic changes in the participants' behavior, changes in price, or preferences on the market. The accumulation of transactions over time can also prove to be problematic. The accumulation of transactions, especially when it occurs over a longer period of time, can bring about the phenomenon of "becoming accustomed to a trend." Participants cease to look for new information because the previous observed accumulation of information (number of transactions) over a short period of time can lead to a conviction concerning the certainty of judgments. In these cases, the arithmetic mean of a price set will be stable and only confirmed by standard deviation. The lack of data, information gaps, and accumulation of information pose a challenge for many methods of real-estate valuation.

The real-estate market is subject to constant development, which makes it similar to the socioeconomic development of a given country or region. Real estate is an integral part of an environment that includes the economic, social, and natural environments. This means that they cannot be treated as secluded (from the rest of the environment) formations. Real estate is subject to the same trends, processes, and procedures as other socioeconomic subsystems. These include ecodevelopment, environmental protection, natural resource deficits, or the financial crisis. All of these factors affect real estate in various ways, and their influence should not only be noticed but also taken into account during valuation processes.

The Participants (Entities) of the Real-Estate Market

As already observed in the previous subchapter, the real-estate market is formed, among others, by entities. The notion of an entity should be understood broadly. One can list whole groups of professionals who operate in the sphere of real estate. From the perspective of the conducted analyses, it is practical to divide these entities into three groups: individuals (microscale – small residential houses), small organizations (mezzo scale – the real estate of a given administrative district or property developer), and large organizations (macroscale – large property developers, investment funds, international corporations). Each of these subjects has a slightly different view on the real-estate market and the value of real estate. They assign different functions to real estate, treat the risk connected with the sphere of real estate differently, and finally, behave differently, thereby taking part in creating the diverse depiction of the real-estate market. These entities also treat valuation processes differently, assigning different levels of importance to the quality, reliability, or completeness of a valuation.

Real-estate market participants (entities) are independent and work in their own interest. This means that each of these entities is characterized by different preferences, expectations, has a different aversion to risk, and so forth, thus creating his/her own image of the market. This is important to the market system since diversity constitutes a factor that leads to development. The diversity of actions signifies the lack of routine, a focus on obtaining new information, making profits, minimizing the risk of loss, and so forth. These factors create the previously mentioned complexity of the real-estate market.

This complexity and the factors indicated earlier naturally lead to various expectations of the employer and increase the contractor's responsibility in valuation processes. With different expectations held by the indicated entities, the valuation process is at risk of dangerous unlawful behavior or that which falls outside the accepted norms of conduct.

Real-estate valuation professionals should be immune to such actions (non rational behaviour, e.g. anchoring selling prices to past market situation, buyers being targeted based on neighbourhood sentiment, proximity to one's family and own definition of prestige).

In an information society, information is the main causative factor. Under the specific conditions observed within the real-estate market, in addition to technical, economic, and other kinds of market information, whole sets of significant information that characterize the individual or collective behavior of real-estate market participants also exist. The previously mentioned individualized expectations and needs of market participants are changed into information streams, which, when flowing into the real-estate market system, evoke certain reactions, the results of which we experience on a day-to-day basis. Is such information important in real-estate valuation processes? The answer to this question is not simple and depends on the scale of operation accepted by the valuer and the object of his/her appraisal. Information describing the influence of the market participants' actions and behaviors is often omitted in the analyses connected with real-estate valuation. On the microscale, their influence at the strategic level is large; however, at the operational level, it is often overlooked. Determining the value of a building lot at the center of a residential district does not necessitate obtaining information regarding the activities of investment funds in the real-estate market of a given country. If, however, we wish to assess the value of real estate that belongs to a globally operating oil concern, then leaving out information regarding generalized trends and behaviors at the macroscale can lead to major factual errors.

The behavior of market participants is often unpredictable, dictated by subjective judgment and often by the lack of access to fitting information or not possessing adequate knowledge. In such a case, the observed state of the real-estate market ought to be treated as the actual state. The real-estate valuer cannot disregard the existence of such behaviors or treat them as a bad thing. The valuer should be aware that reproduction of such behaviors is necessary to achieve the desired quality and accuracy of valuation results and, at the same time, know that the accepted valuation method will be able to cope with such phenomena.

Real Estate and Its Characteristics

The unique features that describe real estate have been the subject of frequent research efforts. Each of them contains whole sets of features describing the objects on the real-estate market. All of these works lead to one timeless message – we view real estate (objects on the real-estate market) through a prism of attributes that describe their functional, technical, spatial, economic, ecological, and so on, values. This is where timeless problems, which have accompanied humans from the moment the very first scientific research and analysis were carried out, arise. Does the method of selecting descriptive features, the way in which these features are described, the accepted levels of description, and so forth, have an influence on valuation processes and, if so, to what extent? We are not going to attempt to answer this question since the answer itself can be treated, by standards of measurement, as a suggested solution. Subjectivity, similarity, and comparability of objects and real-estate markets should, however, be mentioned in the categories of real-estate valuation.

The subjectivity of real estate and markets results directly from the unique features that describe real estate. Attention should, however, be paid to the fact that this subjectivity is directly projected onto the similarity of the valuated objects and brings about specific problems in the comparability analysis of real estate. Subjectivity is not always a bad thing. We can even take this a step further and write that the subjectivity of real estate is a manifestation of individual and social freedom. The thing about freedom is that different behaviors are granted equal rights, including the subjective processes of creating real estate. Everyone can create real estate according to his or her own views, needs, and expectations. In the case of valuation processes, this is, of course, troublesome, but are we to restrict the freedom of subjective creation because of it?

Similarity is one of the most important notions in the real-estate valuation processes. Its function stems from, above all, the fact that the majority of methods for assessing the value of real estate are based on determining the degree of similarity (on the level of descriptive features) between the transactions made in the market sphere and the entity for whom the value is being assessed. In this case, similarity plays a key role. It is impossible to determine the value of real estate without referring to what is happening in the market sphere. However, if we refer to it, the valuation methods should give us the ability to replicate what is happening on the market and so allow us to shape the value of real estate in such a way that it is similar in the specified spheres of similarity. The same situation holds true for real-estate markets.

Comparability is directly connected with similarity. It is easy to compare objects that are similar. What happens, however, when we have to compare dissimilar objects? How can we assess the moment in which the decreasing similarity of objects makes them impossible to compare. Pinpointing this moment is incredibly difficult. It seems obvious that the human factor should be of assistance at this point. People deal with such problems far better than many advanced calculation methods or techniques implemented on the computer. In this case, the same categories apply to writing about the real-estate market.

Data and information constitute the main problem in real-estate valuation processes. Laconic as this statement may be, it is all very true. Data, as raw observations and information, as processed data, are the basis of all appraisal processes. Their lack, insufficiency, incompleteness, outdatedness, unavailability, and so on cause extensive perturbations in the valuation processes.

Methods, complex as they may be, do not work if they have nothing to work on – there is no data or information. We are faced with an opposite situation when the lack of data results from other causes, for example, brought about by the lack of data registration, collection, or gathering systems. Yet, another problem occurs in the real-estate valuation processes when data gaps are a result of incorrect or inadequate descriptions in the light of dynamic changes observed in the real-estate market sphere.

The complexity and intricacy of the real-estate market necessitate the construction and operation of efficient and effective systems for gathering information about real estate and the real-estate market. Such systems would greatly simplify the appraisal process and contribute to increasing the quality and reliability of the obtained results. Data and information should be regularly updated, while mistakes and imperfections corrected. It should be emphasized that these systems should be subjected to constant updating of software and structural upgrading so that they can keep up with the changing situation in the real-estate market sphere.

Algorithms and procedures used in the valuation of real estate should cope with multiple aspects pertaining to the analysis of data and information. They should take into account, among others, the means of coding and the amount and quality of data and information. In addition, they should identify and analyze the dynamics of changes registered within the data and information.

The level of knowledge about the market and its participants is an important aspect of a properly operating real-estate market. This problem should be considered on two planes.

Every market participant should, at the very least, understand the basics of how the market functions and the effect its participants have on it. He or she should be familiar with the basic features that describe the structure of the market and its functions. Thanks to this kind of knowledge, the decision-making processes of individual entities would be more rational and, therefore, a bit easier to determine in real-estate valuation processes. Market participants should also possess some basic knowledge regarding the application of methods used for valuating real estate and be familiar with the limitations of their use. This would make the valuation processes more acceptable to market participants. A higher level of awareness on this topic among real-estate market participants would eliminate, for example, problems stemming from the various understandings of market scope in the spatial sense.

From a different perspective, this problem comes down to gathering data regarding the level of knowledge, behaviors, and skills of individual participants who operate in this market. Thanks to this, it would be possible to analyze the quality of processes realized in real-estate market. This, in turn, would raise the reliability of substantive analyses regarding such phenomenon on the real-estate market as follows: fashion, prospects of development, typical and atypical behaviors, risk-increasing behavior, analysis of the entities' knowledge, the entities' motivations, subjectivity, similarity, and comparability of objects and markets, and so on. The analysis of knowledge and skills would enable the analysis of behavioral factors and the professionalism of individual market participants.

Research and Analytical Methods

The complexity of market behaviors and complication of characteristic functions in the market sphere require the application of appropriate analytical and research methods. Phenomena are most frequently expressed in the form of an analytical model, in accordance with the Bertalanffy theory (1984), where the only reasonable way of studying an organization is to study it as a system, with the model constituting the description of a given system.

Although every mathematical model is an oversimplification, according to the Bertalanffy theory (1984), when it is good (i.e., among others, is not deprived of all the relevant parts that comprise the phenomena), it allows for the necessary deductions, which often lead to unexpected results, which would not have been obtained using "common sense" methods. Problems, however, should first be intuitively recognized before being mathematically formalized. Otherwise, mathematical formalism may interfere with the study of very "real" problems, since, according to Rao (1994), the only and proper justification of such a mathematical solution is the expectation that it will work in practice.

From an analytical point of view, the problem lies in, among others, selecting an appropriate method for the analysis of available information and not (as often witnessed in practice) adapting the information to fit the applied market analysis methods, for example, econometric models. Here, we can often see a commonly occurring problem mentioned in the introduction, that is, "[a] gap exists between the current situation … and state-of-the-art valuation theory, standards and practices" (see page 2).

In the age of globalization of the twenty-first century, we ought to seek quick and standardized solutions (procedures, algorithms) that will enable objectivity and increase the people's trust in the results of research carried out on the real-estate market. These solutions should be of a general nature and, at the same time, account for the local character of the analyzed markets and information derived from them. This ensures that the local character of the created solutions will be considered, all the while accounting for the influence of external factors of a global nature on a given market scale.

A method that is appropriate for analyzing the real-estate market ought to be adapted not only to the specifics of a given piece of real estate but also to the type of market, purpose of valuation, and degree to which the information and results are generalized. The market, entity, object, and purpose of appraisal, define the choice of research methods and techniques. Research methods applied in the analyses connected with the real-estate sector have different origins, character, accuracy, and so on. Among them are the methods that are directly derived from the real-estate sector, for example, comparative methods (methods based on similarity and comparability), methods derived from the science of economics and statistics (econometric methods), or methods originating from many other fields and branches of science (theory of systems, mathematics, physics, etc.). The analysis of methods alone will not prove to be very useful if it is performed separately from the research topic, that is, real estate and the real-estate market.

The real-estate sector does not develop many of its own research methods and techniques in the scope of science fields. Good examples of such methods in this field are the aforementioned comparative methods. The development and application of these methods on the real-estate market are subjected to constant processes of improvement. Numerous other methods that have been applied in the analysis of the real-estate market are borrowed, and their application is connected with many formal and factual restrictions. This directly relates to the issue presented in the introduction, that is, of valuers usually blindly applying valuation theories and approaches adopted from finance. And more often than not, this research tradition copes with the specificity of real estate.

Taking into account the previously mentioned problem-causing factors, one ought to think comprehensively about the practical applicability of research methods and techniques in real-estate valuation. The listed problem-causing factors allow certain general conditions of the applicability of real-estate valuation methods to be determined. They allow certain general conditions and application possibilities to be specified.

When considering the market as a system, one should keep in mind its complicatedness and complexity expressed by numerous factors, especially by spatial scope, the number of transactions, the complexity of subjects and objects, purpose of the carried out analyses, as well as their accuracy and quality.

The scope of the market can be divided into three categories: microscale, mezzo scale, and macroscale (Fig. 4.1). The indicated scopes of the market cannot be specified for this level of generality. These can either spatial scope or scope expressed in the market space by the number of transactions. In many cases, this does not have to be done. The significance of the proposed division is of visual nature. Each entity (market participant) can be easily qualified (separately) at a certain level. It may also be qualified under many levels, in the case of possessing a diverse source of entities.

The analysis of the microscale real-estate market (Fig. 4.1 displays the sample aims for this scale) requires the highest precision and accuracy of analysis results. This is

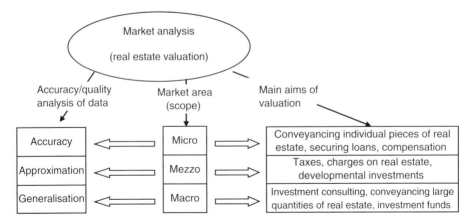

Figure 4.1 Market areas, quality and accuracy of market analyses.

due to the assumptions made by employers regarding the similarity and comparability of objects (single valuation of real estate). At the considered level, the set of requirements for valuation methods are, above all, as follows: high precision, accuracy of the results in the light of individual transactions, and simplicity of the applied analysis tool (the employer wants to understand the result, since it has a large impact (capital intensity) on his or her economic situation). Subjective and objective determinants cause the microscale analyses, in this perspective, to pertain to a situation in which, on the one hand, there are markets in which many transactions are made and, at the same time, markets with very little available data and information. The high precision of the results is connected with a high demand for accurate data and information.

By changing the scale of market analyses to mezzo, the precision of analyses falls to a level of "approximate value." Analyses at this level do not require as much accuracy as at the micro level. This results from, above all, the purposes behind conducting such analyses (see Fig. 4.1). From the perspective of subjective and objective determinants, the change of market scope (including spatial scope) most often causes an increase in the number of transactions along with a simultaneous increase in the number of factors that are to be analyzed. The increase in the number of transactions and value-creating attributes is not always a beneficial solution. In many cases, an increased number of attributes creating real-estate value signifies a higher complexity of analyses, which goes along with increased uncertainty regarding the determined value of real estate.

Analyses that concern large markets (large spatial scope of a market, many transactions) allow for decreasing the accuracy of the analysis results to a generalized level. The increase in scope allows for analyses to be expanded to a level of generalizations that are essential for the purposes shown in Figure 4.1. The macroscale consists of analyses carried out by large, methodologically advanced entities. The actual analyses pertain to large resources of real estate or organized real-estate groups that belong to a single entity or organization.

The division of the market into the previously mentioned scales,: micro, mezzo, and macro, can also be done when looking into the various numbers of transactions (data and information) that are necessary for the analyses and selection of the number of attributes that influence the value of real estate. The authors assume that the valuation result risk (R) and the accuracy of this result (D) on the specified markets are linked to each other and have their own permissible (sufficient and, at the same time, required) values (Fig. 4.2).

Risks (R_1, R_2, and $R_{3)}$) always occur in real-estate analyses and real-estate valuation processes. In accordance with the diagram presented in Figure 4.2, the total risk (R) for all analyses can be expressed by the following equation:

$$R = f(R_1, R_2, R_3) \qquad (4.1)$$

The conduction of analyses at a given level, for example, mezzo, does not exempt the expert from taking another level, which may result in a different kind of risk, into consideration.

As illustrated by this figure, the highest accuracy of results (D_1) and, at the same time, the lowest risk (R_1) occur on the micro market, due to the individual nature of determining the point value of real estate (at a given place and time) and less data necessary for analysis. In addition, creating the result is directly supervised by the employer. This means a relatively low risk in the context of creating results. This issue may present itself

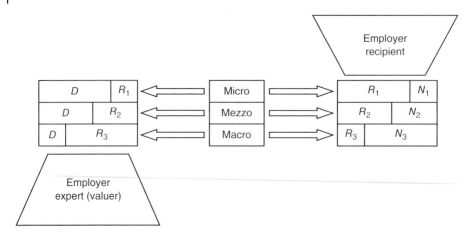

Figure 4.2 Permissible risk and sufficient accuracy of the result at individual levels.

differently from the employer's perspective. His or her direct supervision in the valuation process guarantees high accuracy and precision of determining the result. This same factor should result in preparing the results of the analysis in such a way that they are understandable to the employer. The N_1 variable in Figure 4.2 indicates the level of the employer's lack of knowledge in relation to the accepted level of analyses.

Generally, the larger the market (mezzo- and macroscale), the higher the risk and the lower the required accuracy along with an increasing lack of knowledge possessed by employers or analysis recipients. The increase in risk results from taking a larger scope of the market into consideration, considering larger amounts of data and information (transactions as well as variables). Risk is also affected by determining the value of real estate not only at a given time and place but also dynamically, taking into account the perspectives and possibilities of development (especially at the macroscale). In such cases, a decrease in accuracy should not be treated as something negative. This process is unavoidable in situations where valuation is performed for the purpose of taxing (assessment) or consulting. We want the results to fulfill our expectations in terms of comparability, not at an individual level but at a level of "approximate value." In such cases, the recipient's ignorance regarding the process of creating the result increases. This is a natural process. The wider the scope of the analysis (more advanced methods) and the higher the level of result generalization, the lower is the level of knowledge regarding the principles of creating results displayed by the average recipient. It should also be noted that an individualized level of risk carried by the recipients decreases along with passing over to the mezzo and macro level. In such a case, the responsibilities connected with making a mistake are not scored and do not pertain to individual transactions but rather extend over time and pertain to processes that are often characterized by a collective nature. For example, investment consulting at the mezzo level is performed by taking numerous variants into account, often accompanied by detailed risk analysis, and so forth.

The larger the market and the less specific the purpose of the valuation (in terms of a single piece of real estate), the broader the spectrum of factors (attributes) that are and ought to be looked into. When it comes to making investments and forecasting the value of real estate, the valuation of real estate includes more attributes, the so-called nontechnical ones, but carries a higher risk of making an error. The general division into technical attributes (normally stable in terms of time and easier to predict) and nontechnical attributes (difficult to define and quantify), which have a direct effect on the value of real estate, is presented in Table 4.1. Some of the listed factors are difficult to qualify under the given groups because of the multiple sides of the issue.

Why do classical methods of real-estate valuation have low reliability on the real-estate market? It is commonly believed that a different kind of real-estate valuation method should be chosen for each type of market. However, experience shows that applying numerous methods, as has been the case until now, does not yield effective results. The issue of whether or not we should continue to look for a single valuation method, which will constitute a kind of core – factual base – and then, depending on the type of market and purpose of the valuation, be modified and combined with the use of other real-estate valuation methods, remains open. Looking at this issue from a different perspective, perhaps we should not feel compelled to look for other "100 per cent accurate" methods by force. Maybe it is better to rely on methods that will be compatible with the realistic expectations of employers and practical possibilities (connected with, e.g., the ability to obtain data and information). The issue of the methodology and methods of valuation is an open one. Referring back to the earlier observations concerning the appearing symptoms of evolution or revolution in valuation processes, searching for new solutions should be a priority.

As indicated by the specifics of the real estate market and real estate itself presented earlier, commonly applied methods of analysis (mainly statistical) continue to be relatively inefficient and ineffective. The application of methods and procedures from other fields should take into account the imperfections of information on real estate, for example, the lack of data, a small number of transactions, large differentiation of scales for coding attributes, and nonlinear relationships between the analyzed information and the type of market subjected to them. These methods should be appropriate and chosen so as to allow performance analysis at a potential (theoretical) and an actual (applied) level.

The complicatedness and complexity of situations observed on the real-estate market incline one to contemplate the possibility of applying combined solutions, methods, and algorithms. These methods are based on the ability to create a single supersolution by using a few individual solutions. Proof (theoretical and practical) put forward by the world of science and practitioners is often very promising. This approach is based on a thesis tested in other fields: various methods – various results – a single answer. Combined methods allow us to lower the risk of flawed results and increase the precision of the obtained results. They are, in a way, the natural consequence of using large information sets and creating numerous, frequently contending solutions. The application of these methods, thanks to modules of often heuristic or expert interpretation, in many cases, lead to results that would be unobtainable by means of other methods.

Independent of computer power or the capacity of databases, the application of real-estate valuation methods and techniques is always realized by considering humans as experts. Certified property valuators, investors, or real-estate analysts as well as ordinary people rely on themselves when making the final decision. They are the "creators of solutions," and the questions of whether or not valuation will take place, how it will be conducted, and what effects will be attained depend on them.

Table 4.1 Attributes influencing the value of residential real estate.

Technical attributes of real estate	Nontechnical attributes			
	Social	Economic	Political	Behavioral/ Hedonic – soft
Price	Unemployment	Inflation	Taxes	Fashion on the real-estate market
Date	Migration	GDP	Fees/charges	Market trends
Lot size	Number of transactions	Accessibility to loans	Infrastructural projects	Tradition of "settlement"
Number of lots	Demand for real estate	Planning concepts		Individual motivations
Type of ownership	Average level of income	Supply of real estate		Prestige of possessing real estate
Front	Population growth	Perspectives for area development		Fulfilling needs by young families
Depth		Availability of (undeveloped) land		Public feeling
Shape				Speculativeness
Location	Programs facilitating demand for real estate, for example, "Rodzina na swoim" (Family on its own – state program support young families to buy home), subsidies for equipping real estate with renewable energy sources			Safety/renown of neighborhood
Technical infrastructure devices	Fulfilling basic needs connected with living standards including own dwelling	Price of gas (influence on suburban expansion)		Proclamation of changes in legislation connected with the real-estate market
The lay of the land		Price of fuels connected with maintenance of real estate: energy, gas, coal, and so on		Global macroeconomic feeling (e.g., rating agency rankings, demand for risky investments)
Drive and access		Prices of building materials	Approval of government policies	
Neighborhood nuisances: roads, railways, other (e.g., factories)				
Zoning				
Form of transaction				
Attractiveness of location: for example, wooded areas, parks, bodies of water				
General location: proximity of major shops and services, distance from the city center, general accessibility				

Source: Own study.

Currently, thanks to the wide application of computer techniques, the role of people as decision-makers is limited. The answer to the question of whether or not we should continue down that road and head toward further exclusion of people and restriction of their "decision-making power" is justified and deliberate. Building solutions based on artificial intelligence is a fact. Nobody or nothing is going to stop it. We have become too connected and addicted to the computing units that computers today are. At the present time, it is impossible to set a notebook-sized computer aside on a shelf, as it has become indispensible in just about every aspect of our lives, including real-estate valuation processes.

People are often omitted, as individuals who subjectify solutions, guided by individualized approaches to real-estate valuation (Fig. 4.3). Is that really the case though? Maybe this subjectivity is a merit, enabling us to distinguish facts and analyze little understood and seemingly meaningless factors and variables. Perhaps, when engaging computers to perform calculations, we should appreciate the selected aspects of the human versus computer rivalry in real-estate valuation processes. Who will win in such a competition? Of course, the human! In the context of the aforementioned assumptions, searching for new methods, or rather new applications for existing methods, can significantly contribute to the change and modernization of the means by which real-estate value is presented. In order for such changes to happen, it is necessary to work out clear rules and procedures connected with the analysis of the real-estate market and, in consequence, change the social awareness (those who create value as well as its recipients) and, next, disseminate the calculated results and new implementations. Therefore, for as long as linear regression will continue to be the method commonly recognized as correct for determining mass valuation, there will be no room for new solutions. This does not mean that the authors completely negate linear regression as a useful tool; they only

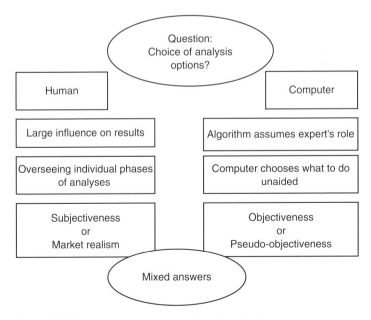

Figure 4.3 Man versus computer in real-estate valuation.

wish to point out that, oftentimes (as seen in scientific research), it does not illustrate the most probable market reality.

The authors, therefore, suggest solutions to valuating real estate by utilizing the rough set theory (RST) and neural networks as competition or an alternative to solutions commonly applied in real-estate analysis (Byrne, 1995; Renigier-Biłozor and Wiśniewski, 2011a,b).

RSTs were chosen over others as one of the better tools for market analysis for a number of reasons, which allow analyses to be effectively conducted while accounting for the aforementioned imperfections of markets, which stem from the genesis of this method (Pawlak, 1997; Polkowski, 2010; Renigier-Biłozor, 2011). It was created in order to describe and study vague knowledge, uncertain in modeling approximate reasonings, decision-making systems, and systems of identifying attributes and classification (Komorowski *et al.*, 1999; Pawlak 1982). When considering the so-called classical–statistical methods of market data analysis and those based on the RST, certain disadvantages of one method and advantages of the other can be found. The common disadvantage of applying classical–statistical analyses is the fact that they are time-consuming and costly (equipment for gathering the adequate, usually large quantities of representative observations) and involve the high complexity of the applied procedures, composed of a so-called preliminary analysis, that is, checking the assumptions of the randomness of variables, testing the probability distribution and correctness of the statistical analysis result interpretation, as well as the ability to conduct and interpret statistical tests. In many cases, this results in fitting the data to the given model rather than the model to the data, as should be done in reality.

When applying methods based on RSTs, the observations "speak for themselves" and are not corrected under any circumstances, neither prior to the application of the method nor during the conduction of analyses. Moreover, the method based on the RST is not restricted when compared to regression models, neither in terms of the quantity of representative observations collected (the sample of observations can be very small as well as very large), nor is it necessary to construct a statistical model; decisions are made based on the dependency: if the specified conditions are met, then the decision is made (as concluded by Boolowski). The presented method does not call for complicated control regulations of the analyzed features or analysis results. The significance of attributes determined in relation to the decisional attribute and established decisional guidelines is controlled by only two main indicators: quality and accuracy, very easy to apply and interpret.

4.2

Economic Sustainability, Valuation Automata and Local Price Development

Tom Kauko

In this chapter, my argument, backed by empirical material from Trondheim (Norway) using a method based on self-organising map (the SOM) and time windows, is that abnormal price development trends need to be recognised with respect to the spatial distribution. From a practical point of view, data/modelling outcomes have tremendous usability: if the indicator is valid, it makes an excellent economic sustainability indicator; if not, it still diagnoses a problem.

Introduction

The magnitude and pace of the recent financial meltdown in the world economy have taken us by surprise. At the end of the summer of 2008, it was mainly about crisis in the United States and then in the United Kingdom, but 2 months later, it had already reached global proportions. In many European countries, financial institutions got into serious troubles and a number of local governments lost the worth of their investments. Furthermore, outside the Eurozone, the currency was devalued until September 2009, and in many countries, the tone of government policymakers became a hopeless one. On the other hand, speaking about the United States, the leader of the world economy, a homeowner confidence survey by Zillow found out that 62% of American homeowners believed that the value of their house has increased or stayed the same during a year, when in reality, 77% of US homes actually declined in value (AVM News, 2008a)! Apparently, consumers still tend to overvalue their assets with it-happens-to-others-but-not-to-me mentality. It is reasonable to believe that similar attitudes prevail on this side of 'the pond' as well.

Given that immovable property (i.e. real estate) was central for the occurrence of the latest financial crisis that begun in year 2008 (UN, 2010), we may have reason to ponder if the development of property value and market modelling tools is an endeavour worth embarking on. Has room now, thanks to the economic downturn, been created for merging the 'sustainable development' and 'market modelling' paradigms? Such a union would constitute a measured response to identified pitfalls on either side. Sticking to the latter paradigm, apparently, the current theory of measuring house prices and mapping the markets is inadequate. This concerns, on the one hand, the price-setting process in relation to the development of affordability, and on the other hand, the price-setting process in relation to more static price factors tied to fundamental quality variables including location-specific amenities such as the physical and social environment or transport infrastructure (see the notions of my chapter in Part 3).

While this topic is important in general socio-economic terms, as witnessed through the established urban housing market research tradition (see e.g. Ball and Kirwan, 1977; Maclennan, 1977; Maclennan and Tu, 1996; Watkins, 2001; see also Meen and Meen, 2003, for a somewhat alternative approach), a more particular issue is now open to speculation, namely, given the pivotal role of the housing bubble in the subsequent credit crunch, could the global financial crisis be moderated or even avoided if prudent property valuations had been made at the time of issuing bank loans and if governments and other institutions were concerned about raising the quality of property market information? Do automatic valuation models/methods (AVMs, automated, often computerised procedures for carrying out the task of valuing one or more properties) help us in mortgage-lending problems? And if we do not believe they do, what are the valid grounds for their criticism? Here, we may select between two different lines of analysis: we may, based on empirical evidence, argue for or against a direct empirical modelling application; alternatively, we may look at a more qualitative, rhetorical way of convincing either for or against the general use of AVM in this research area.

Whereas the valuation process was the topic of Part 3, the contributions in this part and chapter target the actual or hypothetical market context – possibly extended towards non-market aspects such as sustainability. In doing so, the aim of this study is defined in relation to *mass appraisal* (AVM in particular), as opposed to single property valuation which is judgemental (even in the United Kingdom, AVMs are increasingly popular); in other words, from the point of view of aggregate price data accumulation rather than looking at individual property relations. It is to observe that, in this line of analysis, any sustainability or other issue of long-term relevance will be factored into the application rather than the methodology.

Martin (2011) suggests that examining 'early-warning' diagnostics of price bubbles would be a viable research line and that geographers in particular could make a significant contribution here. Perhaps so, geography, similarly to history, is omnipresent. However, it is somewhat unlikely that the editorial 'we' could come up with a methodology to capture the turning points in market development, because we simply cannot grasp these events beforehand, even when we think we recognise one. While may be able to produce better forecasts to mitigate the fall, this will only be a partial success as the ethical dimension remains (Mooya, 2011). Nonetheless, if the risk cannot be eliminated, the following question is asked: how can the risk be managed? In other words, it may be impossible to prevent bubbles from occurring – and indeed bursting. Thus, we can only limit the damage, and perhaps, AVMs are suitable for this.

On the other hand, at the country level, there is a clear positive correlation between large variations in house prices and a widespread use of AVMs, mostly for property taxation purposes, which would tempt us to conclude the opposite.[1] We must also recognise

---

1 Based on the discussion with the audience (including Christine Whitehead and Steve Malpezzi) in the European Network of Housing Research (ENHR) conference, Prague, 28 June–1 July, 2009, where an earlier version of this paper was presented.

that the AVMs have even been partly blamed for causing the sub-prime crisis in the United States (Mooya, 2011).This view of the potential usability of AVMs is, however, restricted to monitoring price development and designing tax assessment applications. When property price estimations are related to other kinds of data set and subsequently automated, this outcome can be developed further into an economic sustainability metrics applicable for many other potential uses in relation to sustainability assessment and implementation (cf. Sayce *et al.*, 2007).

In other words, besides monitoring and evaluation of the price development, other aspects of the price setting can be involved: affordability, quality, variation and so on. To connect the sustainability of the built environment with housing market viability is arguably an important topic today, given the impossibility to separate the physical structure of cities from their economic and social structure (see Jones *et al.*, 2009). However, mainstream market theory offers little help here. Thus, the search needs to be directed towards heterodox economic (i.e. institutional, evolutionary, behavioural and economic theory perspectives) or purely practical approaches instead, such as the development of AVM for mass appraisal (see Kauko and d'Amato, 2008). The aim of the present study then is to show 'how' (or 'why not' if one is a sceptic) an AVM approach to house price analysis is feasible (or unfeasible), given the situation where the market and the whole economy are distorted and (at best) recovering from the financial crises.

This contribution discusses the aspects of general feasibility and presents an empirical application. The aim here is to evaluate as to whether AVMs are useful in handling mortgage lending problems. While AVMs are being seen as an attractive proposition within this competitive realm, the fact that the increasing popularity of AVMs has unfortunately not yet led to an increasing interest in interrogating the foundation of such tools remains (Mooya, 2011). This chapter addresses the aforementioned issues in two ways: on the one hand, it presents an empirical modelling application for local housing markets; on the other hand, it examines more qualitative, rhetorical arguments for the use of AVMs in this field. Currently, it can be observed that mass appraisal is becoming increasingly popular around the world. The argument is that, to avoid a new crisis, a more normative approach is proposed and that it would incorporate sustainability. That would be logical given that the sustainable development paradigm also has an economic dimension. Finally, an empirical illustration of this thinking is provided from Trondheim, Norway. However, before beginning the discussion on valuation methodology, a discussion on the housing market is necessary in order to describe the context where the task of residential valuation takes place.

The Need for a Sustainable Housing Market

As with the more general notion of sustainable development, within a real-estate context too, sustainability is defined through the three dimensions pertaining to environmental, social and economic aspects. In the real-estate paradigm, the key is to understand market processes – hence, the emphasis inevitably falls on the economic sustainability. When we define this concept more clearly, we note that, in general, it is a state of affairs that enables/secures the investment of extra profits for the long term and for the society at large. Several factors such as value stability and product diversity are included in this concept (see Kauko, 2010). Value stability means that the property is not overpriced (or underpriced for that matter) in relation to its objective quality or to the modal incomes. This concept was developed by Kauko (2010) and emphasises consumer protection, on the one hand, and affordability, on the other, and is a part of a broader economic sustainability argument (see Chapter 3.1 in this volume). Value stability may, however, be in sharp disagreement with other kinds of sustainability concepts – even within the economic sustainability category.

In the evolution of the functioning of neighbourhoods, the importance of local housing markets is crucial, as shown by Bramley *et al.* (2008). On the other hand, these authors maintain the importance of house prices having a high responsiveness to income and supply and indirectly being influenced by various planning measures (see Evans and Hartwich, 2005). These factors are to a certain extent time-varying (see Jones *et al.*, 2009). When taking a closer look at this, it is reasonable to assume that both macro- and micro-level factors influence urban housing markets. This turbulence can be for better or for worse, depending on the economic and institutional starting conditions. Concerns about financial stability implications of developments in the housing market when house price dynamics become disconnected from developments in underlying fundamentals of housing demand and supply are particularly serious in the case of Central and Eastern European (CEE) countries, given the strong role of interest rate fluctuations, demographic and labour market movements, development of wages and establishment of new market and financial institutions (see Égert and Mihaljek, 2008).

Within the framework of a typical Keynesian critique of monetarism, Baker (2008) presents how the financial market is both cause and effect of the housing bubble in the United States. He rightly notes that 'the expectation that prices would continue to rise led homebuyers to pay far more for homes than they would have otherwise'. He cites Robert Shiller, who showed that, prior to 1995, in the United States, real house prices were unchanged for 100 years, but by 2002, about 30% overpriced speculative bubble completely detached from the fundamentals of the housing market was evident. Subsequently, however, the bubble burst – by the end of 2007, real house prices had fallen by over 15% from their peak, which, according to Baker, amounts to almost 50% of GDP. Baker blames, above all, the appraisers, who had a strong incentive to, instead of valuing an honest appraisal, adopt 'a high-side bias in their appraisals'. Among the reasons, he notes the complex web of finance that concealed the risk that was building in the financial structure'; a large supply of housing being placed for sale; and a dampened demand as a result of the stress in financial markets. He finally notes that financial bubbles, in principle, could be contained (but accuses Alan Greenspan for not doing his job).

Sapir (2008), however, adds the institutional dimension to the criticism in the sense that, if a country is, to a sufficient extent, detached from the global financial system, it is capable of dampening the effects of crises and thereby remains unaffected by the credit crunch. The emerging economies, on the one hand, and the continued social-democratic welfare states, on the other, are such countries. Arguably, to be able to design better policies compared to the current ones, we cannot rely on neoclassical economic (NCE) theory, but we need to study more realist and heterodox economic theory (see also Keen, 2009; Söderbaum, 2009).

Elsewhere, human geographer Aalbers (2008) sets up the following argumentation that much resonates with those of heterodox economists Baker and Sapir (cf. MacDonald, 1996; Martin, 2011):

- Financialisation occurs when profit-making occurs in different parts of the economy (including real estate) through financial channels rather than through trade and commodity production.
- Risks in any finance-led regime become risks for all actors involved in any specific industry; hence, mortgage loans fuel house prices.
- Mortgage markets are today not only 'a means to an end' but 'an end in itself'.
- Today, the real-estate markets are more than ever dependent on the financial markets.
- *Vice versa*, the development of financial markets is also dependent on the development of the real estate and housing markets.
- Most homeowners depend on mortgage markets, and this fuels the economy both directly and indirectly.
- This crisis is not limited to the United States: many other mortgage markets are increasingly financialised, and, in fact, a ripple effect to Europe was anticipated.
- The importance of the secondary mortgage market (i.e. investors can buy mortgage portfolios from lenders) has increased since the late 1990s.
- Given the high risk and exploitative character of the mortgage loans, many of the borrowers should never have received a mortgage loan.
- Not only is 'global' tied to 'local' through financialisation of the mortgage market, but also the financial and the built environment have become tied together through this mechanism.

As Aalbers shows, the analysis of individuals is used as a basis for credit scoring and risk-based pricing. The key to the crisis is still in understanding the credit scoring of lenders. However, it is not clear why such a criterion could not be based on the product itself – the real estate, instead of the personal traits of the lender (see RICS, 2007). In such a case, the role of appraisals is important.

When evaluating inflationary effects against sustainability criteria, an additional qualification has to be noted. While in countries where the overall demand has risen strongly in recent decades due to increased incomes (e.g. Norway), there is a total negative impact on a sustainable market. Indeed, it is true that when house price inflation is higher than the development of incomes and the consumption index, the situation is categorised as unsustainable – at least economically – using the definitions of the present study. However, in a normal market situation, after a lag of a few years, the new stock will be adjusted upwards in terms of quantity and quality, which then moves the situation towards sustainability again, albeit at functionally and spatially varying rates.

A quick review of NCE (mainstream theory) and its criticism already showed that this line of conceptualisation is outmoded and misleading as it comprises 'autistic' research results. It is to observe that only in NCE-based models do we need to clean up the anomalies (Kauko and d'Amato, 2008). Three arguments can be brought up here:

1) In recent years, AVMs have in fact performed better than the more eloquent and orthodox NCE-based models.
2) Both types of NCE approaches have their problems: time-series-based macroeconomic modelling tends to 'fall short of fool explanation', whereas cross-sectional models – while obviously providing more detailed analysis than the former – are improvable only insofar as the spatial and other 'chaotic' aspects of the distribution are taken in consideration.

3) Risk in relation to the eligibility of borrowers has seriously undermined current value modelling practices, as discussed earlier.

The gist of the story is to identify certain economic sustainability elements in real-estate locations. In this interrogation the attention of the paper turns to AVMs and empirical application of large data sets and sophisticated modelling technology.

The New Paradigm of Modelling Value – Is AVM the Solution?

The comments in the previous section suggest that the way we understand and explain property value might be undergoing a paradigm change. However, several issues mark this (plausible) change, and to dwell on all of them is beyond the scope of this contribution. The way 'value' and 'market' are understood from an epistemological or ontological point of view must nevertheless be of concern here, given our ambition of improving the methodological basis for valuation. For pedagogical purposes, let us distinguish between 'old' and 'new' paradigms. In the old paradigm, the separation of the various dimensions (economic, physical, social, cultural, etc.) was acceptable because being able to use equilibrium economic models such as the hedonic model, which would not have been possible otherwise, was considered the goal of the application. In the new paradigm, the methodology might be pragmatic instead of formal, but that is not the point; the point is to avoid a totally artificial separation of dimensions as is the case with the models and methods of the old paradigm. In other words, the motive is holism rather than reductionism. As the sheer complexity involved is huge, the following question arises: what kinds of opportunities (if any) emerge for the application of valuation automata?

Given the often doubted relevance of AVMs for valuation and market analysis, a good starting point is the recent literature survey on automated valuation models by Downie and Robson (2007). From their comprehensive literature review, Downie and Robson find that traditional valuation approaches are being increasingly replaced by the cheaper and quicker AVMs and that this development goes together with the need to control loan decisions. They identify, however, potential problems due to inaccuracy and the fact that AVMs have not yet been fully tested in a housing market slump, although some evidence from the United States indicates that circumstances of market downturn do not cause invalidity. Furthermore, in a more established market, best practice guidance is being developed about when and how AVMs are to be used. Finally, Downie and Robson argue that human valuers will not become obsolete even if many valuations are carried out electronically, as the US experience shows. They conclude that standardisation of AVM procedures and features is the crucial issue that determines the direction of R&D in this respect and that there is potential for proving the benefit of AVMs for stakeholders in less-established markets.

To get some insight into the discourses being recreated within this realm, the following brief review of currently available American and British commercial AVM options is indicative of the challenges and trends to deal with. A variety of notes, columns and adds written with post-bubble hindsight, that is to say, since the summer of 2008, in the recently established e-newsletter AVM News (2008a,b,c, 2009, 2012) are used as a source. While this documentation is largely opinion-based, the first fact to note is that the Obama Administration had already included appraisal and valuation components in its guidelines for the Home Affordable Refinance program, and a number of federal agencies have jointly issued the following comment:

> Volatility within certain real estate markets and associated credit risk underscore the importance of independent and reliable collateral valuations.

Elsewhere, it is clarified that lenders are apparently more interested in the capability of the potential borrower to repay the loan than on the current market value of the property. The AVM development framework furthermore seems to be a local rather than national issue according to some experts; this is after all understandable, given that housing markets are granular and localised.[2] Anthony Garritano, Editor of Mortgage Technology Magazine, points out that it is ultimately the investor who determines the value and that technology cannot work alone without the control of lenders and servicers because the risk in relinquishing the collateral values to a model or third party is too high. He states that, while there is a role for predictive models, the role for solutions that provide transparency and data management capabilities is even greater and that 'the real need is for accurate analytically based valuations combined with solutions that allow users to understand the different value opinions'. It is furthermore noted that several different tools or methods should be used for valuing the same property or to support a particular lending activity and that one should not select simply the one that provides the highest value, but instead establish criteria where property type, location and the nature of transaction are all taken into consideration. Finally, it is speculated that the future of valuation lies in a blend of 'traditional human evaluations' and 'automated products'.

In the United States, several technology and database companies have taken the AVM technology on board. Zaio provides an instant predicted market value as well as an estimated value based on the assessed value of the property using digital photographs of the property. This can be used as a tool to check property values. They maintain a database of 140 million properties. Their goal is photographing every home in major cities and metropolitan areas. The alliance between FNC and IntelliReal gives a sophisticated option for AVMs as this product utilises multiple listing data from 77 million property records nationwide. Visre is a company active in imaging of country government tax reassessment projects in Louisiana and Georgia. Their vehicle-mounted camera arrays that enable imaging 4000 parcels a day offer a service for reducing the risk levels of the valuation. Realtor.com offers yet another tool that utilises multiple listing services. Lender Processing Services (LPS) is a particularly interesting option as they have announced a launch of a system for value forecasting at the neighbourhood level, including delinquency and inventory trends for the immediate neighbourhood surrounding a specified property. LPS thereby has a solution for understanding not only the property's current value but also its likely direction in the near future, given that individual property values are substantially influenced by neighbourhood characteristics. Other appraisal systems worth mentioning here are 'the three leading home valuation sites': Zillow.com, Cyberhomes.com and Trulia.com; MDA DataQuick based in San Diego; Boxwood Means; Patriot; Integrated Asset Services (IAS); and – this

---

2 Sustainability is arguably also a local issue insofar as it requires knowledge of a local market and competence of local planning; this, despite some authors such as Goering (2009) claiming otherwise.

seems somewhat obscure even within the esoteric AVM community – a cooperation between the firm Smithfield & Wainwrights and an anonymous 'Florida State University alumnus'.

Various AVM solutions have become increasingly common also in the UK residential mortgage markets due to a rise in demand for mortgage products for which lenders require a more time-efficient and cost-efficient valuation approach than the physical inspection undertaken by surveyors which hitherto has been the standard practice (cf. Op't Veld *et al.*, 2008, on the corresponding situation in the Netherlands, a third country with sophisticated AVM systems). UK Valuation, the UK's pioneering provider of AVMs, reports that its AVM solution is performing robustly despite the continuing decline in UK house prices: their largest observed undervaluation of test portfolios during an over two-and-a-half-year period was just 0.5%. Besides this merit, their parent company First American recoded an overvaluation of only 1.7% during a half-year period of falling house prices. Moreover, their market-leading AVM solution Mortgage Brain has launched a systems' integration where users get instant access to its AVM using innovative data modelling techniques to enable provision of residential property valuations in service characterised as highly accurate, fast, efficient, complete, simple and easy to use. Moody's modelling approach also quantifies the risk associated with the use of different AVMs in Residential Mortgage-Backed Securities (RMBS) transactions. Hometrack, which claims to have 95% of the AVM market in the United Kingdom, is claiming to reach acceptable levels of accuracy irrespective of whether the market is rising or falling. Last (but not the least), Zoopla has added a 'knowsiest neighbours' module to their system: interestingly, where homeowners have regularly checked the value of their property and neighbouring properties also turn out to be relatively expensive locations and streets; conversely, in streets and locations where residents do not bother with such activity, the price levels are systematically much lower (see AVM News, 2012). [As for a more balanced evaluation and critical comment on AVMs, see AVM News (2010) and (2011).] The key point in the critical comments seems to be that an AVM model based on actual data can create false expectations if the ideal conditions of the data that were used to generate the model are not met.

Based on this documentation of the practitioners' state of the art – sometimes referred to as 'the dark side' by academic researchers – there seems no end in sight in the drive to establish innovative solutions for AVM, and if anything, the crisis has only accelerated this development. Such aspirations align with the aim of this paper, designing an empirical approach to determine the degree of housing market sustainability. The next task is therefore to look at the issues at stake from a 'more scientific' point of view. We stress that no claim is made here about one method being the best. The option purported in the next section here for empirical purposes is only one of many options. In the last instance conventions, experience and tastes matter in the methodological selection.

Designing an Empirical Modelling Method

A similar ingenuity as the practitioners have is yet to be seen on the academic side. Within the residential sector, two different broad scientific approaches or perspectives to valuation and market analysis exist: one, hedonic, which has been extended in recent years; two, the alternative or non-market perspective which is yet in a testing stage. The approach propagated in the current paper falls in between those two but is closer to the latter. Drawing on prior contributions (see d'Amato and Kauko, 2008; Kauko, 2001, 2004a,b, 2008a,b), the point here is that context is an important precondition to take into account when selecting/designing valuation methodology in relation to specific changes in the market environment.

In latter-day methodological perspectives to house price analysis and modelling, the market is considered idiosyncratic with respect to one or more of its fundamentals, in which case, the differences across locations and housing bundles are more qualitative than quantitative by nature. This way, the urban location is possible to analyse using either a simple equilibrium or a more context-specific model, based on multiple equilibria. There are, however, no clear guidelines for when to apply what kind of model or method. The question to answer is how physical, socio-demographic, financial and administrative factors shape the housing choices of individual households and, this way, the urban form? As already noted, these factors are interlinked. If we want to perform empirical tests on these issues, we need simplifications.

The selection of modelling approach is the key to success when the criterion is 'realisticness' as opposed to formal elegance. This principle is not difficult to grasp: what kind of market – that kind of method (see d'Amato and Kauko, 2008). The SOM (Kohonen Map) is one example of a promising approach within this realm of realistic but less elegant modelling techniques (several other comparable techniques exist, e.g. genetic algorithms and case-based reasoning, see Kauko and d'Amato, 2008). Using machine learning and adaptive computation jargon, the SOM is a type of unsupervised neural network with competitive network architecture. The neural network is a sophisticated semi-parametric statistical method that captures non-linear, but regular associations (i.e. patterns) within a data set without a predefined model. The SOM is best defined as a mapping from a high-dimensional data space onto a (usually) two-dimensional lattice of points (see Fig. 4.4). This way, disordered information is profiled into visual patterns, forming a landscape of the phenomenon described by the data set.

The overall principle of the learning process in the SOM is to 'train' the output lattice (map surface, feature map) based on the input data and some externally manipulated parameters in such a way that each original observation is matched with a unit (node, neuron) on the map surface where the numerical values measured in the dimensions of the observation are as close to those of the input observation as possible (see Fig. 4.5). When this matching proceeds iteratively, we eventually obtain a projection of the input data. In this projection, the topology between items is preserved rather well from the original data. The result is when the SOM, after a predefined amount of iterations, has then produced a feature map of nodes, each of which represents a characteristic combination of attribute levels. In the training procedure of the algorithm, the matching is usually determined by the smallest Euclidean distance between observation

Figure 4.4 The situation of the nodes in a three-by-two (3 × 2) map.

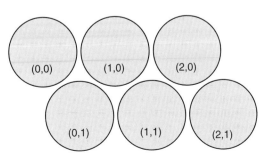

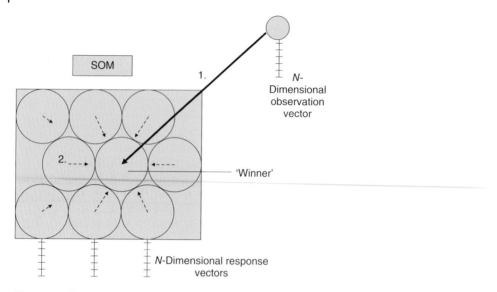

SOM

1.

N-
Dimensional
observation
vector

2.

'Winner'

N-Dimensional response
vectors

Figure 4.5 Illustration of the learning process of the SOM in two steps: in Step 1, the winner is determined, and its numerical value subsequently adjusted towards the observation vector; in Step 2, the numerical values of the other nodes are adjusted towards this winner, and the further they are situated on the map surface, the lesser is this adjustment.

and response. The results are strongly dependent on the data – all necessary guidance to the analyses is obtained from the sample we feed the network and from the compulsory network parameters.

The SOM-based methodology having a black box nature is not a problem anymore as a posteriori explanations of the resulting clustering patterns can be used (see Spielman and Thiel, 2007). Nonetheless, here too the strive is for validity, reliability and feasibility (Kauko, 2004c; Kauko and d'Amato, 2008). Mooya (2011) goes as far as to suggest that the ontological underpinnings of market value are violated for both traditional valuation and AVMs. Without entering debates as philosophical as that, the argument here is that the SOM fulfils reasonable validity, reliability and feasibility requirements to a sufficient extent and will therefore fit the bill insofar as our purposes are concerned.

There are obvious limitations with this method, however. As shown in Figures 4.4 and 4.5, the SOM only performs cross-sectional analysis – of price or any other variable or combination of variables. However, apart from the question of 'where?', the other interesting question to answer here is 'when?' Thus, the answer cannot be provided merely by results of one model only. Because the objective of the present study is price movement, as opposed to cross-sectional price analysis, the SOM has to be used in a repetitive manner. Carlson's (1998) method of fixed time windows is suited for this purpose. It is a quasi-dynamic modelling device which can illustrate changes in the modelling outcome or in one particular variable such as price without using the time of sale as a variable. This is illustrated in Figure 4.6 (see also Kauko, 2009a,b). It is to note that the labels of the nodes are for identification only: each node with 'hits' obtains the most frequent label of the observations it has 'won'.

The results from a prior study serve to illustrate the possibilities (cf. prior analyses on Budapest housing markets by the same author, see Kauko, 2006, 2009a,b). As shown in Figure 4.6, the SOM output identifies the dynamics in terms of the change in dominant

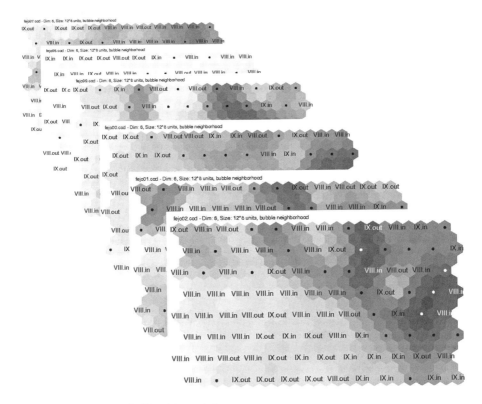

Figure 4.6 The method of fixed time windows.

house type and the change in price level, concerning two inner city areas in Budapest, Hungary. However, in the present study, the variable of interest is economic sustainability of real-estate price development approximated through the affordability indicator: transaction prices divided by income. How are data on the long-term development of prices and affordability indicators related to each other? This is yet an uncharted territory within the fields of market/price modelling and AVM.

Data Preparation

The particular aim of this project is to compare house prices with an affordability indicator. Relevant information for the study is assembled from the Norwegian property registry[3] [property transaction price, dwelling format (i.e. house type) and location (geographical coordinates, street and ward)], on the one hand, and from the income statistics, on the other hand (the income variable comprises median gross income for the municipality based on the taxation of residents over 17 years old). The administrative city area of Trondheim is isolated from the data which results in 36,613 sales transactions for the years 1993–2007. These are the years for which we obtained aggregate

---

3 The data was originally acquired from Norsk Eiendomsinformasjon AS.

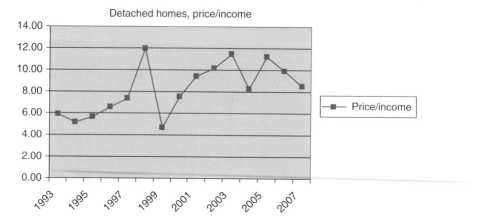

Figure 4.7 Development of prices in relation to incomes in Trondheim for the detached house type.

income data as well. Suspicious cases such as those with prices lower than 150,000 kr (ca. 18,000 EUR) or containing (other) clear errata as well as non-residential use (offices, warehouses, shops, farms, public buildings, etc.) were subsequently removed from the data set. The data cleansing operation did not, however, end here (i.e. in preparing a data set for all dwelling formats).

When different indicators are considered, it should be stressed that we must operate on the best possible data we get, while acknowledging the limits in comparability and compatibility between different data sets and variable definitions. Valid property value data is easy to find in some countries and difficult/impossible in others. For example, in Italy, such registers do not exist at all; in the Netherlands, their existence depends on the municipality in question; in England and Wales, such data has only recently become available for research purposes, whereas it was previously available only in Scotland or Northern Ireland. In Norway, such data does exist in large quantities, but the majority of it is unreliable due to limitations in the register system: namely, the accurate information about the physical description of the dwelling unit sold is not recorded consistently. Hence, after a careful examining of the data set, it turned out that most of the data was not applicable, which was lamentable but not surprising. The data for other dwelling formats than the detached house type turned out to be unreliable as observations can be about several dwellings sold in one transaction without being coded comprehensively by the authorities (Tinglysning) who register this data from the transactions. Because of this, building features could not be included as input variables in the analysis. In the end, 5260 transactions (between 183 and 735 observations for each cross section) were applicable for the analysis. The descriptive trend is shown in Figure 4.7. It is to note that the graph shows socially and (using our definitions) economically unsustainable peaks for the years 1998, 2003 and 2005.

The Results of the Analysis

Next, the price development was analysed using the SOM and its extension, the method of fixed time windows. By examining successive feature maps of cross sections from 1993 to 2007, the price-to-income signals are seen as a trend. This way, it can be established which cases have become the most expensive ones in relative terms, using location and, if necessary, other available property descriptors as identification. When such a piece of analysis is carried out on a year-by-year cross-sectional basis, it can be seen which house types and locations are more and less sustainable in terms of the upwards (i.e. decreased sustainability) and downwards (i.e. increased sustainability) signals when measured through the price/income indicator identifiable from the yearly SOM outputs. This is a pragmatic approach in the sense that we look for a locally adequate viable solution for a problem without the need for general laws.

Hence, each feature map represents the transactions in 1 year and can be analysed with respect to three direct dimensions: price, land area included in the transaction and location of the transaction. In addition, each map can be analysed in terms of other, latent dimensions, such as topographic features of the terrain (and thus, having pleasant view), good access to various services or special architectural/design characteristics of the house or neighbourhood – but these factors are not directly recorded among the input variables. The map layer depicting the price of the property is picked for further scrutiny for all 16 annual feature maps (see Appendix). Together, these 16 diagrams make up the time-window application and are analysed as follows. (The corresponding diagrams for the other three map layers: size of plot, northing and easting are obtainable from the author upon request.) The same information would also be possible to be shown in numeric format – the graphic format is selected here due to convenience reasons.

In most cases, the extremely high priced, that is to say, from a value stability point of view, unsustainable, area remains the same through time: the output reveals the same five or six adjacent neighbourhoods in Byåsen, the suburban district in the western part of the town. Towards the end of this period, the high-priced areas, however, pop up also in other parts of the city; a suburban location, Jakobsli, in the eastern part of town as well as three locations in the inner city (or immediately adjacent to the inner city), Nidar southwest of the city core and Rosenborg and Nedre Berg southeast of it, are the only locations that show up in at least two maps – a single-family home in the inner city is obviously 'a rare butterfly'. For example, two suburban locations, Eberg and Stokkan, both in the eastern part of town, show up in one map only, as do other outliers/anomalies. In such cases where it is obvious that the exceptionally high price of one property is due to a specific unrecorded reason (e.g. in 2005, a house in Lademoen, and otherwise unfashionable inner city, sold for over 7 Mkr, and the only recorded fact that supports the high price is that an area of about 1200 m^2 is included in the transactions). In other cases, the computations have been robust; for example, in 2003, Rosenborg represents by far the most expensive transactions, and this case is actually backed up by 272 comparable properties (in fact, more than every third observation in the cross section) which landed in the same node. The increase in prices in Rosenborg is in fact contributed to the completion of a nearby shopping area and Waterfront development in Nedre Elvehavn, which improved both the status and accessibility of this neighbourhood.

Moreover (apart from the Lademoen case mentioned earlier), there is not much association/overlap between the size of the plot and price – especially not for the earlier years; the only continuous interval when the largest areas also happened to be relatively expensive properties was during the years 2000–2002. However, these cases are not the most expensive ones for any year during this period.

It is difficult to see any systematics for the data overall; in some years, certain locations are overpriced, and in other years, other locations are overpriced. Thus, no connection with plot size can be confirmed and also not with location, beyond the tendency of being situated in Byåsen. Here, we must add that the notable price premiums might be explained by the fact that Byåsen also has some of the best panoramas in town. Hence, the SOM output ought to be supported by domain knowledge and expert information. Some of the findings are contributed to 'rational' neighbourhood effects, for example, the aforementioned Rosenborg case, whereas other findings require more nuanced behavioural explanations about the long-term motives of the risk-averse investors, who speculate about the future development of the area. However, exciting as further speculation might be, the aim here is only to demonstrate the usefulness of the method, rather than to delve further into the empirical findings.

The Principle of Smoothing the Value Using a SOM Approach

It can be argued that avoiding excessive peaks and lows in the trend (i.e. the procedure known as smoothing) is one of the necessary steps towards economic sustainability. This is because it avoids the most drastically myopic valuations that caused the financial crisis – as the big problem is mortgage underwriting decisions being made by merely mirroring the actual price trends, as argued earlier. The main idea then becomes normative: to reduce the price estimate when it is an unsustainable trend and increase it when a sustainable trend is detected. These adjustments have to be determined empirically, however, and this is where the SOM becomes topical.

The SOM approach proceeds iteratively in two steps as follows:

1) Take an arbitrary observation (i.e. home sale) in year t, and feed it to the already generated map as input.
2) See which node on the map it is won by, and record its numerical values with regard to all input dimensions (including value).

After that, perform the same for subsequent years until we have a smoothed value trend for this category of observation (in terms of price, plot size and location) to compare with the corresponding original trend of initial values.

Used in this way, the SOM could be seen as a smoother of noisy data sets. Let us demonstrate the point with Trondheim data. The following three cases are picked up for demonstration of this point. They represent different neighbourhoods in Trondheim and comprise administrative units at the most detailed level (i.e. wards). The data is the same as earlier: that is to say, single-family homes sold between 1993 and 2007, with recorded variables for the price, the plot size, Eastings and Westings. Rosenborg 6 is a traditional working-class area on the outskirts of the inner city which underwent strong gentrification during this period. Stokkan 16 is a middle-class neighbourhood developed since 1982 on previously Greenfield land, about 7 km from the city centre. Utsikten is an inner suburb with a magnificent panorama over the city and the fjord – this is a location comprising wealthy people. Note that the data set does not cover one or two of the selected cases for all years (see Figs 4.8–4.10).

The mid-1990s were characterised by increasing prices until a period of stagnation around the turn of the millennium and early noughties – presumably the consequence

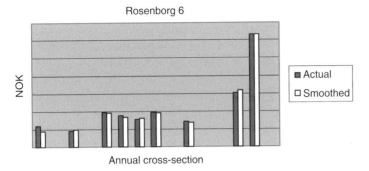

Figure 4.8 Development of actual and smoothed prices in Rosenborg 6 (NOK/m² for detached homes estimated with the SOM for annual cross sections).

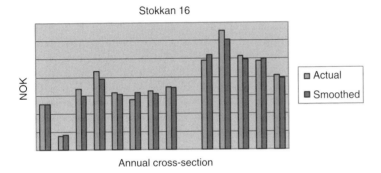

Figure 4.9 Development of actual and smoothed prices in Stokkan 16 (as in Fig. 4.8).

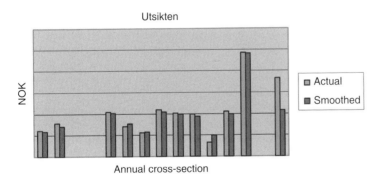

Figure 4.10 Development of actual and smoothed prices in Utsikten (as in Fig. 4.8).

of the Asian financial crisis in 1997 and the burst of the dot-come bubble in 2000. Besides these general trends, there are considerable upward and downward movements which are not synchronised across the three cases. The magnitudes and exact years vary, however, considerably across the three locations. It is to note that the financial crisis from the period 2007–2008 onwards is not covered by the data.

The figures show that, for the majority of the cases, the smoothed price estimate is below the actual price paid, as theory would predict. For Rosenborg 6, in 5 of the 9 years with recorded price information, the actual price paid is higher than the SOM estimation of the same price. For Stokkan 16, the corresponding ratio is 7 out of 13. For Utsikten, it is 8 out of 12. The same systematic price difference applies for mean differences, albeit for Stokkan 16 and especially Rosenborg 6, the actual prices are only slightly higher than the estimated ones on average.

On the other hand, we cannot distinguish any systematic relationship between the size of the spread (actual minus smoothed) and market situation (i.e. increasing or decreasing price trend), namely, when we examine this ratio for assumed peak, falling and rising price trend, we note the following comparison across the following three locations:

- Rosenborg 6: apart from the first recorded cross section (1993), which is in a period of a falling trend, the differences between actual and smoothed are rather minuscule.
- Stokkan 16: for the two peak prices (1996 and 2003, respectively), the differences between actual and smoothed are substantial; also 1998, in a stable period, show considerable differences, with smoothed prices higher than the actual ones.
- Utsikten: only for the last year of observing, and in a falling period, the difference is substantial (and in the predicted direction, namely, the actual price being above the smoothed price).

Conclusions and Discussion

As cyclic price developments worldwide have shown, issues related to the economic sustainability of local housing markets cannot be tackled satisfactorily by the mainstream housing market research community. Instead, the agenda needs to be reset. In doing so, it is argued here that we might look at heterodox economists, on the one hand, and practitioners, on the other, to find helpful ideas, concepts and research attitudes. Transdisciplinarity, that is, when a science discipline makes an effort to not only connect with other disciplines but also with lay knowledge, opens new avenues, when the old ones are found misleading (cf. Gibbons *et al.*, 1994; Cotgrave, 2003; Kersloot and Kauko, 2004). At any rate, connecting the discussions on housing market viability with the discussions on built-environment sustainability is fruitful according to the argument proposed in this contribution.

Consistently applying valuation automata on local house prices and other complex databases over several years will help us develop various economic sustainability metrics, which in turn are vital for setting the appropriate incentives for sustainable real-estate investments and justifications for government policies (cf. Sayce *et al.*, 2007). In the AVM, other kinds of quantifiable data such as income or real-estate quality indicators may be worth combining with the price data. Subsequently, less-tangible criteria and indicators can be incorporated into the outcome of the automated modelling of real-estate value. Finally, the resulting metrics based on long-term and partial criteria make a convenient basis for real-world decisions concerning economic sustainability. This principle is illustrated diagrammatically in Figure 4.11. The current study has dealt with the upper half and mainly left-hand side of the diagram.

The purported argument about abnormal price development trends needing to be recognised in terms of their spatial distribution is backed by empiry from Trondheim (using the SOM method of fixed time windows). From a practical point of view, data

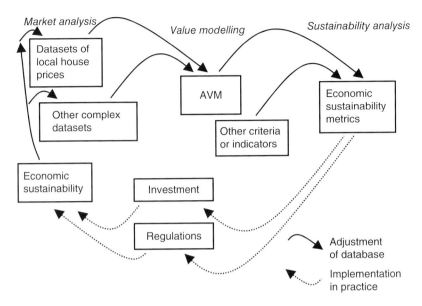

Figure 4.11 The proposed sequence of procedures for the development and implementation of economic sustainability metrics.

modelling outcomes have tremendous usability: if the indicator is valid, it becomes an excellent economic sustainability indicator; if not, it still diagnoses a problem. It is important to understand that AVMs are not the whole solution but only part of it, as the example from Trondheim illustrates. There should also be set incentives for advocating more qualitative thinking in the form of additional longer term criteria relating to sustainability.

Given the backdrop of the current financial crisis worldwide and housing market downturn in most Western countries, regions and cities,[4] the list of practical AVM applications launched for valuation is astonishing. Throughout the community of leading commercial AVM developers, various innovative solutions are being tested 'as we speak' – it is all about going forwards in this problem field regardless of any doom-and-gloom scenarios. This really is an unexpected finding. The present study has attempted to catch some of this attitude and keep distance from the current conservatism of the academia in this research area. The fact that the frontier of valuation research is moving forwards so rapidly is an embarrassing finding for us academic housing market and real-estate analysts. This brings to mind the conclusion by Söderbaum (2009), who argues that we academics cannot escape the blame for causing the economic downturn, because one of the roles of the science and university is to inform actors and governments about the right decisions to make. In particular, NCE has contributed to legitimate neoliberal policies and, as these policies have failed, so has the teachings of the economics departments. While the hardest criticism can be levied on the general economists, to a lesser extent, the same applies within the applied fields of real estate and housing economics.

---

4 This was written between 2009 and 2012.

However, we need to be constructive here: if market sustainability is a goal, what kind of methods and models should we then aim at? The desired level of empirical model performance depends not only on the context but also on the preferred balance in the trade-off between conceptual soundness and accuracy. This is why the sufficiently accurate linear hedonic regression modelling of the housing market has proven reasonably successful. On the other hand, alternative approaches allow researchers to capture the complex nature of the housing market relationships (cf. Chapter 3.1 of this volume).

Due to its pragmatic and nonlinear nature, the quasi-dynamic 'modelling approach' illustrated with Trondheim housing market data and the fixed time-window approach based on the SOM seems promising. Given the increasing significance of the sustainability discourse within planning, the findings also have policy implications: using innovative empirical housing market modelling as an analytic tool enables planning for sustainable land use on an urban and regional scale. A further, more practical implication of all this is that all properties could in principle be 'sustainable', and this is not only with regard to the physical aspects but also with regard to socio-economic aspects. That said, for some academics, this approach might seem too different from an economic mainstream approach (see Lorenz et al., 2008). Therefore, one is well advised to thread with caution. As stated at the outset, the ambition level probably should be reduced from developing tools to capturing the turning points in market development and eliminating the risk involved to tools that merely manage the unfavourable situation. Data quality poses further requirements to this project. While this obviously is not 'rocket science', an intellectual breakthrough could be achieved by reaching out towards discussions evolving elsewhere such as those pertaining to the definitions and criteria for creating a sustainable built environment.

4.3

Evaluation of Selected Real-Estate Markets – A Case Study from Poland

Malgorzata Renigier-Bilozor and Radoslaw Wisniewski

Introduction

It is possible to examine local real-estate markets (market areas) without using deterministic functions. This work provides a contribution to real-estate analysis using an approach based on socio-economic and demographic indicators from the largest Polish cities (areas). It relies on the same methodology that we successfully applied in Chapter 3.3, in order to define the determinants of different types of land use.

This study addresses a common problem encountered during advanced analyses of real estate, namely the choice and use of analytical and research methods that account for the specific nature of real-estate data. The following factors contribute to the difficulty in evaluating local real-estate markets:

- Significant variations in the quantity of available information, subject to the type of the analysed market (region)
- Complex methods of data description (differences in the scale of attribute description) – the same attribute can be described in a variety of ways using different evaluation scales
- Significant differences between real estates (no two real estates are identical)
- Various criteria for using real estate (every real estate can be used and managed in a variety of ways)
- Lack of comprehensive information (due to the lack of homogeneous systems for gathering real-estate data which results in limited and incomplete knowledge about real estate and market prices)
- Inaccurate and 'fuzzy' character of real-estate data (caused by stochastic factors which reflect random processes that escape the generally acknowledged cause-and-effect market relationship)
- Absence of homogeneous functional dependencies between real-estate attributes
- Decision-making strategies represented by the value, function and method of real-estate management.

This analysis is only a preliminary attempt at determining real-estate market analysis in Poland using non-deterministic functions. The results showed that classifications of the real-estate market analysis focus particularly on two indicators:

(1) average wage (HA)/average price per square metre (GW) (HA/GW), directly showing the flexibility of the market in adjusting the price of real estate to the capacity of its buyers in the light of a spreading crisis. We can see that markets which increase the demand capacity of the market faster are more effective. (2) The next indicator, in turn, shows the population (PO) per one real-estate transaction (RET) (PO/RET) which indicates the supply on the real-estate market and unfailing demand despite the increasingly difficult economic situation of a country.

Perfect versus Imperfect Real-Estate Markets

According to Kucharska-Stasiak (2005) and Bryx (2006), a perfect market has the following attributes:

- There is a large number of buyers and sellers – no participants have sufficient 'market power' to set the price of a product, buyers and sellers have to be dispersed.
- Product homogeneity (uniformity and full substitution) – when products are homogeneous, the decision to buy a given product will be determined by the price rather than variations in the product's nature.
- Perfect information (market transparency) – prices and quality of products are assumed to be known to all consumers and producers.
- Utility and profit maximisation – in addition to maximising their profits, decision-makers attempt to maximise their security or significance.
- Zero entry or exit barriers – a competitive market is freely available to all participants; owners can move their capital to market segments generating higher revenues; the capital market is marked by a high degree of liquidity.

The following factors contribute to real-estate market imperfections making real-estate market analysis difficult within the traditional deterministic framework (MRA, etc.):

- Speculation
- Monopolistic practices, such as the policies adopted by municipalities
- Large spread between prices quoted for similar real estates
  - the prices on local markets, in particular weakly developed markets, may differ even several-fold due to
    o unavailability of information,
    o specific features of a transaction,
    o specific features of real estate,
    o financing method,
    o subjective evaluation of real estate's utilitarian value,
    o underestimation of prices in property deeds,
    o low asset liquidity – real estate is difficult to sell at a price equal to its market value,
  - sporadic market equilibrium – on the real-estate market, supply and demand are usually out of balance due to
    o market outlook,
    o fluctuations in return rates,

- o specificity of the local market,
- o the return on alternative investments,
- o situation on the construction market,
- o state policy,
- o frequent legislative changes,
- o small number of transactions – real-estate turnover is low,
- non-rational behaviour – buyers' and sellers' decisions are influenced by factors other than the price, including trends, neighbourhood, tradition and advertising. Non-rational behaviour may result from
- o subjective evaluation of real estate's utilitarian value,
- o unequal access to market information,
- o mutual dependencies between parties,
- o acting under coercion,
- o insufficient information, and
- o differences in interpreting data.

It often happens that real-estate market analysis suffers from a lack of data and few organised databases. This is a serious issue to the reach towards more sustainable real-estate markets. It is also difficult to interpret without extensive analyses of functional dependencies between various attributes of real estate. The determination of the effect that real-estate attributes have on a selected decision (e.g. price) may also prove to be problematic.

From a different perspective, the ineffectiveness of the Polish real-estate market has a number of positive outcomes, including above-average profits and rates of return on real-estate investments. Transactions usually entail the conviction that real estate is worth more than the price paid upon acquisition and that is worth less that the price paid upon sale. High profits and high rates of return on real-estate investments would be very difficult to achieve on an effective market.

Analysis of Selected Real-Estate Markets in Poland – Case Study

Due to the strong emphasis placed on the statement that a simplified analysis created by the authors to evaluate local markets using an expert system based on the rough set theory (the approach based on the principles of Boolean logic) has been presented as follows. This method was chosen due to the specific area of research that the real-estate market constitutes and so the need to develop a different approach to real-estate analysis than that provided by classical financial economics.

Data from various real-estate markets in Poland for 2008–2010 are presented in Table 4.2 with reference to population statistics. The analysed data constitute a benchmark for measuring the size and affordability of the real-estate markets in selected Polish cities, and it accounts for the population, unemployment rate, average gross monthly wages, area in square kilometres, number of real-estate transactions separately for land plots and apartments and the average price per square metre of apartment area. At this stage of the analysis, the choice of data was dictated by the ease of acquisition and the availability of the relevant information. The real number of transactions on a

Table 4.2 Real-estate market analysis in Poland.

No.	City	Population	Unemployment rate	Gross monthly wage in PLN	Area (km²)	No. of transactions		Average price PLN/m²	Population/no. of transactions [PO/RET]	Average wage/average price per square metre [HA/GW]
						Land plots	Apartments			
1	Olsztyn	176,457	4.5	2,830	88.33	224	717	4,765	188	0.59
2	Słupsk	97,331	9.2	2,667	43.15	91	816	3,783	107	0.70
3	Suwałki	69,448	13.4	3,645	66.00	270	124	4,433	176	0.82
4	Ciechanów	45,270	5.7	2,994	32.51	131	182	2,503	145	1.20
5	Wrocław	632,162	5.0	3,415	292.82	159	2661	6,740	224	0.51
6	Działdowo	21,644	6.6	2,546	11.47	17	60	2,401	281	1.06
7	Inowrocław	76,137	20.4	2,789	30.42	11	25	3,443	2,115	0.81
8	Gdańsk	456,591	5.1	4,053	261.68	26	1728	6,215	260	0.65
9	Cracow	755,000	4.6	3,424	326.00	127	2298	7,260	311	0.47
10	Koszalin	106,987	4.7	2,932	98.33	258	805	4,112	101	0.71
11	Kętrzyn	27,942	27.5	2,423	10.35	9	31	2,345	698	1.03
12	Toruń	193,115	8.3	3,175	115.75	49	252	4,666	642	0.68
13	Gołdap	13,514	5.7	2,361	17.20	4	5	2,432	1,501	0.97
14	Poznań	554,221	3.3	3,669	261.85	83	1292	5,800	403	0.63
15	Łódź	742,387	9.5	3,159	293.25	251	2165	4,666	307	0.68
16	Bydgoszcz	357,650	7.3	2,830	175.98	61	1235	4,125	276	0.69
17	Zielona Góra	117,503	7.5	3,060	58.00	12	615	3,446	91	0.89
18	Ełk	57,579	12.2	2,584	21.00	72	252	2,990	178	0.86
19	Elbląg	127,954	16.5	2,521	38.94	87	821	3,894	141	0.65
20	Białystok	294,685	11.6	3,145	102.00	74	324	4,660	740	0.67

Source: Own research based on: http://www.stat.gov.pl/cps/rde/xbcr/gus/PUBL_PBS_transakcje_kupna_sprzedazy_nieruch_2008.pdf
http://www.mi.gov.pl/2-492414ae09dd9-1793287-p_1.htm; www.money.pl; www.egospodarka.pl, www.gratka.pl, www.oferty.net.pl, http://www.stat.gov.pl/cps/rde/
xbcr/gus/PUBL_ik_obrot_nieruchomosciami_2009.pdf, information given by municipal housing departments.

given local market (city) proved to be most problematic. It could be postulated that the level of difficulty with acquiring the relevant data was reversely proportional to city size (population and area). According to the authors, the aforementioned theory is supported by the following arguments:

- Lack of data gathering systems in the public domain.
- Lack of data sorting algorithms in units and departments responsible for data accumulation.
- Lack of advanced systems for updating, processing and releasing data.
- The units and departments responsible for gathering public information are reluctant to create access to the data.

Access to information is an important yet not the only factor determining market analysis.

In Table 4.2, available data (for 2008–2010) are presented as conditional attributes denoted as $c_1, c_2, c_3, c_4, c_5, c_6$, representing population, unemployment rate, average gross monthly wage (PLN), area (km^2), number of transactions (land plots + apartments) and average price (PLN) per square metre of apartment area, respectively.

The data were used to analyse real-estate market. At this stage of the analysis, the choice of data was dictated by the ease of acquisition and the availability of the relevant information. The determination of the real number of transactions on a given local market (city) proved to be most problematic as the units and departments responsible for gathering such information are reluctant to create access to the data, and there are no advanced and standardised systems for updating, processing and releasing market data. It appears that the level of difficulty with acquiring the relevant data was reversely proportional to city size (measured in population and area). If the Polish real-estate markets were to be evaluated based on the criterion of data availability, the majority of Polish cities would receive low or very low marks.

Based on the assumption that the data in Table 4.2 are credible, the following four decision attributes (denoted as D_1, D_2, D_3, D_4 in Table 4.3) were computed with the use of the rough set theory: number of transactions (conditional attribute for decisions D_2 and D_4), average price (PLN) per square metre of apartment area (conditional attribute for decisions D_1 and D_3), **PO/RET** – population per real-estate transaction and HA/GW – housing area in square metres that can be purchased with an average gross monthly wage.

In the analysis of real-estate data with the use of the rough set theory (Renigier, 2006, Renigier, 2008), the values v of attribute domains $D(v \in VD)$ are referred to as decision classes. Since $V = \underset{d \in D}{\cup} V_D$ [2] (where V_D – attribute domain $d \in D$), the following domains were adopted for the decision classes presented in Table 4.3:

$V_{D1} = \{1, 2, 3, 4\}$, where 1, 2, 3, 4 – number of transactions on a given real-estate market – are:

1 – up to 100
2 – from 101 to 500
3 – from 501 to 1000
4 – above 1001

Table 4.3 Decision attributes on selected real-estate markets.

No.	City	Decision attributes							
		D_1		D_2		D_3		D_4	
		Number of transactions (land plots + apartments)	Decision classes	Average price (PLN) per square metre of apartment area	Decision classes	Population/number of real-estate transactions [PO/RET]	Decision classes	Average gross monthly wage/average price (PLN) per square metre of apartment area [HA/GW]	Decision classes
1	Olsztyn	941	3	4765	2	188	1	0.59	1
2	Słupsk	907	3	3783	2	107	1	0.70	1
3	Suwałki	394	2	4433	2	176	1	0.82	2
4	Ciechanów	213	2	2503	1	145	1	1.20	3
5	Wrocław	2820	4	6740	3	224	2	0.51	1
6	Działdowo	77	1	2401	1	281	2	1.06	3
7	Inowrocław	161	2	3443	2	2115	2	0.81	2
8	Gdańsk	1754	4	6215	3	260	2	0.65	1
9	Kraków	2425	4	7260	3	311	2	0.47	1
10	Koszalin	1063	4	4112	2	101	1	0.71	2
11	Kętrzyn	40	1	2345	1	698	3	1.03	3
12	Toruń	301	2	4666	2	642	3	0.68	1
13	Gołdap	9	1	2432	1	1501	3	0.97	3
14	Poznań	1375	4	5800	3	403	2	0.63	1
15	Łódź	2416	4	4666	2	307	2	0.68	1
16	Bydgoszcz	1296	4	4125	2	276	2	0.69	1
17	Zielona Góra	627	3	3446	2	91	1	0.89	2
18	Ełk	324	2	2990	1	178	1	0.86	2
19	Elbląg	908	3	3894	2	141	1	0.65	1
20	Białystok	398	2	4660	2	740	3	0.67	1

Source: Own research based on: http://www.stat.gov.pl/cps/rde/xbcr/gus/PUBL_PBS_transakcje_kupna_sprzedazy_nieruch_2008.pdf
http://www.mi.gov.pl/2-492414ae09dd9-1793287-p_1.htm; www.money.pl; www.gospodarka.pl, www.gratka.pl, www.oferty.net.pl,
http://www.stat.gov.pl/cps/rde/xbcr/gus/PUBL_ik_obrot_nieruchomosciami_2009.pdf, information provided by municipal housing departments.

$V_{D2} = \{1, 2, 3\}$, where 1, 2, 3 – average price (PLN) per square metre of apartment area – are:

1 – up to 3000
2 – from 3100 to 5000
3 – above 5100

$V_{D3} = \{1, 2, 3\}$, where 1, 2, 3 – population per real-estate transaction (PO/RET) – are:

1 – up to 200
2 – from 201 to 500
3 – above 501

$V_{D4} = \{1, 2, 3\}$, where 1, 2, 3 – housing area in square metres that can be purchased with an average gross monthly wage HA/GW – are:

1 – up to 0.7
2 – from 0.71 to 0.9
3 – above 0.91

Based on the aforementioned assumptions, the indiscernibility relation for the decisions listed in Table 4.3 was divided into the following equivalence classes of U:

$D_1 - U/\text{IND}_{TD}(d) = \{X_1 = \{6, 11, 13\}, X_2 = \{3, 4, 7, 12, 18, 20\}, X_3 = \{1, 2, 17, 19\}, X_4 = \{5, 8, 9, 10, 14, 15, 16\}\}$

$D_2 - U/\text{IND}_{TD}(d) = \{X_1 = \{4, 6, 11, 13, 18\}, X_2 = \{1, 2, 3, 7, 10, 12, 15, 16, 17, 19, 20\}, X_3 = \{5, 8, 9, 14\}\}$

$D_3 - U/\text{IND}_{TD}(d) = \{X_1 = \{1, 2, 3, 4, 10, 17, 18, 19\}, X_2 = \{5, 6, 7, 8, 9, 14, 15, 16\}, X_3 = \{11, 12, 13, 20\}\}$

$D_4 - U/\text{IND}_{TD}(d) = \{X_1 = \{1, 2, 5, 8, 9, 12, 14, 15, 16, 19, 20\}, X_2 = \{3, 7, 10, 17, 18\}, X_3 = \{4, 6, 11, 13\}\}$

The applied computational procedure, which relies on the rough set theory and the valued tolerance relation (d'Amato, 2007, 2008; Renigier-Biłozor and Biłozor, 2007, Renigier-Biłozor, 2008a, 2008b; Renigier-Biłozor and Biłozor 2009a) and accounts for the regular entry of conditional attributes, supported the determination of the overall sum matrix for four decision attributes:

$$R_j(x, p) = \max\left(\sum_{j=1}^{n} R_j(x, p)\right) \tag{4.2}$$

where R_j is the valued tolerance relation, x the analysed property's attribute, p the attribute in the conditional segment of the investigated decision rule and n the number of property attributes in the conditional segment of the decision rule. A sample matrix for decision attribute D_1 – number of transactions – is presented in Table 4.4.

The equivalence classes of the indiscernibility relation were determined based on the similarity between the analysed properties at a minimum level of 60% (due to the specific character of the real-estate market, the number of the analysed properties and differences in attribute description). If five conditional attributes are analysed, indiscernible (similar) properties are those for which the sum matrix determined based on the matrix of the valued tolerance relation (equation 4.2) is higher than 3.0 (since 60% of 5.0 is 3.0). Properties with approximated assumed similarity are marked in bold in the first column of Table 4.4.

Table 4.4 Sum matrix determined based on the matrix of the valued tolerance relation for decision attribute D_1.

	1	2	3	4	5	6	7	8	9	10	11	12	13	14	15	16	17	18	19	20
1	5.00	2.46	2.13	2.41	0.92	1.70	2.05	0.90	0.98	3.92	0.80	3.24	1.50	1.08	1.40	2.57	2.57	1.37	2.07	2.64
2	2.46	5.00	2.54	2.51	0.32	2.76	3.29	0.33	0.25	2.91	1.89	2.19	2.24	0.04	1.33	2.10	3.41	3.41	3.44	1.66
3	2.13	2.54	5.00	1.60	0.50	1.31	1.96	0.11	0.52	2.33	1.32	2.05	1.33	0.99	1.20	0.79	2.08	2.34	2.64	2.31
4	2.41	2.51	1.60	5.00	0.97	3.51	2.75	0.90	0.88	2.85	2.62	1.82	3.68	0.61	1.02	1.38	3.38	2.61	1.64	1.07
5	0.92	0.32	0.50	0.97	5.00	0.73	0.00	2.63	3.75	0.95	0.00	0.94	0.89	2.91	2.26	0.63	0.82	0.00	0.00	0.41
6	1.70	2.76	1.31	3.51	0.73	5.00	2.35	0.75	0.67	1.70	3.66	1.09	4.33	0.45	0.54	1.27	2.32	3.37	2.27	0.36
7	2.05	3.29	1.96	2.75	0.00	2.35	5.00	0.00	0.00	2.47	2.06	1.05	1.99	0.00	0.34	1.43	2.99	3.07	2.81	0.84
8	0.90	0.33	0.11	0.90	2.63	0.75	0.00	5.00	1.60	0.93	0.00	0.48	0.90	3.18	0.99	1.46	0.61	0.00	0.00	0.35
9	0.98	0.25	0.52	0.88	3.75	0.67	0.00	1.60	5.00	0.99	0.00	0.85	0.82	1.86	2.27	0.56	0.73	0.00	0.00	0.39
10	3.92	2.91	2.33	2.85	0.95	1.70	2.47	0.93	0.99	5.00	0.88	2.99	1.72	0.77	1.33	2.63	3.39	1.55	2.32	2.36
11	0.80	1.89	1.32	2.62	0.00	3.66	2.06	0.00	0.00	0.88	5.00	0.37	3.68	0.00	0.00	0.11	1.44	2.98	2.12	0.16
12	3.24	2.19	2.05	1.82	0.94	1.09	1.05	0.48	0.85	2.99	0.37	5.00	0.95	0.39	2.77	2.49	2.93	0.95	1.50	3.86
13	1.50	2.24	1.33	3.68	0.89	4.33	1.99	0.90	0.82	1.72	3.68	0.95	5.00	0.61	0.38	0.74	2.21	2.91	1.99	0.26
14	1.08	0.04	0.99	0.61	2.91	0.45	0.00	3.18	1.86	0.77	0.00	0.39	0.61	5.00	1.16	0.77	0.32	0.00	0.00	0.20
15	1.40	1.33	1.20	1.02	2.26	0.54	0.34	0.99	2.27	1.33	0.00	2.77	0.38	1.16	5.00	1.54	1.61	0.56	0.46	2.62
16	2.57	2.10	0.79	1.38	0.63	1.27	1.43	1.46	0.56	2.63	0.11	2.49	0.74	0.77	1.54	5.00	2.03	0.87	1.24	2.31
17	2.57	3.41	2.08	3.38	0.82	2.32	2.99	0.61	0.73	3.39	1.44	2.93	2.21	0.32	1.61	2.03	5.00	2.34	2.47	2.18
18	1.37	3.41	2.34	2.61	0.00	3.37	3.07	0.00	0.00	1.55	2.98	0.95	2.91	0.00	0.56	0.87	2.34	5.00	2.08	1.21
19	2.07	3.44	2.64	1.64	0.00	2.27	3.18	0.00	0.00	2.32	2.12	1.50	1.99	0.00	0.46	1.24	2.47	3.08	5.00	1.42
20	2.64	1.66	2.31	1.07	0.41	0.36	0.84	0.35	0.39	2.36	0.16	3.86	0.26	0.20	2.62	2.31	2.18	1.21	1.42	5.00

Source: Own research.

In view of the aforementioned assumptions, equivalence (indiscernibility) classes were determined for conditional attributes. For the data in Table 4.4, the equivalence classes are as follows:

I – 1, 10, 12; II – 2, 17, 18, 19; III – 3; IV – 4, 6, 13, 17; V – 5, 9; VI – 4, 6, 11, 13, 18; VII – 2, 7, 18, 19; VIII – 8, 14; IX – 5, 9; X – 1, 10, 17; XI – 6, 11, 13; XII – 1, 12, 20; XIII – 4, 6 11, 13; XIV – 8, 14; XV – 15; XVI – 16; XVII – 2, 4, 10, 17; XVIII – 2, 6, 7, 18, 19; XIX – 2, 18, 19; XX – 12, 20.

At the next stage of the procedure, conditional rules were determined for all the configurations of the analysed data, assuming full covering of the sets of conditional and decision attributes. Only those whose lower and upper approximation was equal to 100% were selected. The quality of approximation was calculated (Mrózek and Płonka, 1999; Pawlak, 1982, 1991; Słowiński, 1992) based on the assumption that the approximation quality of family F in approximation space S relative to the set of attributes C is

$$\gamma_{\tilde{C}}(F) = \frac{\text{card}(POS_{\tilde{C}}(F))}{\text{card}(U)} \qquad (4.3)$$

where the numerator is the number of properties contained in the lower approximation of the set (counting once recurrent objects in particular subsets in the indiscernibility classes of decision attributes) (Pawlak, 1982; Mrózek and Płonka, 1999), and the denominator is the number of all properties belonging to a given indiscernibility class.

For instance, the approximation quality of decision attribute D_1 (number of transactions) shows that real-estate markets no. 6, 11 and 13 can be found in approximation class X1 (up to 100 transactions). Thus, there is a maximum of three observations (numerator in equation 4.3), and only market no. 11 is contained in the lower approximation (denominator in equation 4.3) since, as shown in Table 4.4, the other two observations (6 and 13) correspond to markets with different decision attributes. At a similarity level of 60% (above 3.0), $X_1 = \{6, 11, 13\}$, therefore VI – **4**, 6, 11, 13, **18**; XI – 6, 11, 13; XIII – **4**, 6, 11, 13. The observations marked in bold can be ruled out as members of the analysed equivalence class X_1 for attribute D_1. Only rule XI can be deterministically classified as belonging to the aforementioned equivalence class. Table 4.5 presents the decision rules that can be considered useful for real-estate market analysis.

In the first decision group D_1 (number of transactions), in equivalence class X_1 (up to 100 transactions), rule XI (Kętrzyn) is representative:

if $(c_1 = 27942)$ **and** $(c_2 = 27.5)$ **and** $(c_3 = 2423)$ **and** $(c_4 = 10.35)$ **and** $(c_5 = 2345)$ **then** $(c = 1)$,

in equivalence class X_2 (from 101 to 500 transactions), rules III (Suwałki) and XX (Białystok) are representative:

if $(c_1 = 69448)$ **and** $(c_2 = 13.4)$ **and** $(c_3 = 3645)$ **and** $(c_4 = 66.00)$ **and** $(c_5 = 4433)$, **then** $(c = 2)$

if $(c_1 = 294685)$ **and** $(c_2 = 11.6)$ **and** $(c_3 = 3145)$ **and** $(c_4 = 102.00)$ **and** $(c_5 = 4660)$, **then** $(c = 2)$,

in equivalence class X_3 (from 501 to 1000 transactions), rule XIX (Elbląg) is representative:

if $(c_1 = 127954)$ **and** $(c_2 = 16.5)$ **and** $(c_3 = 2521)$ **and** $(c_4 = 38.94)$ **and** $(c_5 = 3894)$, **then** $(c = 3)$

Table 4.5 Decision rules for real-estate market analysis.

No. of decision attributes	Equivalence classes	C-approximation quality	No. of decision rules
D_1	X1	1/3	11
	X2	2/6	3, 20
	X3	1/4	19
	X4	5/7	8, 9, 14, 15, 16
D_2	X1	3/5	6, 11, 13
	X2	5/11	1, 10, 12, 16, 20
	X3	3/4	5, 8, 14
D_3	X1	4/8	3, 10, 17, 19
	X2	6/8	5, 8, 9, 14, 15, 16
	X3	1/4	20
D_4	X1	7/11	5, 8, 9, 14, 15, 16, 20
	X2	1/5	3
	X3	1/4	13

Source: Own research.

in equivalence class X4 (above 1001 transactions), rules VIII (Gdańsk), IX (Kraków), XIV (Poznań), XV (Łódź) and XVI (Bydgoszcz) are representative:

if $(c_1 = 456591)$ and $(c_2 = 5.1)$ and $(c_3 = 4053)$ and $(c_4 = 261.68)$ and $(c_5 = 6215)$, then $(c = 4)$

if $(c_1 = 755000)$ and $(c_2 = 4.6)$ and $(c_3 = 3424)$ and $(c_4 = 326.00)$ and $(c_5 = 7260)$, then $(c = 4)$

if $(c_1 = 554221)$ and $(c_2 = 3.3)$ and $(c_3 = 3669)$ and $(c_4 = 261.85)$ and $(c_5 = 5800)$, then $(c = 4)$

if $(c_1 = 7422387)$ and $(c_2 = 9.5)$ and $(c_3 = 3159)$ and $(c_4 = 293.25)$ and $(c_5 = 4666)$, then $(c = 4)$

if $(c_1 = 357650)$ and $(c_2 = 7.3)$ and $(c_3 = 2830)$ and $(c_4 = 175.98)$ and $(c_5 = 4125)$ then $(c = 4)$.

In the remaining decision groups, representative decision rules can be determined in the same way.

Two indicators were computed based on the assumption that the acquired data are credible:

PO/RET – population per one real-estate transaction

HA/GW – housing area in square metres that can be purchased with an average gross monthly wage.

The two indicators can be used to perform a simplified analysis of the real-estate markets in Poland.

The first indicator, PO/RET, indicates the size of the local population per one real-estate transaction, and the higher its value, the lower the relative transaction activity of the local market. The second indicator, HA/GW, is a price-to-income

Table 4.6 Indicator: population size per one RE transaction.

No.	Real-estate market	Population/no. of transactions [PO/RET]
1	Zielona Góra	91
2	Koszalin	101
3	Słupsk	107
4	Elbląg	141
5	Ciechanów	145
6	Suwałki	176
7	Ełk	178
8	Olsztyn	188
9	Wrocław	224
10	Gdańsk	260
11	Bydgoszcz	276
12	Działdowo	281
13	Łódź	307
14	Cracow	311
15	Poznań	403
16	Toruń	642
17	Kętrzyn	699
18	Białystok	740
19	Gołdap	1502
20	Inowrocław	2115

Source: Own research.

ratio that measures the affordability of real estate, and the higher its value, the more affordable real estate is within this market. The value of the second indicator illustrates the correlation between real-estate prices and incomes on the local market.

Real-estate markets are ranked according to the adopted indicators listed in Tables 4.6 and 4.7. An analysis of the data in Table 4.6 indicates that a given market's place in the ranking is not determined by the size of the city, its population or the unemployment rate. The ranking is topped by medium-sized cities with a population nearing 100,000 – Zielona Góra, Koszalin and Słupsk. Table 4.7 suggests a certain trend, namely that real-estate prices are more affordable in smaller cities: in this case, Ciechanów, Działdowo and Kętrzyn. An analysis of both the tables shows a certain analogy as regards similar positions occupied by Bydgoszcz, Łódź, Suwałki and Ełk.

The aforementioned analysis is only a preliminary attempt at determining real-estate market analysis in Poland using non-deterministic functions. The results showed that classifications of the real-estate market analysis focuses particularly on two indicators such as average wage/average price, directly showing the flexibility of the market in adjusting the price of real estate to the capacity of its buyers in the light of a spreading crisis. We can see that markets which increase the demand capacity of the market faster are more effective. The next indicator, in turn, shows the population per one transaction

Table 4.7 Indicator: real-estate affordability – the number of square metres that can be purchased with average monthly wages.

No.	Real-estate market	Average wage/average price per square metre of housing area [HA/GW]
1	Ciechanów	1.20
2	Działdowo	1.06
3	Kętrzyn	1.03
4	Gołdap	0.97
5	Zielona Góra	0.89
6	Ełk	0.86
7	Suwałki	0.82
8	Inowrocław	0.81
9	Koszalin	0.71
10	Słupsk	0.71
11	Bydgoszcz	0.69
12	Toruń	0.68
13	Łódź	0.68
14	Białystok	0.67
15	Gdańsk	0.65
16	Elbląg	0.65
17	Poznań	0.63
18	Olsztyn	0.59
19	Wrocław	0.51
20	Cracow	0.47

Source: Own research.

which indicates the supply on the real-estate market and unfailing demand despite the increasingly difficult economic situation of a country.

The Use of the Rough Set Theory in Real-Estate Market Analysis

According to the authors, popular analytical methods (mostly statistical) are relatively ineffective in weak-form efficient real-estate markets. The preferred methods and procedures should account for the following defects in real-estate data: absence of data, small number of transactions, significant variations in attribute coding, non-linear relations between the analysed data and the type of the underlying market. The applied methods should support market analysis at the potential (theoretical) and actual (applied) levels. The following solutions (Table 4.8) that rely on the rough set theory may offer an effective alternative to popular analytical methods. References to detailed studies are indicated in parentheses.

The process of managing real-estate resources is problematic due to the specificity of real-estate information. Owing to the complexity and diversity of data sets, the

Table 4.8 The use of the rough set theory (RST) for improving real-estate market analysis.

The RST-based methods for analysing the real-estate market		
General problem	Detailed problem	Solution
Selection of methods for managing and using buildings and apartments (Renigier, 2006)	Analysis of the real-estate market using various methods for registering real-estate attributes without data loss (Renigier, 2008b)	Option for analysing data sets without the risk of data loss when quantitative attributes are replaced with qualitative attributes
Real-estate appraisal on markets characterised by limited resource availability (Renigier, 2008a)	Real-estate appraisal involving limited data sets (Renigier, 2008b)	Real-estate appraisal based on expert data sets, with high confidence in results
Selection of functions assigned to land on ineffective real-estate markets (Renigier-Biłozor and Biłozor, 2009a,b)	Determining the significance of real-estate attributes without the use of statistical methods (Renigier-Biłozor and Biłozor, 2009a,b)	Reliable verification of the significance of attributes adopted based on a limited data set
	Determining weighting factors for real-estate prices (Renigier-Biłozor and Biłozor, 2009)	Determining the significance of attributes without the use of statistical tests
Real-estate appraisal based on limited market data (Renigier-Biłozor, 2010)	Supplementing the missing real-estate attributes (Renigier-Biłozor, 2010)	Determining the value of the missing real-estate attributes based on the analysed data set
Analysis of real-estate markets (Renigier-Biłozor, 2011; Renigier-Biłozor and Wiśniewski, 2012)	Classifications of the real-estate market focus particularly on information availability (Renigier-Biłozor, 2011; Renigier-Biłozor and Wiśniewski, 2012)	Determining the availability of information in real-estate markets

decision-making process in managing the resources of the largest property owners in Poland, such as municipalities or Polish State Railway companies, is wrought with problems. The greater the responsibility, the more difficult is this process which affects not only the owner's financial performance but also the spatial, economic and social development of urban areas. The authors have concluded that the application of the rough set theory in real-estate market analyses may deliver positive results (compare with Table 4.5). As demonstrated in Table 4.5, the use of the rough set theory for developing decision trees could enhance the effectiveness of the decision-making process in real-estate management.

As demonstrated by the results of studies referenced in Table 4.8, market analyses can produce reliable results even when the number of transactions is small and when different attribute description is applied. The procedure proposed by the authors does not require the development of complex models, preliminary analyses or the adjustment of the available data sets. In the approach based on the rough set theory, decisions are made based on 'raw data' in line with the principles of Boolean logic; that is to say, a given decision (real-estate value) is made, if the given conditions (real-estate attributes) are fulfilled.

Real estate attributes possess diversity and imprecision, the scope of data is extensive and complex, and the variability of real estate decisions over time is relatively high. As a consequence, these decisions become difficult and burdened with considerable risk. The use of the rough set theory and the valued tolerance relation in the decision-making process produces satisfactory results. Problems that cannot be tackled by statistical analyses alone may be solved with the involvement of the proposed method whose outcomes are easy to implement and interpret.

The application of the rough set theory also supports the identification of the key attributes and core characteristics of real estate based on the available data. As demonstrated by the studies referred to in Table 4.8, the proposed procedure can be applied to investigate the effect of real-estate attributes on the analysed decision-making problem.

The lack or unavailability of data poses one of the greatest obstacles hindering the exploration of real-estate market information. Table 4.5 cites a quick and simplified procedure for supplementing the missing information in the data sets used for market analyses. It is based on the principles of the rough set theory aided by the valued tolerance relation. This solution is particularly suitable for markets that are weak-form efficient as regards information availability.

Conclusions

An evaluation of real-estate market areas is possible using an approach based on socio-economic and demographic indicators. Using such an approach, this paper identifies factors that influence real-estate markets and, consequently, the entire market system in Poland. The venture point for every analysis of real market is the selection of adequate research methods that account for the market's specific attributes and produce results applicable to other local markets. Owing to their individual character, local markets require suitable analytical tools, such as the proposed method based the rough set theory which was initially developed to analyse 'difficult', fuzzy and inaccurate data. Methods based on the principles of the rough set theory and the valued tolerance relation may constitute a valuable tool for evaluating the real-estate markets.

4.4

Cyclical Capitalization

Maurizio d'Amato

Introduction[5]

An article in the Wall Street Journal referring to Lehman Brothers explained that "When it failed the estates of the collapsed investment bank listed its real estate holding as valued at 23 billion of dollars … The 23 billion of dollars has been written down substantially. In all, Lehman expects to receive some of 13.2 billion dollars between 2011 and 2014 …." (Brown, 2011) It would be interesting to understand how the large real-estate position of one of the most important investment banks has been valued. At the moment, we know that Lehman Brothers was one of the most important players in commercial property before it collapsed. We know also that Lehman Brothers was compelled to appraise properties at fair value following the accounting principle of mark-to-market value indicated in the Financial Accounting Standard n. 157. It is well known that at the moment of the crisis, the real-estate market cycle was affected by an impressive downturn. In this contribution, the necessity of a clear improving role of property market cycle in the valuation process is highlighted. On the third anniversary of its bankruptcy, Lehman Brothers remained the most important owner and seller in this property market segment in the largest and most transparent real-estate market in the world. In particular, the attention is focused on cyclical capitalization models that integrate income approach with the time series of the real-estate market cycle.

In particular, as a possible solution that might help to change the attitude toward property valuation, in this chapter, I propose a generalization of the Cyclical Dividend Discount Model introduced previously in d'Amato (2003), d'Amato (2004), and d'Amato (2015). The main focus of the chapter is not to provide an exhaustive analysis of cyclical capitalization modeling but to show the weak and strong points of their application. At this stage, a few empirical applications are available, but according to the formal robustness of the models and the emergent role of property market cycle, especially after the nonagency mortgage crisis, they may give an added value to valuation practice. More empirical applications can be provided only in a more transparent market where it is possible to collect net operating income (NOI) and price time series at a

5 This chapter is based on a presentation of the author to the American Enterprise Institute on the 31st of July 2013 in Washington. The author is grateful to CRIF for the financial aid to the research.

neighborhood level. Time-series analysis represents a necessary but not a sufficient condition to cyclical capitalization application. Price and rent forecasts may also be based on an expectation analysis. In both the cases, market transparency is a fundamental issue for a more professional and more sustainable real-estate market. The remainder of the paper is structured as follows. A brief literature review on real-estate market cycles is presented in the first section. An outline of the "classic" income approach method for real-estate valuation is given in the second section. In the third section, an introduction to cyclical capitalization is offered, and in the fourth section, application to London office market data is discussed. Final remarks are offered at the end.

Real-Estate Market Cycle

There is a large body of literature analyzing the property market cycles. One of the first real-estate cycle researchers is an American named Roy Wenzlick. By charting cycles of US housing transactions from 1795 to 1973, he found that the average length of the long cycle is 18 and 1/3 years. A pioneering work on real-estate cycles was conducted by Kuznets (1930). Real-estate market cycle literature can be approached from different points of view (Rottke and Wernecke, 2002). From a macroeconomic viewpoint, real-estate cycle as a part of construction sector and, from a microeconomic perspective, variables such as rent levels, vacancy, and absorption rate are relevant. From a finance point of view, the relationship between market cycle and several variables of Modern Portfolio Theory models such as interest rate, correlation of return, and risk premiums is analyzed. The last point of view is the management point of view involving concept related to life cycle of real estate. An analysis of the rental rate cycle (Wheaton, 1987) was carried out to analyze the market trend of rent. Although not recent, one of the most broad and comprehensive papers on this subject is by Pyhrr and colleagues (1999). It synthesizes most of the relevant research and commentary on real-estate cycles as well as presents a basic theory of cycles with some models to support the investors' and portfolio managers' decisions.

An extensive literature review on real-estate cycles is beyond the scope of this paper; in the remainder of this section, just some important contributions on real-estate cycles are cited. Therefore, the interested reader looking for an excellent introduction is recommended to refer to Pyhrr and colleagues (1999). In the same year, Grissom and De Lisle (1999) demonstrated the possibility to model cyclical change at an overall industry level. Pritchett (1984) studied the US investment-grade real-estate market and, among other things, discovered that the best indicator of the cycle phase is vacancy rate. Hekman (1985) analyzed the office sector in 14 cities over the 1979–1983 period, and it was shown that the construction sector is cyclical. Clear indications of cyclic vacancy rates and market differences between metropolitan areas are shown in Voith and Crone (1988), by analyzing the office market vacancy rates in 17 large metropolitan areas in the United States for the period from June 1980 through June 1987. Wheaton and Torto (1988) confirmed that office vacancy rates and real rents are cyclical, while the effect of the business cycle on the cycle of real-estate asset performance was examined in Sagalyn (1990).

Pyhrr *et al.* (1990) and Pyhrr and Born (2006) provided a seminal outlook on the role of market cycle in real-estate market analysis. Roulac (1996) performed a qualitative study on important cyclical relationships and concluded that real-estate markets are influenced by the economy, office demand, office construction, property values, volume of transactions, capital for real estate, investor interest, and tax climate factors. Studying the determinants of Canadian commercial property prices, Clayton (1996) suggested that such prices may be forecast and that major market cycles may be detectable in advance, potentially leading to arbitrage opportunities. Mueller *et al.* (1994) and Mueller and Pevnev (1997) analyzed rent distributions in different alternative market cycles. Kaiser (1997) studied long cycles as well as short cycles and concluded that the former better explain the behavior of the real-estate markets. Other important contributions not included in Pyhrr and colleagues (1999) are by Case and Shiller (1989), Borio *et al.* (1994), Abraham and Hendershot (1996), Case *et al.* (1997), and Wheaton (1999), all of which give evidence on the cyclical nature of real-estate prices. Another interesting review article that focuses on the role of speculation in real-estate cycles is by Malpezzi and Watcher (2005), which also examines whether land speculation is primarily a cause of, or a symptom of, property cycles. The importance of property cycles has been stressed in several recent contributions in the literature. Reed *et al.* (2010) highlighted the necessity of a deeper knowledge on property market cycle.

In this work, cycle of observation is closely integrated with professional valuation practice. The models proposed here belong to the income approach and rely on the existence and observation of real-estate cycles. In particular, the models integrated the observation of real-estate market rent with the local trend analysis in order to include local market value in the opinion of value.

Income Approach and International Valuation Standards

Property valuation professional activity is subject to International Valuation Standards and is based on three approaches: market, income, and cost. The market approach is based on the selection of appropriate comparables to the property to be valued. Therefore, they can be used in several ways (Multiple Regression Analysis, Adjustment Grid Methods) to appraise the value of a property. Commercial properties without a set of comparables as income-producing properties may be appraised using a direct relation between market value and income. The direct relationship between income and market value is based on different models rooted in the financial mathematics. The International Valuation Standards considers the income that an asset will generate over its useful life and indicates value through a capitalisation process. Capitalisation involves the conversion of income into a capital sum through the application of an appropriate discount rate (IVS 2011 Framework; para. 60). Income approach is composed of three different groups of methodologies: income capitalization, (yield capitalization) discounted cash flow, and various option pricing models (IVS 2011 Framework para. 61). Two theoretical appraisal models are based on the income approach (IVSC, 2011a,b,c; IVS 230; C6–C21): the former is direct capitalization, which is a process that transforms an infinitive group of rents into a value, and the latter is yield capitalization, which is a process that transforms a finite group of rents into a value. The so-called Discounted Cash-Flow analysis is normally included in the yield capitalization. In formal terms, a direct capitalization is indicated in equation 4.4 for constant rents:

$$V = \frac{\text{NOI}}{R_o} \tag{4.4}$$

Here, V is the value of a property to be valued, NOI or Net Operating Income is the rent (in this case, the net rent, but it may also be gross rent), while R_o is the overall capitalization rate. The International Valuation Standard states that "… The income approach requires the estimation of a capitalisation rate when capitalising income…" (IVS 2011; para C24). The future growth of the rent is included in the capitalization rate estimation. In fact, IVS 2011 indicates that "…In capitalisation methods that do not employ discounting, expected growth is normally reflected in the capitalisation rate…" (IVS, 2011; para C25). If the rent is supposed to grow, it is normally applied in the Dividend Discount Model as shown in equation 4.5:

$$V = \frac{\text{NOI}}{Y - \Delta a} \tag{4.5}$$

Here, NOI is the Net Operating Income, Y the appropriate rate, Δ the "…total relative change in income and value over the projection period, and a the annualizer or conversion factor…" (The Appraisal of Real Estate 13th edition, p. 532); Δa is usually expressed as g or growth factor, which represents the compound growth of the capital during the holding period. In fact, IVS states that "…in methods that employ discounting, expected growth may be explicitly considered in the forecasted income or cash flow…" (IVS 2011; para C25). This g factor may be increasing or decreasing. This is the methodological consequence of the false myth of the ever-growing trends for real-estate prices: "…Mr. Greenspan, needless to say, had a lot of help from Wall Street, Washington…and just as the contempt for risk that made possible the gross extravagances in housing and the financial market was sustained by confidence that Mr G would always bail out the participants" (Abelson, 2007, p. 2). Both equations 4.4 and 4.5 refer to an infinite number of rents and can be considered for two different models of direct capitalization. The valuation of income-producing properties for a limited number of years or the valuation of a fractional interest requires a different approach. The valuation of a property having constant rent for a limited number of years is shown in equation 4.6:

$$V = \frac{\text{NOI}}{R_o} \frac{(1 + Y)^n - 1}{(1 + Y)^n} \tag{4.6}$$

Here, NOI is the Net Operating Income, Y the appropriate discount rate, R_o is the overall capitalization rate, and n the number of annual rents considered in the valuation. If the rents are limited and grow at g (or Δa) rate, the equation becomes

$$V = \text{NOI} \frac{1 - \left(\frac{1+\Delta a}{1+i}\right)^n}{Y - \Delta a} \tag{4.7}$$

Equation 4.7 is valid by assuming $Y > \Delta a$. If $Y < \Delta a$, then, the equation becomes

$$V = \text{NOI} \frac{\left(\frac{1+\Delta a}{1+i}\right)^n - 1}{\Delta a - Y} \tag{4.8}$$

In Equations 4.7 and 4.8, NOI is the net operating income, Y the discount rate, the g factor or Δa the growth factor previously defined, n is the number of annual rents considered in the valuation. Equations 4.6–4.8 can be considered as yield capitalization because they allow the appraisal of a limited number of rents. Another model widely used is the Discounted Cash-Flow Analysis. In this case, the valuer discounts a limited number of rents. Technical Information Paper 1 of IVSC describes the application of DCF at point 6 "…The DCF Method results in an indication of value whereby forecasted cash flows are discounted back to the valuation date, resulting in a present value of the asset or business. A terminal value at the end of the explicit forecast period is then determined and that value is also discounted back to the valuation date to give an overall value for the asset or business….". In formal terms, the general equation of DCF is indicated as follows:

$$V = \sum_{t=1}^{n} \frac{NOI_t}{(1+Y)^t} + \frac{NOI_{n+1}}{R_o(1+Y)^{n+1}} \tag{4.9}$$

Here, NOI means Net Operating Income, Y is the discount rate, n the holding period, and R_o the overall capitalization rate. Equation 4.9 can be rewritten as follows:

$$V = \sum_{t=1}^{n} \frac{NOI_t}{(1+Y)^t} + \frac{NOI}{(Y-\Delta a)(1+Y)^n} \tag{4.10}$$

Here, the second term in equation 4.9 is replaced by the application of Dividend Discount Model. The second term in Equations 4.9 and 4.10 is defined in several ways: scrap value, terminal value, or going-out value. The brief introduction to income approach highlights an important problem: the valuer needs to provide a forecast for the future rents in terms of capitalization rate, discount rate, or g factor. For this reason, "…An appraiser must consider the future outlook both in the estimate of income and expenses and in selection of the appropriate capitalization methodology to use…" (The Appraisal of Real Estate 13th Edition, p. 469). Therefore, a question can be raised as to how future rents are taken into account. According to the equation presented in this section, a graphical description of the relationship between NOI and time of the valuation process of income approach is provided by Figure 4.12. As one can see, the figure shows how valuers deal with the future. Each approach to the valuation process is denoted by a line. The future is denoted as a straight line in Equation 4.4, as a constant decreasing or increasing rent as in equation 4.5, a limited constant line as in Equation 4.6, a limited increasing (or decreasing rent), an increasing limited rent as in the line referring to Equation 4.7, and finally, a two-stage rent as in the line referring to Equation 4.10 (Fig. 4.12).

Probably, we should be honest. The myth of ever-increasing real-estate market is not a strange recurring idea, but it is based on our valuation approaches. It is based on valuation methods that do not take into account the relationship between income and a local market cycle. Neglecting the property market cycle is probably a bug in the everyday task of valuers.[6]

Cyclical Capitalization

There is a lack of information about the cycle appraising income-producing properties even if the IVS GN 1 states at 5.12.1 that "The income capitalization approach is based on the same principles that apply to other valuation approaches In particular, it

---

6 This bug can be defined as 'looking glass bug'.

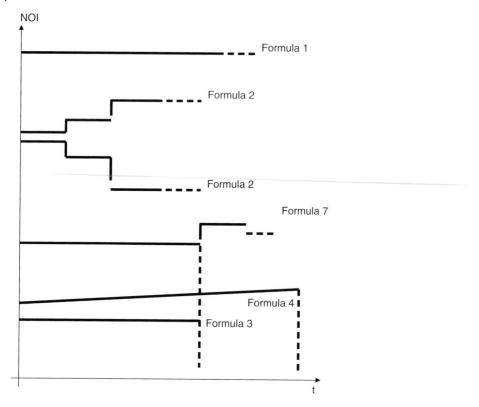

Figure 4.12 Relationship between NOI and time in the principal valuation models income-oriented.

perceives value as created by the expectation of future benefits (income streams)" The questions are as follows: Do our present set of models take into account the expectation of future benefits? How to do this? We suspect that market expectations, which draw into a bubble, are also amplified by a group of methods that do not take into account the important role of the real-estate market cycle. Cyclical capitalization is proposed to integrate property market cycle analysis with property valuation. It is a family of valuation methodologies belonging to income approach based on the Cyclical Dividend Discount Models (d'Amato, 2003; d'Amato, 2004). A specific field of application of cyclical capitalization are the income-producing properties where information about the property market cycle is known. The model was applied for the first time in Italian and Spanish Residential Property Markets. The following section presents four different groups of cyclical capitalization dubbed (in Latin): defined as primum group, secundum group, tertium group, and quartum group. The order is chronological. The primum group integrates the traditional Dividend Discount Model with market cycle analysis, the secundum group integrates the traditional direct capitalization modeling with real-estate market cycle analysis, the tertium group is composed of models including cyclical capitalization in the calculation of exit value, and finally, the quartum group also includes a fixed interval of vacancy of the property in the calculation of the value. All the models presented here deal with freehold properties. It is possible to develop specific cyclical capitalization modeling for leasehold properties.

The Primum Group of Cyclical Capitalization

The primum group of Cyclical capitalization methodologies is based on CDD models. CDD models are based on a simple variation of the original Dividend Discount Model (Gordon and Shapiro, 1956; Gordon, 1962). In this model, the appraiser deals with a rent that increases and decreases cyclically with more than two g factors. It is very important to introduce meaning of g factor in terms of real-estate before approaching the cyclical capitalization modeling of the primum group.

The Meaning of g Factor or Δa

Before analyzing the proposed cyclical capitalization, it is necessary to understand the nature of the growth factor g or Δa indicated in equations 4.5, 4.7, 4.8, and 4.100. The growth factor shown also as Δa is a product between two parts. The former Δ is also assumed to be the "total relative change in property income and value" (The Appraisal of Real Estate, 13th Edition, p. 532). The second component can be defined as an "annual sinking fund factor or an annual recapture rate, to convert the total relative change in income and value into an appropriate periodic rate of change" (The Appraisal of Real Estate, 13th Edition, p. 532). Income approach models exposed in paragraph 1 identify only Δa. In practical terms, it is possible to define the product as follows:

$$\Delta a = \Delta \frac{Y}{(1+Y)^n - 1} \tag{4.11}$$

Here, the change in income and property value is a sinking fund factor for an appropriate periodic rate of change. As a consequence, this rate of change is a synthesis of future change in property value and property rent. Cyclical capitalization proposes a different approach to the problem. Both Δ and a are related to a rate of change specific property market phases. Therefore, the relative change is not referred to the whole life of the property but to the life of the property in a specific phase of the market. In the cyclical capitalization, the rate of change is calculated based on the real data during the temporal length of the single phase of the cycle.

Appraisers must select an appropriate backward holding period between 10 and 15 years in which they will calculate the rate of change of rent in different real-estate market phases. The term backward holding period is proposed to distinguish this particular type of holding period from the well-known holding period adopted in the DCF (here referred to as forward holding period). As a consequence, there is not only one but more terms according to the specific time of valuation with respect to the real-estate market cycle. It is still possible to deal with expectations instead of time series when determining the g factors.

The Primum Group

In this valuation method, the appraiser considers more than one g factor or Δa by taking into account the real-estate market cycles. The value of the property in a cycle is obtained by summing up the value of the property in the Recovery Recession phase and the same value in the Expansion Contraction phases. Therefore,

$$V_{PG1} = \frac{NOI}{Y - \Delta a_{RR}} - \frac{NOI}{Y - \Delta a_{RR}} \frac{1}{(1+Y)^{t_{rr}}} + \frac{NOI}{Y - \Delta a_{EC}} \frac{1}{(1+Y)^{t_{rr}}}$$
$$- \frac{NOI}{Y - \Delta a_{EC}} \frac{1}{(1+Y)^{t_{ec}+t_{rr}}} \tag{4.12}$$

Considering an n number of phases and assuming $t_{rr} = t_{ec} = n$, then

$$
\begin{aligned}
V_{PG1} &= \frac{NOI}{Y - \Delta a_{RR}} - \frac{NOI}{Y - \Delta a_{RR}} \frac{1}{(1+Y)^n} \\
&+ \frac{NOI}{Y - \Delta a_{EC}} \frac{1}{(1+Y)^n} - \frac{NOI}{Y - \Delta a_{EC}} \frac{1}{(1+Y)^{2n}} \\
&+ \frac{NOI}{Y - \Delta a_{RR}} \frac{1}{(1+Y)^{2n}} - \frac{NOI}{Y - \Delta a_{RR}} \frac{1}{(1+Y)^{3n}} \cdots
\end{aligned}
\tag{4.13}
$$

In the first version of the model, we make a quite strong assumption that $t_{rr} = t_{ec} = n$. In fact, it means that the property market cycle has two phases with equal temporal length. The equation above can be expressed as follows:

$$
\begin{aligned}
V &= \frac{NOI}{Y - \Delta_{RR} a_{RR}} \left(1 + \frac{1}{(1+Y)^{2n}} + \frac{1}{(1+Y)^{4n}} + \frac{1}{(1+Y)^{6n}} \cdots \right) \\
&- \frac{NOI}{Y - \Delta_{RR} a_{RR}} \left(\frac{1}{(1+Y)^n} + \frac{1}{(1+Y)^{3n}} - \frac{1}{(1+Y)^{5n}} \cdots \right) \\
&+ \frac{NOI}{Y - \Delta_{EC} a_{EC}} \left(\frac{1}{(1+Y)^n} + \frac{1}{(1+Y)^{3n}} - \frac{1}{(1+Y)^{5n}} \cdots \right) \\
&- \frac{NOI}{Y - \Delta_{EC} a_{EC}} \left(\frac{1}{(1+Y)^{2n}} + \frac{1}{(1+Y)^{4n}} - \frac{1}{(1+Y)^{6n}} \cdots \right)
\end{aligned}
\tag{4.14}
$$

Equation 4.14 presents four infinitive geometric progressions of rate $r = \frac{1}{(1+Y)^{2n}}$ in the second part. The term r is within the interval $-1 < r < 1$; therefore, progression tends to the following equation:

$$
\sum_{i=1}^{\infty} r_i = \frac{1}{1-r} \quad \text{where } r = \frac{1}{(1+Y)^{2n}}
\tag{4.15}
$$

The value of the perpetuity can be calculated as follows:

$$
V_{PG1} = \frac{(1+Y)^n}{(1+Y)^n + 1} \left[\frac{NOI}{Y + \Delta a_{RR}} + \frac{NOI}{Y - \Delta a_{EC}} \frac{1}{(1+Y)^n} \right]
\tag{4.16}
$$

The opinion of value may be referred to a limited number of years as in the case of a fractional interest. In this case, the geometric progression may be limited. In this case, starting from equation 4.16 and assuming that the number of years equals k, the equation will be the sum of a limited number of geometric progressions whose progression rate r is equal to $-1/(1+Y)^n$. Therefore, the geometric progression can be rewritten in two ways. Assuming a decreasing geometric progression, the final equation is

$$
Sn = a \frac{1 - q^k}{1 - q}
\tag{4.17}
$$

where a is the first term, k the term number, and q the progression rate. The application of this equation to equation 4.18 allows us to define a different cyclical capitalization model:

$$
\begin{aligned}
V &= \frac{NOI}{Y + \Delta a_{RR}} \left[1 - \frac{1}{(1+Y)^n} + \frac{1}{(1+Y)^{2n}} - \frac{1}{(1+Y)^{3n}} \cdots \right] \\
&+ \frac{NOI}{Y - \Delta a_{RR}} \left[\frac{1}{(1+Y)^n} - \frac{1}{(1+Y)^{2n}} + \frac{1}{(1+Y)^{3n}} - \frac{1}{(1+Y)^{4n}} \cdots \right]
\end{aligned}
\tag{4.18}
$$

Then,

$$V = \left[\frac{\text{NOI}}{Y + g_{\text{RR}}} + \frac{\text{NOI}}{Y - g_{\text{EC}}} \frac{1}{(1+Y)^n} \right] \left(1 - \frac{1}{(1+Y)^n} + \frac{1}{(1+Y)^{2n}} - \frac{1}{(1+Y)^{3n}} \right)$$

(4.19)

Finally,

$$V = \left[\frac{\text{NOI}}{Y + \Delta a_{\text{RR}}} + \frac{\text{NOI}}{Y - \Delta a_{\text{EC}}} \frac{1}{(1+Y)^n} \right] \left\{ \frac{(1+Y)^{kn} + 1}{(1+Y)^k [(1+Y)^n + 1]} \right\}$$

(4.20)

where k is the progression term number, and n indicates the length of the phase of the cycle. Equation 4.16 indicates the first model of cyclical capitalization belonging to primum group. It can be used if there are only two phases of property market cycle, having a similar length. It may occur that the length of a property market phase is composed of more than two different phases. As a rule of thumb, four equal-length temporal intervals can be considered. In this case, we have

$$V = \frac{\text{NOI}}{Y - \Delta_{\text{RR1}} a_{\text{RR1}}} \left(1 - \frac{1}{(1+Y)^{4n}} + \frac{1}{(1+Y)^{8n}} + \cdots \right)$$

$$- \frac{\text{NOI}}{Y - \Delta_{\text{RR1}} a_{\text{RR1}}} \left(\frac{1}{(1+Y)^n} + \frac{1}{(1+Y)^{5n}} - \frac{1}{(1+Y)^{9n}} \cdots \right) +$$

$$+ \frac{\text{NOI}}{Y - \Delta_{\text{RR2}} a_{\text{RR2}}} \left(\frac{1}{(1+Y)^n} + \frac{1}{(1+Y)^{5n}} + \frac{1}{(1+Y)^{9n}} \cdots \right)$$

$$- \frac{\text{NOI}}{Y - \Delta_{\text{RR2}} a_{\text{RR2}}} \left(\frac{1}{(1+Y)^{2n}} + \frac{1}{(1+Y)^{6n}} - \frac{1}{(1+Y)^{10n}} \cdots \right)$$

$$+ \frac{\text{NOI}}{Y - \Delta_{\text{EC1}} a_{\text{EC1}}} \left(\frac{1}{(1+Y)^{2n}} + \frac{1}{(1+Y)^{6n}} - \frac{1}{(1+Y)^{10n}} \cdots \right)$$

$$- \frac{\text{NOI}}{Y - \Delta_{\text{EC1}} a_{\text{EC1}}} \left(\frac{1}{(1+Y)^{3n}} + \frac{1}{(1+Y)^{7n}} + \cdots \right)$$

$$+ \frac{\text{NOI}}{Y - \Delta_{\text{EC2}} a_{\text{EC2}}} \left(\frac{1}{(1+Y)^{3n}} + \frac{1}{(1+Y)^{7n}} + \cdots \right)$$

$$- \frac{\text{NOI}}{Y - \Delta_{\text{EC2}} a_{\text{EC2}}} \left(\frac{1}{(1+Y)^{4n}} + \frac{1}{(1+Y)^{8n}} + \cdots \right)$$

(4.21)

Here, there are eight geometric progressions whose rate of progression is always the same, and it is indicated in equation 4.22:

$$r = \frac{1}{(1+Y)^{4n}}$$

(4.22)

Clearly, the progression rate r is included in the interval $-1 < r < 1$, and assuming the cycle as always being constant along the life of the property, the third part of the equation can be expressed as a geometric progression of rate. Equation 4.23 can be considered the third model of primum group of cyclical capitalization (d'Amato, 2003).

$$V_{PG3} = \frac{NOI}{((1 + Y)^{2n} + 1)((1 + Y)^n + 1)}$$

$$\times \left(\frac{(1 + Y)^{3n}}{Y + \Delta_{RR_1} a_{RR_1}} + \frac{(1 + Y)^{2n}}{Y + \Delta_{RR_2} a_{RR_2}} + \frac{(1 + Y)^n}{Y - \Delta_{EC_1} a_{EC_1}} + \frac{1}{Y - \Delta_{EC_2} a_{EC_2}} \right)$$

(4.23)

It is possible to also consider an opinion of value for a fractional interest, assuming a property market cycle with more than one recession recovery phase having the same g_{RR} or Δa_{RR} and more than one expansion contraction phase with the same g_{EC} or Δa_{EC}. Therefore, the value of the property in the first complete cycle is

$$V = \frac{NOI}{Y - \Delta_{RR1} a_{RR1}} \left(1 - \frac{1}{(1 + Y)^{4n}} + \frac{1}{(1 + Y)^{8n}} + \cdots \right)$$

$$- \frac{NOI}{Y - \Delta_{RR1} a_{RR1}} \left(\frac{1}{(1 + Y)^n} + \frac{1}{(1 + Y)^{5n}} - \frac{1}{(1 + Y)^{9n}} \cdots \right) +$$

$$+ \frac{NOI}{Y - \Delta_{RR2} a_{RR2}} \left(\frac{1}{(1 + Y)^n} + \frac{1}{(1 + Y)^{5n}} + \frac{1}{(1 + Y)^{9n}} \cdots \right)$$

$$- \frac{NOI}{Y - \Delta_{RR2} a_{RR2}} \left(\frac{1}{(1 + Y)^{2n}} + \frac{1}{(1 + Y)^{6n}} - \frac{1}{(1 + Y)^{10n}} \cdots \right)$$

$$+ \frac{NOI}{Y - \Delta_{-EC} a_{EC1}} \left(\frac{1}{(1 + Y)^{2n}} + \frac{1}{(1 + Y)^{6n}} - \frac{1}{(1 + Y)^{10n}} \cdots \right)$$

$$- \frac{NOI}{Y - \Delta_{EC1} a_{EC1}} \left(\frac{1}{(1 + Y)^{3n}} + \frac{1}{(1 + Y)^{7n}} + \cdots \right)$$

$$+ \frac{NOI}{Y - \Delta_{EC2} a_{EC2}} \left(\frac{1}{(1 + Y)^{3n}} + \frac{1}{(1 + Y)^{7n}} + \cdots \right)$$

$$- \frac{NOI}{Y - \Delta_{EC2} a_{EC2}} \left(\frac{1}{(1 + Y)^{4n}} + \frac{1}{(1 + Y)^{8n}} + \cdots \right)$$

(4.24)

If the cycle is supposed to be always the same along the life of the property, then the value in the fourth version of the model belonging to the primum group can be expressed as

$$V_{PG4} = \frac{\left(1 - \frac{1}{(1 + Y)^{4n}} \right)^k}{1 - \frac{1}{(1 + Y)^{4n}}} \left[\begin{array}{l} \frac{NOI}{Y + \Delta a_{RR1}} 1 - \frac{NOI}{Y + \Delta a_{RR1}} \frac{1}{(1 + Y)^n} \\ + \frac{NOI}{Y + \Delta a_{RR2}} \frac{1}{(1 + Y)^n} - \frac{NOI}{Y + \Delta a_{RR2}} \frac{1}{(1 + Y)^{2n}} \\ + \frac{NOI}{Y - \Delta a_{EC1}} \frac{1}{(1 + Y)^{2n}} - \frac{NOI}{Y - \Delta a_{EC1}} \frac{1}{(1 + Y)^{3n}} \\ + \frac{NOI}{Y - \Delta a_{EC1}} \frac{1}{(1 + Y)^{3n}} - \frac{NOI}{Y - \Delta a_{EC1}} \frac{1}{(1 + Y)^{4n}} \end{array} \right]$$

(4.25)

The property market cycle is formed by four t equal-length temporal intervals. It is evident that the third part of the equation can be expressed as a geometric whose progression rate is equal to $1/(1+Y)^{4n}$. This geometric progression can be expressed by recalling equation 4.17 as follows:

$$V_{PG4} = \frac{(1+Y)^{4nk}-1}{(1+Y)^{n+k}[(1+Y)^n+1][(1+Y)^{2n}+1]}$$

$$\left[\begin{array}{c} \dfrac{NOI}{Y+\Delta a_{RR1}} + \dfrac{NOI}{Y+\Delta a_{RR2}}\dfrac{1}{(1+Y)^n} + \dfrac{NOI}{Y-\Delta a_{EC1}}\dfrac{1}{(1+Y)^{2n}} \\ + \dfrac{NOI}{Y-\Delta a_{EC2}}\dfrac{1}{(1+Y)^{3n}} \end{array}\right] \tag{4.26}$$

where a is the first term, k is the term number, and q the progression rate previously indicated. Equations 4.7 and 4.8 generate another group of cyclical capitalization methodologies. The general idea is always the same, adhering to an opinion of value based on an income approach whose rent varies cyclically. Beginning from equation 4.7

$$V = NOI\frac{1-\left(\dfrac{1+\Delta a}{1+i}\right)^n}{Y-\Delta a} \tag{4.27}$$

One can consider that the income is not limited, but the variation of the income can be described as the sum of different accumulations with more than one g factor or Δa as in equation 4.28:

$$V = NOI\frac{1-\left(\dfrac{1+\Delta a_{EC}}{1+i}\right)^n}{Y-\Delta a_{EC}} + \frac{1-\left(\dfrac{1+\Delta a_{RR}}{1+i}\right)^n}{Y-\Delta a_{RR}}\frac{1}{(1+Y)^t}$$

$$+ \frac{1-\left(\dfrac{1+\Delta a_{EC}}{1+i}\right)^n}{Y-\Delta a_{EC}}\frac{1}{(1+Y)^{2t}} + \frac{1-\left(\dfrac{1+\Delta a_{RR}}{1+i}\right)^n}{Y-\Delta a_{RR}}\frac{1}{(1+Y)^{3t}}$$

$$+ \frac{1-\left(\dfrac{1+\Delta a_{RR}}{1+i}\right)^n}{Y-\Delta a_{EC}}\frac{1}{(1+Y)^{4t}}\cdots \tag{4.28}$$

We can write

$$V = NOI\left[\begin{array}{c} \dfrac{1-\left(\dfrac{1+\Delta a_{EC}}{1+i}\right)^n}{Y-\Delta a_{EC}}\left(1+\dfrac{1}{(1+Y)^{2t}}+\dfrac{1}{(1+Y)^{4t}}\cdots\right) \\ + \dfrac{1-\left(\dfrac{1+\Delta a_{RR}}{1+i}\right)^n}{Y-\Delta a_{RR}}\left(\dfrac{1}{(1+Y)^t}+\dfrac{1}{(1+Y)^{3t}}\right) \end{array}\right] \tag{4.29}$$

Therefore

$$V = \text{NOI} \left[\frac{1 - \left(\frac{1 + \Delta a_{\text{EC}}}{1 + i} \right)^n}{Y - \Delta a_{\text{EC}}} \left(1 + \frac{1}{(1 + Y)^{2t}} + \frac{1}{(1 + Y)^{4t}} \cdots \right) + \frac{1 - \left(\frac{1 + \Delta a_{\text{RR}}}{1 + i} \right)^n}{Y - \Delta a_{\text{RR}}} \left(\frac{1}{(1 + Y)^t} + \frac{1}{(1 + Y)^{3t}} \right) \right] \quad (4.30)$$

We can see two different infinitive geometric progressions having the same rate $1/(1 + Y)^{2t}$. The final equation is

$$V_{\text{PG5}} = \text{NOI} \frac{(1 + Y)^{2t}}{(1 + Y)^{2t} - 1} \left[\frac{1 - \left(\frac{1 + \Delta a_{\text{EC}}}{1 + Y} \right)^n}{Y - \Delta a_{\text{EC}}} + \frac{1 - \left(\frac{1 + \Delta a_{\text{RR}}}{1 + Y} \right)^n}{Y - \Delta a_{\text{RR}}} \frac{1}{(1 + Y)^t} \right] \quad (4.31)$$

One can start from equation 4.8. In this case, the final result is

$$V_{\text{PG6}} = \text{NOI} \frac{(1 + Y)^{2t}}{(1 + Y)^{2t} - 1} \left[\frac{\left(\frac{1 + \Delta a_{\text{EC}}}{1 + Y} \right)^n - 1}{\Delta a_{\text{EC}} - Y} + \frac{\left(\frac{1 + \Delta a_{\text{RR}}}{1 + Y} \right)^n - 1}{\Delta a_{\text{RR}} - Y} \frac{1}{(1 + Y)^t} \right] \quad (4.32)$$

The six models presented, which can appraise income-producing properties with a variable rent, are summarized in Table 4.9.

The choice among different models of the primum group is conditioned by a regular cycle. In this case, the valuer may choose a specific model according to the length of the cycle and the relationship between the discount factor and the growth rate.

The Secundum Group of Cyclical Capitalization Methods

The models listed in Table 4.9, plot the cycle by applying the original Dividend Discount model (Gordon and Shapiro, 1956) with more than one g factor or Δa term. Cyclical capitalization can also be applied using the traditional direct capitalization. In this case, it is possible to calculate an overall capitalization rate that is not based on the dividend discount model but on the ratio between rent and price (gross or net) in each phase of the cycle. Therefore, replacing the $Y-g$ in different property market phases with the overall capitalization rate R represents a secundum group of models of cyclical capitalization based on the direct capitalization. Equation 4.16 would be modified as follows:

$$V_{\text{SG7}} = \frac{(1 + Y)^n}{(1 + Y)^n + 1} \left[\frac{\text{NOI}}{R_{\text{o RR}}} + \frac{\text{NOI}}{R_{\text{o EC}}} \frac{1}{(1 + Y)^n} \right] \quad (4.33)$$

This kind of replacement is considered in all six formulas listed in Table 4.9. Table 4.10 lists the equations representing the secundum group of the cyclical capitalization models.

Table 4.9 Premium group of cyclical capitalization models.

Cyclical capitalization, primum group, first model

$$V_{PG1} = \frac{(1+Y)^n}{(1+Y)^n + 1} \left[\frac{NOI}{Y + \Delta a_{RR}} + \frac{NOI}{Y - \Delta a_{EC}} \frac{1}{(1+Y)^n} \right]$$

Regular cycle and no more than two different g factors for the upturn and downturn phases. *Unlimited number of years*

Cyclical capitalization, primum group, second model

$$V_{PG2} = \frac{NOI}{(1+Y)^{3t} + (1+Y)^{2t} + (1+Y)^t + 1}$$
$$\times \left(\frac{(1+Y)^{3t}}{Y + \Delta a_{RR_1}} + \frac{(1+Y)^{2t}}{Y + \Delta a_{RR_2}} + \frac{(1+Y)^t}{Y - \Delta a_{EC_1}} + \frac{1}{Y - \Delta a_{EC_2}} \right)$$

More than one g factor in the cycle. *Unlimited number of years*

Cyclical capitalization, primum group, third model

$$V_{PG3} = \left[\frac{NOI}{Y + \Delta a_{RR}} + \frac{NOI}{Y - \Delta a_{EC}} \frac{1}{(1+Y)^n} \right]$$
$$\times \left\{ \frac{(1+Y)^{kn} + 1}{(1+Y)^k[(1+Y)^n + 1]} \right\}$$

Regular cycle and no more than two different g factors for the upturn and downturn phases. *Limited number of years*

Cyclical capitalization, primum group, fourth model

$$V_{PG4} = \frac{(1+Y)^{4nK} - 1}{(1+Y)^{n+k}[(1+Y)^n + 1][(1+Y)^{2n} + 1]}$$
$$\times \left[\frac{NOI}{Y + \Delta a_{RR1}} + \frac{NOI}{Y + \Delta a_{RR2}} \frac{1}{(1+Y)^n} \right.$$
$$\times \left. + \frac{NOI}{Y - \Delta a_{EC1}} \frac{1}{(1+Y)^{2n}} + \frac{NOI}{Y - \Delta a_{EC2}} \frac{1}{(1+Y)^{3n}} \right]$$

Regular cycle and no more than two different g factors for the upturn and downturn phases. *Limited number of years*

Cyclical capitalization, primum group, fifth model

$$V_{PG5} = NOI \frac{(1+Y)^{2t}}{(1+Y)^{2t} - 1}$$
$$\times \left[\frac{1 - \left(\frac{1 + \Delta a_{EC}}{1 + Y} \right)^n}{Y - \Delta a_{EC}} + \frac{1 - \left(\frac{1 + \Delta a_{RR}}{1 + Y} \right)^n}{Y - \Delta a_{RR}} \frac{1}{(1+Y)^t} \right]$$

Regular cycle and no more than two different overall cap rates for upturn and downturn phases. *Unlimited number of years. The rent grows (decreases at Δa ratio)*

Cyclical capitalization, primum group, sixth model

$$V_{PG6} = NOI \frac{(1+i)^{2t}}{(1+i)^{2t} - 1}$$
$$\times \left[\frac{\left(\frac{1 + \Delta a_{EC}}{1 + i} \right)^n - 1}{\Delta a_{EC} - Y} + \frac{\left(\frac{1 + \Delta a_{RR}}{1 + i} \right)^n - 1}{\Delta a_{RR} - Y} \frac{1}{(1+i)^t} \right]$$

Regular cycle and no more than two different overall cap rates for upturn and downturn phases. *Unlimited number of years. The rent grows (decrease at Δa ratio)*

Table 4.10 Secundum group of cyclical capitalization models.

Cyclical capitalization, secundum group, seventh model	
$$V_{SG7} = \frac{(1+Y)^n}{(1+Y)^n + 1} \left[\frac{NOI}{R_{o\,RR}} + \frac{NOI}{R_{o\,EC}} \frac{1}{(1+Y)^n} \right]$$	Regular cycle and no more than two different overall cap rates for the upturn and downturn phases. *Unlimited number of years*
Cyclical capitalization, secundum group, eighth model	
$$V_{SG8} = \frac{NOI}{(1+Y)^{3t} + (1+Y)^{2t} + (1+Y)^t + 1}$$ $$\times \left(\frac{(1+Y)^{3t}}{R_{o\,RR_1}} + \frac{(1+Y)^{2t}}{R_{o\,RR_2}} + \frac{(1+Y)^t}{R_{o\,EC_1}} + \frac{1}{R_{o\,EC_2}} \right)$$	More than one cap rate in the cycle. *Unlimited number of years*
Cyclical capitalization, secundum group, ninth model	
$$V_{SG9} = \left[\frac{NOI}{R_{o\,RR}} + \frac{NOI}{R_{o\,EC}} \frac{1}{(1+Y)^n} \right] \left\{ \frac{(1+Y)^{kn} + 1}{(1+Y)^k [(1+Y)^n + 1]} \right\}$$	Regular cycle and no more than two different overall cap rates for the upturn and downturn phases. *Limited number of years*
Cyclical capitalization, secundum group, tenth model	
$$V_{PG4} = \frac{(1+Y)^{4nK} - 1}{(1+Y)^{n+k} [(1+Y)^n + 1][(1+Y)^{2n} + 1]}$$ $$\times \left[\frac{NOI}{R_{RR1}} + \frac{NOI}{R_{RR2}} \frac{1}{(1+Y)^n} + \frac{NOI}{R_{EC1}} \frac{1}{(1+Y)^{2n}} + \frac{NOI}{R_{EC2}} \frac{1}{(1+Y)^{3n}} \right]$$	Regular cycle and no more than two different cap rates for upturn and downturn phases. *Limited number of years*
Cyclical capitalization, secundum group, eleventh model	
$$V_{SG11} = NOI \frac{(1+Y)^{2t}}{(1+Y)^{2t} - 1} \left[\frac{(1+Y)^n - 1}{R_{EC}(1+Y)^n} + \frac{(1+Y)^n - 1}{R_{RR}(1+Y)^n} \frac{1}{(1+Y)^t} \right]$$	Regular cycle and no more than two different overall cap rates for upturn and downturn phases. *Unlimited number of years.* The rents are constant.

This methodology may be applied in those contexts where there is information on the rent and price and the market growth of rent and price is meaningless.

The Tertium Group of Cyclical Capitalization Methods

This group is based on an integration between the DCF models and cyclical capitalization. In particular, cyclical capitalization may be a useful tool to deal with the terminal value determination. Starting from equation 4.9, it is possible to add a new model by replacing the second term of the equation with a terminal value calculated with an appropriate cyclical capitalization model as in the following equation:

$$V_{TG12} = \sum_{p=1}^{k} \frac{NOI_p}{(1+Y)^p} + \left\{ \begin{array}{l} NOI \frac{(1+Y)^{2t}}{(1+Y)^{2t} - 1} \left[\frac{(1+Y)^n - 1}{R_{EC}(1+Y)^n} \right. \\ \left. + \frac{(1+Y)^n - 1}{R_{EC}(1+Y)^n} \frac{1}{(1+Y)^t} \right] \end{array} \right\} \frac{1}{(1+Y)^{k+1}} \quad (4.34)$$

Table 4.11 The tertium group of cyclical capitalization models.

Cyclical capitalization, tertium group, twelfth model

$$V_{TG12} = \sum_{p=1}^{k} \frac{NOI_p}{(1+Y)^p}$$

$$+ \left\{ NOI \frac{(1+Y)^{2t}}{(1+Y)^{2t}-1} \left[\frac{\frac{(1+Y)^n-1}{R_{EC}(1+Y)^n}}{+\frac{(1+Y)^n-1}{R_{EC}(1+Y)^n}\frac{1}{(1+Y)^t}} \right] \right\} \frac{1}{(1+Y)^{k+1}}$$

DCF model whose terminal value is based on cyclical capitalization and constant rent

Cyclical capitalization, tertium group, thirteenth model

$$V_{TG13} = \sum_{p=1}^{k} \frac{NOI_p}{(1+Y)^p}$$

$$+ NOI \frac{(1+i)^{2t}}{(1+i)^{2t}-1} \left[\frac{1-\left(\frac{1+\Delta a_{EC}}{1+i}\right)^n}{Y-\Delta a_{EC}} + \frac{1-\left(\frac{1+\Delta a_{RR}}{1+i}\right)^n}{Y-\Delta a_{RR}}\frac{1}{(1+i)^t} \right] \frac{1}{(1+i)^{k+1}}$$

DCF model whose terminal value is based on cyclical capitalization and growing or decreasing rent

In this equation, NOI means the Net Operating Income, Y is the discount rate, k the holding period, and t the temporal length of the phase. The terminal value is not ever-growing or ever-decreasing. The terminal value will deal with the future in a cyclical way. In a similar way, equation 4.10 can be replaced by the following equation:

$$V_{TG13} = \sum_{p=1}^{k} \frac{NOI_p}{(1+Y)^p} + NOI \frac{(1+i)^{2t}}{(1+i)^{2t}-1}$$

$$\left[\frac{1-\left(\frac{1+\Delta a_{EC}}{1+i}\right)^n}{Y-\Delta a_{EC}} + \frac{1-\left(\frac{1+\Delta a_{RR}}{1+i}\right)^n}{Y-\Delta a_{RR}}\frac{1}{(1+i)^t} \right] \frac{1}{(1+i)^{k+1}} \qquad (4.35)$$

Table 4.11 summarizes the synthesis of different cyclical capitalization models (Fig. 4.13).

The choice among different models depends on several aspects: the specific market situation or real-estate price and rent time series, the characteristics of the property to be appraised, the nature of the data, the nature of contractual and market rent and the issue of the valuation. All these considerations must be analyzed by the appraiser before the application of a cyclical capitalization model. In Figure 4.13, it can be seen how the cyclical capitalization models deal with the future in terms of the relationship between NOI and time.

Comparing Figures 4.12 and 4.13, it is quite clear how different the approach to real-estate appraisal is in using cyclical capitalization.

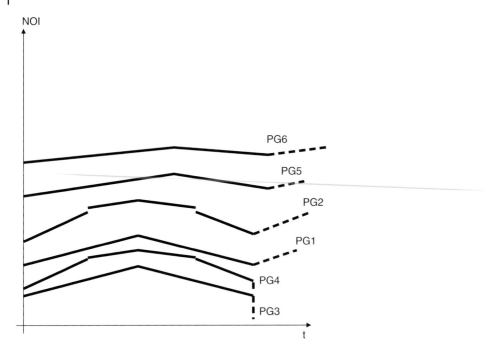

Figure 4.13 Relationship between NOI and time in the cyclical capitalization models belonging to the primum group.

The Quartum Group of Cyclical Capitalization Methods

The quartum group includes a period of vacancy in the calculation of the cycle, in the model. In this case, between two phases, there is a vacancy period; therefore, equation 4.14 becomes

$$V_{QG1} = \left(\frac{NOI}{Y + \Delta a_{RR}} - \frac{NOI}{Y + \Delta a_{RR}} \frac{1}{(1+Y)^n} \right)$$

$$+ \left(\frac{NOI}{Y - \Delta a_{EC}} \frac{1}{(1+Y)^n} - \frac{NOI}{Y - \Delta a_{EC}} \frac{1}{(1+Y)^{2n}} \right)$$

$$+ \left(\frac{NOI}{Y + \Delta a_{RR}} \frac{1}{(1+Y)^{3n}} - \frac{NOI}{Y + \Delta a_{RR}} \frac{1}{(1+Y)^{4n}} \right) + \dots \tag{4.36}$$

In the analysis, a recurring phase of vacancy equal to n is included in the calculations. The property market cycle is formed by four n equal-length temporal intervals. The second part of the equation can be expressed with two geometric progressions whose rate equals $1/(1+Y)^{3n}$. Considering an n number of phases and assuming trr = tec = n, then finally,

$$V_{QG1} = \frac{(1+Y)^n}{(1+Y)^{3n}+1} \left[\left(\frac{NOI}{Y + \Delta a_{RR}}(1+Y)^n - \frac{NOI}{Y + \Delta a_{RR}} \right)(1+Y)^n \\ + \left(\frac{NOI}{Y - \Delta a_{EC}}(1+Y)^n - \frac{NOI}{Y - \Delta a_{EC}} \right) \right] \tag{4.37}$$

Table 4.12 The quartum group of cyclical capitalization models.

Cyclical capitalization, quartum group, fourteenth model

$$V_{QG1} = \frac{(1+Y)^n}{(1+Y)^{3n}+1} \left[\left(\frac{NOI}{Y+\Delta a_{RR}}(1+Y)^n - \frac{NOI}{Y+\Delta a_{RR}} \right)(1+Y)^n + \left(\frac{NOI}{Y-\Delta a_{EC}}(1+Y)^n - \frac{NOI}{Y-\Delta a_{EC}} \right) \right]$$

Cyclical Capitalization Model based on unlimited number of years, a recurring interval of vacancy n equal to one phase of the cycle. In this case, we have unlimited number of years and the use of direct capitalization through dividend discount modeling.

Cyclical capitalization, quartum group, fifteenth model

$$V_{QG2} = \frac{(1+Y)^n}{(1+Y)^{3n}+1} \left[\left(\frac{NOI}{R_{RR}}(1+Y)^n - \frac{NOI}{R_{RR}} \right)(1+Y)^n + \left(\frac{NOI}{R_{EC}}(1+Y)^n - \frac{NOI}{R_{EC}} \right) \right]$$

Cyclical Capitalization Model based on unlimited number of years, a recurring interval of vacancy n equal to one phase of the cycle. In this case, we have unlimited number of years and the use of direct capitalization.

Using direct capitalization, the results are

$$V_{QG2} = \frac{(1+Y)^n}{(1+Y)^{3n}+1}$$
$$\times \left[\left(\frac{NOI}{R_{RR}}(1+Y)^n - \frac{NOI}{R_{RR}} \right)(1+Y)^n + \left(\frac{NOI}{R_{EC}}(1+Y)^n - \frac{NOI}{R_{EC}} \right) \right]$$

$$(4.38)$$

The use of the quartum group may be advisable in those contexts with vacancy lag in the property market cycle (Table 4.12).

Application of Cyclical Capitalization Models to London Office Market

Cyclical capitalization has been applied using a time series of prime rent in the office sector of London. The data regarding a time series from the third quarter of 1972 to the first quarter of 2008 are particularly important because they consider more than 20 years before the 2008 crisis. They have been provided by CB Richard Ellis London. The data referred to prime rent. Appendix to this chapter explains the meaning of prime rent.

Time-Series Analysis for Cyclical Capitalization Application

The time series is composed of several components. The components are Trends, Cyclical, Seasonal, and Erratic. In order to detect the product Δa in the single phases of the cycle, the attention was focused on the rate of change of prime rent in the time series taken into account, calculated as shown in equation 4.39:

$$d = \frac{R_{t+1} - R_t}{R_t} \tag{4.39}$$

The rate of change applied was calculated for each period of the time series of prime rent of the office market in the area city of London. The application of cyclical capitalization is based on the hypothesis that the rate of change of prime rent is coincident with the rate of change of the property asset in building value and income. Therefore, the cyclical component of the time series of rate of change was isolated using ARIMA models. ARIMA models are a time-series analysis technique based on the integration between autoregressive models and moving average models. Several contributions highlighted the robustness of these methods. ARIMA models have been used for real-estate market analysis in Hong Kong (Tse, 1997) These models have been used to examine the UK office market (McGough and Tsolacos, 1995). ARIMA models have been compared with OLS- and VAR-based models (Stevenson & McGrath, 2000). In Figure 4.14, the cyclical component isolated in the time series of rate of change can be seen.

The cyclical component of the time series provides important information but considers more than 20 years. For this reason, it was reduced to 10 years. This happens because in the application of these models, the appraisers refer to an interval previously defined as backward holding period in order to distinguish it from the well-known holding period used in the Discounted Cash-Flow Analysis. In this way, the time series of rate of change becomes the trend shown in Figure 4.15.

In this way, the appraiser considers only the part of the time series closer to the valuation moment (Table 4.13). As one can see, there is a comparable length of the two phases. In this case, the first one is an expansion–contraction phase. The second is a recession–recovery phase, and in the third case, it is possible to observe again an expansion–contraction phase, which ends after few months with the beginning of the

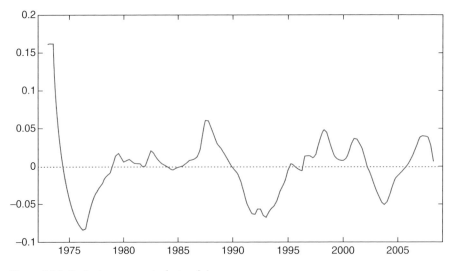

Figure 4.14 Cyclical component of rate of change.

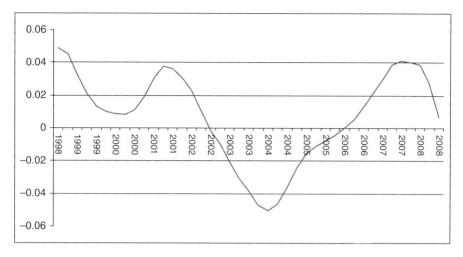

Figure 4.15 Cyclical component of rate of change in the backward holding period.

Table 4.13 Calculation of phase and Δ terms according to the backward holding period.

From	To	Trimestral rate of change	Annual rate of change	Quarter
1998, 1st sem	2001, 4th sem	0.024088438	0.099891513	16
2002, 1st sem	2005, 2nd sem	−0.024595286	−0.094810722	14
2005, 3rd sem	2008, 1st sem	0.023840882	0.09882838	11

crisis. In the backward holding period, it is possible to observe a medium phase of 15 quarter or 3.75 years.

We can approximate the medium length of the phase to four years. In Table 4.13, there is useful information to determine the Δa term indicated in equation 4.11. The Δ term is normally considered "… as the total real percentage loss in building value and income over its remaining economic life or the holding period …" (Smith *et al.*, 1998). In the application of cyclical capitalization, the holding period is represented by the temporal length of the single phase; the real percentage loss (or gain) can be considered as the rate of variation in building value and income. In this chapter, the rate of change is calculated as the mean of the rate of change of the market rent observed in each market phase. Δ is estimated as −0.094810722 in the recession–recovery phase and is equal to 0.099359946 in the expansion–contraction phase of the model (the mean between the two values observed in the first and the third phase). The a term is normally considered as the sinking fund factor for the building's remaining economic life or holding period at the discount rate selected. It must be stressed that while in the application of the traditional Dividend Discount Model, the percentage is normally considered as 100%, because it may be referred to the entire economic life of the property, in this case, the percentage is referred to a specific temporal length of a phase, which may vary according to the single phase of the cyclical component in the backward holding period. In this case, the temporal length of the phase is 4 years; therefore, Δa in the recession–recovery phase is calculated as follows:

$$\Delta a_{RR} = -0.094810722 \frac{Y}{(1+Y)^4 - 1} \tag{4.40}$$

While Δa in the expansion–contraction phase is

$$\Delta a_{EC} = -0.099359946 \frac{Y}{(1+Y)^4 - 1} \tag{4.41}$$

Table 4.14 shows the variation of the overall capitalization rate of the recovery–recession phase of the market assuming a discount rate that varies between 0.15 and 0.055. It also assumes that the temporal length of the recession–recovery phase is equal to 4 years.

In a similar way, Table 4.15 shows the variation of the overall capitalization rate of the expansion–contraction phase of the market assuming a discount rate that varies between 0.15 and 0.055. It also assumes that the temporal length of the expansion–contraction phase is equal to 4 years

Table 4.14 Calculation of overall capitalization rate assuming variable Y between 0.15 and 0.05 and the temporal length of the recovery recession phase equal to 4 years.

	Recession recovery phase					
	Y	Rate of change Δ	Sinking fund factor a	Δa	R_{rr}	t (years)
1	0.15	−0.094810722	0.200265352	−0.018987303	*0.168987303*	4
2	0.145		0.201728872	−0.01912606	*0.16412606*	
3	0.14		0.203204783	−0.019265992	*0.159265992*	
4	0.135		0.20469319	−0.019407109	*0.154407109*	
5	0.13		0.206194197	−0.019549421	*0.149549421*	
6	0.125		0.207707911	−0.019692937	*0.144692937*	
7	0.12		0.209234436	−0.019837668	*0.139837668*	
8	0.115		0.210773881	−0.019983624	*0.134983624*	
9	0.11		0.212326352	−0.020130815	*0.130130815*	
10	0.105		0.213891956	−0.020279251	*0.125279251*	
11	0.1		0.215470804	−0.020428942	*0.120428942*	
12	0.095		0.217063002	−0.0205799	*0.1155799*	
13	0.09		0.218668662	−0.020732134	*0.110732134*	
14	0.085		0.220287893	−0.020885654	*0.105885654*	
15	0.08		0.221920804	−0.021040472	*0.101040472*	
16	0.075		0.223567509	−0.021196597	*0.096196597*	
17	0.07		0.225228117	−0.02135404	*0.09135404*	
18	0.065		0.22690274	−0.021512813	*0.086512813*	
19	0.06		0.228591492	−0.021672924	*0.081672924*	
20	0.055		0.230294485	−0.021834386	*0.076834386*	

Table 4.15 Calculation of overall capitalization rate assuming variable Y between 0.15 and 0.05 and the temporal length of the expansion contraction phase equal to 4 years.

		Expansion contraction phase				
	Y	Rate of change Δ	Sinking fund factor a	Δa	R_{ec}	t (years)
1	0.15	0.099359946	0.200265352	0.019898355	*0.130101645*	4
2	0.145		0.201728872	0.02004377	*0.12495623*	
3	0.14		0.203204783	0.020190416	*0.119809584*	
4	0.135		0.20469319	0.020338304	*0.114661696*	
5	0.13		0.206194197	0.020487444	*0.109512556*	
6	0.125		0.207707911	0.020637847	*0.104362153*	
7	0.12		0.209234436	0.020789522	*0.099210478*	
8	0.115		0.210773881	0.020942482	*0.094057518*	
9	0.11		0.212326352	0.021096735	*0.088903265*	
10	0.105		0.213891956	0.021252293	*0.083747707*	
11	0.1		0.215470804	0.021409168	*0.078590832*	
12	0.095		0.217063002	0.021567368	*0.073432632*	
13	0.09		0.218668662	0.021726907	*0.068273093*	
14	0.085		0.220287893	0.021887793	*0.063112207*	
15	0.08		0.221920804	0.022050039	*0.057949961*	
16	0.075		0.223567509	0.022213656	*0.052786344*	
17	0.07		0.225228117	0.022378654	*0.047621346*	
18	0.065		0.22690274	0.022545044	*0.042454956*	
19	0.06		0.228591492	0.022712838	*0.037287162*	
20	0.055		0.230294485	0.022882048	*0.032117952*	

As the temporal lengths of the phases are quite similar and included in the backward period, the first model belonging to the premium group (equation 4.16) is applied to this case by assuming an NOI equal to 1. Table 4.16 shows the results of the valuation process.

Cyclical capitalization yields results using more than one Δa factor. In this way, the valuer does not interpolate the trend but follows the market phase.

Conclusions

The models proposed are a group of methods that can be helpful in the integration between property valuation activity and real-estate market cycle. These 15 models are a small and generic overview of a great family of income approach procedures considering the property market cycle. The difference between the opinion of value obtained using cyclical capitalization and the traditional dividend discount model increases with the length of the phase. The comparison between Figures 4.12 and 4.13 highlights the different ways of approaching the future in the two models. It may be argued that this kind of method relies on information that cannot be collected. The 2008

Table 4.16 Application of valuation model n.1 of the primum group of cyclical capitalization models, assuming NOI equal to 1 and discount rate variation between 0.15 and 0.055.

	Y	R_{rr}	R_{ec}	t	PG_1
1	0.15	0.168987303	0.130101645	4	6.560998141
2	0.145	0.16412606	0.12495623		6.795369199
3	0.14	0.159265992	0.119809584		7.04779057
4	0.135	0.154407109	0.114661696		7.32049276
5	0.13	0.149549421	0.109512556		7.616098818
6	0.125	0.144692937	0.104362153		7.937716521
7	0.12	0.139837668	0.099210478		8.289058275
8	0.115	0.134983624	0.094057518		8.674599119
9	0.11	0.130130815	0.088903265		9.099787907
10	0.105	0.125279251	0.083747707		9.571334124
11	0.1	0.120428942	0.078590832		10.09760437
12	0.095	0.1155799	0.073432632		10.68918145
13	0.09	0.110732134	0.068273093		11.35967069
14	0.085	0.105885654	0.063112207		12.12689283
15	0.08	0.101040472	0.057949961		13.01470155
16	0.075	0.096196597	0.052786344		14.05584841
17	0.07	0.09135404	0.047621346		15.29668313
18	0.065	0.086512813	0.042454956		16.80524049
19	0.06	0.081672924	0.037287162		18.6859801
20	0.055	0.076834386	0.032117952		21.10864086

subprime crisis probably taught us that this information must be collected. In general terms, transparency of a market has two dimensions. The former is the availability of data at a certain time, while the latter is the availability of time series of data especially for income-producing properties. The model presented relies on this second concept of transparency. Further directions of research may analyze the relationship among the opinion of value (market value estimate), the length of the phase, and the rate of variation. In this case, the rate of variation was coincident with the rate of variation of a prime rent in the local market segment. Here, the necessity to improve the local market analysis in order to link the appraisal process to local market cycle should be stressed. A comparison in terms of valuation variation between the cyclical capitalization and the most frequent capitalization method may help in understanding how cyclical capitalization works. Another important issue is the combination of contractual rent length, vacancy lag, and real-estate market cycle.

Part 5

Towards a More Sustainable Real-Estate Market

5.0

Introduction

Peter Dent

At the outset, this book has sought to address what is perceived as limited understanding of the concept of property value within the valuation profession in the context of a global financial market. The need for value and the determination of value exist under more complex and more demanding circumstances. Financial deregulation, cross-border trade and global environments have created circumstances where both equity and debt markets are significantly influenced by the value of real estate. It can be argued that if the property valuation profession does not interpret the intrinsic linkages between the economic, environmental, social and cultural measures and the components of property value, then there is a danger that either professionals will sell their individual clients (and society) short on the advice given or they will help to create a series of ever-greater crises in financial markets. In exploring the technology and sustainability in asset valuation, PwC may be understating the issue when they observe that 'if real estate players don't understand these new value drivers they'll be at a competitive disadvantage' (PwC, 2014, p. 25). In fact, they could become irrelevant, being replaced by those who not only have a transdisciplinary understanding of the complexity of calculation and interpretation but also can capitalise on the power of technology. It is clear that, in the recent past, whilst many of the micro-drivers have changed little over time (i.e. the physical nature of buildings and their use requirements), the macro-drivers have become more complex (i.e. financial systems/vehicles, technology, environmental requirements, global impacts).

This book has been concerned with trying to find a more sustainable approach to valuation in such an age of complexity. The financial crisis, the energy scarcity challenge and the changing climate all have nonlinear behaviours which lead to 'intractable uncertainty, intermittently long time lags between perturbation and response, and the

Value in a Changing Built Environment, First Edition.
Edited by David Lorenz, Peter Dent and Tom Kauko.
© 2018 John Wiley & Sons Ltd. Published 2018 by John Wiley & Sons Ltd.

potential to "flip" abruptly from one state to another' (Clapp *et al.*, 2009, pp. 31–32). These characteristics give scope for ignoring any advanced warnings of change. So, whilst not a 'real-estate' crisis *per se*, fundamental to the financial crisis was the manner in which the market chose to ignore the warning signs by, at the very least, tempering valuations with caution. The market acted as a reinforcing feedback loop which amplified inaccurate data. In other words, it generated value where there was none, and securitised stock was being bought and sold on the basis of limited substance in a very bullish market where caution was not commercially viable.

However, perhaps more seriously, whilst Commercial Mortgage-Backed Securities (CMBSs) and Collatoralised Mortgage Obligations (CMOs) were allowed to overheat in the few years leading up to the financial crisis, the other macro-driver of concern here (i.e. the climate) has been overheating now for a century, and messages to control it have only recently started to appear as value signals in the market place.

In this new environment, Deloitte (2014) has identified three game changers in this regard. These are (p. 9) as follows:

- *Embedding Environmental, Social, Governance (ESG) risk management into core investment processes to maintain stakeholder confidence.*

To embed means to fix something firmly and deeply in a surrounding mass not simply to attach (i.e. join or fasten). This book questions the long-term effectiveness of traditional methodologies to arrive at market value. Consequently, earlier chapters have considered the use of a risk premium map and regressed DCF methodology (Chapter 3.2) and a 'flexible' version of Rough Set Theory (Chapters 3.3 and 4.3) in an effort to embed financial and environmental risks within the process to advise on value.

- *Improve measurement and reporting to manage sustainability risk.*

AVM models based on self-organising maps (Chapter 4.2) and cyclical capitalisation approaches (Chapter 4.4) are examples where ESG risks can effectively be measured and managed beyond traditional comparative or income methodology. By these means, predictive analytics can be actively used to provide insights into potential future risks.

- *Plan resource efficiency to enhance occupant satisfaction and investment returns.*

Recognising that the professional's role is a commercial, an ethical and a fiduciary role places resource efficiency in its widest sense high on the agenda of advice to clients. Qualitative as well as quantitative judgements are an essential part of a holistic perspective which induces financial, environmental as well as social considerations.

Taking this further, UNEP FI: United Nations Environment Programme Finance Initiatives framework for action (2016) draws attention to the need for property owners and their advisers to develop and execute a material ESG and climate strategy following the Paris Climate Agreement. This includes ongoing assessment of the impact on long-term value.

To ensure, therefore, that the valuation profession does not fall behind, it has to find a way of breaking out of the old mould and address these new value drivers in an inclusive way. This, in itself, raises questions about a new professionalism, trust, risk and, ultimately, education.

5.1

Professional Responsibility

Stephen Hill, David Lorenz, Peter Dent and Thomas Lützkendorf

Introduction[1]

Many professional bodies claim that sustainability is at the core of their activities, yet many professionals remain unclear about how to respond to complex and interconnected environmental, social and economic challenges, in relation to their responsibilities to their clients and their own or clients' interests or 'shareholder value'. The objectives of selected built-environment professional bodies are examined in the following in order to understand their approaches to sustainability as a field of technical expertise and a public interest responsibility. Disabling factors that prevent a change of mindset being translated into new models of practice are identified, including the following:

- The absence of a coherent new paradigm and narrative for sustainability in which to acquire and apply new knowledge and redefine public interest values
- The absence of action-learning cultures in everyday practice
- The erosion of ethical values and social context, as the fundamental guiding principles for interrelated personal and professional behaviours

Analysis of the relationship between knowledge, skills and ethics to models of professional practice suggests a range of propositions for actions by professional bodies and individuals, including the idea of personal responsibility for 'the Other' as the core principle for ethical professional behaviour. This notion of 'the other' beyond ourselves or our clients is considered in more detail later in this section. However, for now, it is pertinent to consider our own responsibilities.

Speaking at a public meeting in London, in January 2012, Professor Richard Sennett urged the audience 'to stop thinking about the political parties as the necessary destination for political action. Think and then just do it yourself' (Sennett, 2012). There is a

---

1 This chapter is derived in part from 'Professionalism and Ethics in a Changing Economy' by the authors, published in *Building Research & Information* in 2013, available online: http://www.tandfonline.com/https://dx.doi.org/10.1080/09613218.2013.736201. It explores the tensions between an emerging change of mindset in favour of more ethical behaviour among built-environment professionals and their attempts to understand what they should be doing to help create a more sustainable world.

sense, therefore, that the burden for action now falls to self-directed individuals and to public interest organisations that have the capacity to provide both disinterested advice and leadership, if societal values, and the markets that can only be derived from stable societies, are to be sustained. Responsibility and accountability can be seen as more diffuse in a global market and now lie with a wider group including professionals and, in particular, professional bodies and organisations, rather than just governments. It should be the overall institutional framework of civil society, of which professional bodies are an integral part, which now needs to lead on realigning market forces with the wider public interest.

However, the prospect for professional leadership does not look promising. For example, in a survey of people employed in international real-estate consultancies, less than 5% of respondents felt that professional bodies had any responsibility for mitigating the impacts of climate change (Dent and Dalton, 2010). This suggests that, despite the efforts to push a sustainability agenda, there are barriers to its implementation. Universities must be the most practical and effective places in which to effect lasting changes in professional behaviour and skill levels, but, whilst some universities have taken a bold lead, efforts are fragmented as the professions 'at work' are not giving a consistent lead about what is needed and expected. Consequently, the feedback loops between universities and the workplace are often not working as effectively as they should (Hartenberger *et al.*, 2013).

These barriers, the ethical and moral bases for responsibility and accountability of professional bodies, and thus, the consequences for individual professionals, are discussed in the following sections, with a focus on the wider built-environment professions.

Built-Environment Professionalism and Professional Bodies

General Guiding Principles and Role within the Institutional Framework

Built-environment professional bodies, being both part of and apart from the market process, are an important element of the overall institutional framework. On the one hand, they 'circumscribe and reinforce workplace skills and practices, develop and control a knowledge base, control entry into the occupation, demand public recognition of professional status and fix the market for professional services. On the other hand, they also offer the promise of a covenant with society to protect it from unscrupulous, unfair or short-term practices through the provision of impartial advice and services', informed by public interest values (Hill and Lorenz, 2011, p. 314).

Davies and Knell (2003) identify four guiding principles for the built-environment professions:

The development of a body of knowledge – This is not only 'codified knowledge', which is increasingly available to all via electronic access but, more particularly, 'tacit knowledge', 'the knowledge that is not consciously on our minds, but acts as an indispensable resource for getting things done'. This is the enabling knowledge built into a professional framework to meet moral and ethic conduct within social boundaries.

Trustworthiness – The role that the professions play is as an intermediary, establishing levels of behaviour in the markets 'with extreme informational asymmetries'. They provide another layer to the market mechanism offering integrity and independence.

Formal association – It is only through formally constituted organisational structures that professional bodies can wield any power or influence. In order to be authentic in their role over and above the market and immediate financial reward, they have to be perceived as 'maintaining high barriers to entry […] [to] ensure that both their body of knowledge and their reputation are secure' (Davis and Knell, 2003, p. 24).

The protection of the public interest – There is a tension here between 'the public-oriented ethos' of a profession and the market mechanism within which its members, as employees of third-party organizations, work. To overcome this, most professional bodies have a code of conduct and a regulatory framework within which their members are expected to work in order to avoid conflicts of interest.

Professional Bodies at Risk

Despite the important role that built-environment professional bodies hold, both within the overall institutional framework and as guardians of their respectable general guiding principles, there is a very real danger that they could lose both their authority and reputation because of the weight of market influences – markets which are more and more focused on the pursuit of short-term financial advantage above all else. In some way, professional bodies need to encourage a shift in market analysis 'from a deterministic, linear, internally defined and therefore supply-led framework, to one which allows for the full breadth of exogenous influences (social, economic, technical and organisational) to be examined' (Guy *et al.*, 1997, p. 134). Equally, the mindset needs to move from a 'retrospective' to an 'anticipatory framework'. This suggests moving from simply discerning trends based on linear progression to acknowledging the discontinuities and complex twists and turns of a non-linear system.

This can be illustrated in the context of sustainable development: a complex concept which is of significant concern to all the built-environment professions. The professions could, and probably should, take a lead in addressing both the technical fix and the behavioural shift needed to mitigate both the impacts of climate change and the loss of important and valued public goods. These threats include privatised and hostile public spaces, occupational diseases, contaminated land, resource exploitation, energy and water insecurity, wastelands within cities and destruction of the countryside (see, e.g. Minton, 2006). So far, among professional bodies and their members, there has been some movement on the first, the technical fix, but very limited activity on the second, the behavioural change. The reasons for this are threefold:

Firstly, technical solutions are based on science. Generally, practitioners are presented with a potentially long-term problem, but they are often only able to produce a short-term solution that does not tackle the underlying causes of the problem. This raises the following question: 'under what conditions do certain sections of human populations develop new fundamental behaviour patterns, rather than merely move between the already constituted patterns they predictably adopt due to their social position?' (Bonta and Protevi, 2004, p. 34). In this case, social position relates to patterns learnt and applied as professional surveyors, planners, architects or engineers.

Secondly, most professions in the built environment have their roots in technical knowledge and the physical sciences. In itself, this is not a problem, but it does encourage attitudes and work practices that concentrate on the concrete rather than the value-laden aspects of the skill set needed to perform the work: 'If one imagines that education, if it is to be of any value at all, is concerned mainly with "things", whether in scarcity or abundance, the whole point is missed [...] both make the mistake of trying to produce wisdom by circumstances instead of circumstances by wisdom' (Snelling *et al.*, 1987). Behavioural change and reaction to natural or man-made factors tend to be a more difficult area to teach and pursue in professional practice, falling outside many professionals' expertise or interests.

Thirdly, sustainability does not lend itself to reductionist approach, in the way that it is possible to assess stress on building materials or cost per square metre of usage. Nor can it be seen in terms of present or, indeed, short-term future usage. Sustainability as a concept has to be seen holistically over space and time. It is essentially an attempt to plan for adaptation for the long run and continuous change. In addition, most people still think of 'sustainability' as meaning only environmental concerns and experience sustainability as a phenomenon that is largely unseen ('day to day the weather stays the same!'), distant ('why should I be concerned about world poverty?') and something to worry about in the long term ('it can be discounted away to virtually no problem at all!').

If sustainability is to have a greater sense of immediacy and meaning, then its broader social and financial consequences, such as social costs, for example, transport, health, security, general well-being, as opposed to value-added marketing, would have to be exposed to more rigorous examination by the professional bodies. But professional bodies have not, at least for the past generation, been too directly involved in these issues. Social justice and equity are rarely taught, examined or debated as part of everyday practice, let alone inform the key strategic concerns of the professional institutions.

Despite professionals' greater proficiency and interest in the scientific and technical aspects of sustainability, the technical fix is, in fact, relatively unimportant if it is not accompanied by accompanying shifts in behaviour. Wasteful resource usage and disposal activities remain the same, or consumption habits and practices continue to accelerate. What is needed is a level of sustainability literacy which enables both the technical and the behavioural aspects of professional advice to be taught, designed and implemented side by side.

Sustainability Literacy in Built-Environment Professionalism

The report *Sustainable Development in Higher Education – Current practice and future development* (HEA, 2006, p. 6) identifies the following skills and knowledge as representing sustainability literacy:

- An appreciation of the importance of environmental, social, political and economic contexts for each discipline
- A broad and balanced foundation knowledge of sustainable development, its key principles and the main debate within them, including its contested and expanding boundaries
- Problem-solving skills in a non-reductionist manner for highly complex real-life problems
- Ability to think creatively and holistically and to make critical judgements
- Ability to develop a high level of self-reflection (both personal and professional)
- Ability to identify, understand, evaluate and adopt values conducive to sustainability
- Ability to bridge the gap between theory and practice; in sustainable development, only transformational action counts

- Ability to participate creatively in interdisciplinary teams
- Ability to initiate and manage change

This list represents a skill set that requires a high level of ability to integrate knowledge of technical, behavioural and ethical issues. These are very different skills from those of the more traditional and technically minded professional. The need for them may appear counter-intuitive to the pragmatic professional who is regularly sought out by clients seeking a finite short-term solution and downplaying the 'non-linearities' and 'surprises'. However, these solutions are often responses based on the partial knowledge about the situation, and its context, and the behaviour of future users of the buildings, on the part of the client or the professional. There is also a world of difference between a building as designed and its performance as built and in use (see Leaman *et al.*, 2010; Bordass, 2011). Such clients and professionals are unlikely to be able to take account of wider issues, whether deliberately or unknowingly. Thus, in the terms of this suggested skill set, they do not respond 'adequately', nor is the response necessarily effective or at its 'highest capacity' (see also Krishnamurti, 1983).

In short, built-environment professionals, as any other professional and citizen, cannot continue to evaluate the world and the choices they make in a 'moral vacuum' (see Judt, 2010, p. 37). However, according to Blake (1999), three key barriers hinder a shift in behaviour from taking place: individuality, responsibility and practicality.

- *Individual barriers* – barriers lying within the person, having to do with attitude and temperament
- *Responsibility barriers* – people who do not act sustainably feel that they cannot influence the situation or should not have to take the responsibility for it
- *Practicality barriers* – the social and institutional constraints that prevent people from acting sustainably regardless of their attitudes or intentions, for example, lack of time, lack of money, lack of information

If the professional bodies can start to address the issue at this level, it may be possible to develop the buildings and places that align with the sustainability agenda, created with sustainable finance and used in a way that helps to realise a sustainable future. But why, how and to what extent should built-environment professional bodies engage in changing behaviour and, thus, in shaping the forces of the market and the free play of private interests?

The Ethics of Built-Environment Professionalism

Professional Disciplines in a Social, Environmental and Economic Context

'It is no longer possible for us to masquerade as disinterested, or objective professionals, applying our techniques with equal ease to those clients we agree with, as well as to those we disagree with. We are, in effect, the client for all our projects, for it is our own society we are affecting through our actions.'

This sounds as a very contemporary assessment of the challenges facing built-environment professionals engaged in championing the principles and promises of sustainability. In fact, it comes from an account of urban renewal in the cities in the United States in the 1960s and 1970s. Robert Goodman's 'After the Planners'

(Goodman, 1972, pp. 249–250) is an exhausting but exhilarating 300-page polemic of sustained anger at the architects, planners and property professionals who had been lured into the urban renewal process and how their values, skills and knowledge were then debased by corporate political and commercial interests. Goodman accused them of abandoning their public interest obligations: in this case, towards the mostly poor urban populations that were displaced by these projects and programmes. Goodman's unforgiving ethical challenge to all built-environment professionals resonates today, both in the context of sustainability and in the light of the 'morning after the night before' feeling of life after the global financial crisis. Did we really let that happen? How?

Professor Michael Sandel from Harvard University echoed this feeling of malaise, a generation later, in his 2009 Reith Lectures on 'The New Citizenship': 'It's [...] a time to rethink the role of markets in achieving the public good. There's now a widespread sense that markets have become detached from fundamental values, that we need to reconnect markets and values' (Sandel, 2009, p. 4). In 2009, his views were not widely held. Now, in the United Kingdom at least, few politicians would dare to deny that 'something needs to be done' about 'the markets', though whether they can or will actually do anything is another matter.

According to Haldane, in 2016, when talking about financial services generally, 'evidence has emerged, both micro and macro, to suggest trust may play a crucial role in value creation' (p. 6). He later qualifies this by suggesting that it is not so much the maximisation of trust amongst consumers but, more significantly, the maximisation of trustworthiness amongst producers that is crucial to value creation. One of his conclusions is that 'culture cannot be regulated or educated; it has to be inculcated among financial firms themselves'. (p. 13). The real-estate industry, as part of financial services, perhaps needs to reflect on this through its professional bodies.

As suggested in Part 3, a higher level of analysis is needed where market signals and structures are the main target of the analysis rather than technical issues in relation to estimation. It is not simply a financial exercise (based on market rent, market yield and/or required rate of return). Nor is it a computational exercise (based on yields, returns, growth expectations). These are relevant, but too often, in the first case, market data is accepted unquestioningly, and in the second case, often too much confidence is placed in the software and not enough in interpretative reasoning. Integrated into this process somewhere there needs to be some reflection of inherent values (both client and agent). Without these, the calculations provide a spot price supported by a cash flow or a cash flow adapted to validate a spot price. Often, financial modelling is used to arrive at real-estate values. Usually, as explained in Part 3, these rely on unrealistic assumptions completely distant from real-estate markets' reality.

Running alongside the financial dimension to evaluation and decision-making, therefore, there needs to be a 'values' dimension. Whilst professional bodies have codes of ethics for their members in the performance of their advice work, there is still a gap between the commercial (financial) and the professional (values/ethics). In the general context of ESG investment, 'the ability to recognize and distinguish between the two motivations is crucial because designing an ESG investment framework entails different investment approaches and implementation considerations.' (Briand *et al.*, 2011, p. 5).

'Ecological Urbanism', published by Harvard University Graduate School of Design (Mostafavi and Doherty, 2010), may sound rather detached from ethics, values and markets, but it goes to the heart of the skills that may be required of an ethical professional with values about what to be and how to act:

'The prevailing conventions of design practice have demonstrated a limited capacity both to respond to the scale of the ecological crisis, and to adapt their established ways of thinking. Ecological urbanism utilises a multiplicity of old and new methods, tool and techniques, in a cross-disciplinary and collaborative approach' (Mostafavi and Doherty, 2010, p. 26).

'Ecological Urbanism' recognises the tensions between disciplinary knowledge and the moral imperative of sustainability; an imperative that can override and undermine the value of professional rigour, by treating sustainability as an unquestionable and static absolute good or as a question to which there is a 'right' answer. Mostafavi and Doherty (2010), and the other 150 contributors, argue that the traditional distinctions between the design professions are breaking down and that generalism is also important and necessary as a productive disciplinary strength. 'Ecological Urbanism' will emerge into a way of professional working that is based on the complexity of human experience and behaviour, both observed and personal, and informed by social justice and ethics, as well as technology and design competence.

Such a vision also implies that clients are bound into that web of complexity and human experience, from which the professional is expected to make some sense of the challenges of climate change, resource depletion, population growth and urbanisation. In this regard, professionals need to understand the difference between truth and reality. The truth is verified through a particular frame of mind which, in its widest sense, is created through the values held by a particular culture. On the other hand, reality is the stuff that exists outside of such cultural definition. Cultures create myths and, as such, give value to reality.

In the context of real-estate pricing, the 'truth' (i.e. the market value) is generally derived through a mechanistic and deterministic interpretation of the world. If we are to acknowledge the reality of existential risks which are non-linear, 'fuzzy' and probabilistic, then hard science and rigid methodologies may undermine rather than determine that truth (i.e. value). Climate change, global trade, footloose financial capital, cross-border terrorism, wealth differentials, resource depletion along with population growth all mitigate against an internally defined, causal deterministic framework. So, what role can individual professionals and their professional bodies play in this regard?

How Ethical Are Professional Codes of Conduct?

In the United Kingdom, the professional bodies are founded with charters, stating their purpose, backed up by Codes of Conduct, regulations and by-laws, which widely regulate the business of the institution, the education, accreditation and the practices of its members, as well as the promotion of the institution's purposes to the world at large. In Germany, similar regulations apply which are contained within the articles, statutes or laws of the respective professional organisations. This is examined briefly in the following, but the main focus lies on some UK professional bodies. In this chapter, the authors have focussed on UK-based institutions, as particularly the Institution of Civil Engineers (ICE) and the Royal Institution of Chartered Surveyors (RICS) have a global reach, with the RICS being the largest organisation for property professionals worldwide. In addition, it seems possible that the UK model of professional institutions could serve as a template for international application:

'It has become almost commonplace to suggest that the professions are at a watershed – or even under siege. That, with the new culture of accountability in society, there is a "crisis of trust", in their conduct and a serious questioning of their continued relevance. Seen as self-serving and insufficiently accountable by a more transparent and less deferential public, they struggle to position themselves and retain peoples esteem. Contrariwise, with a clear set of values, an insightful vision for the future, a strong sense of social responsibility, enlightened leadership, high standards of professionalism and proven performance, and a good dose of common sense and self-confidence, there is every reason to suppose that the British model of professional institutions could, suitably adapted, serve as an exemplar for international application. Arguably, no institution is better placed for this global role than the Royal Institution of Chartered Surveyors.' (Ratcliffe, 2011, p. 6)

UK professional bodies – such as the Royal Institute of British Architects (RIBA), Royal Town Planning Institute (RTPI), ICE and the RICS – are not membership organisations designed to promote the interests of individual members, beyond the overarching purpose of promoting the profession as a whole. Many members do not fully understand the distinction, and the business of the institutions can be compromised by the occasional discontent of members who feel their self-interests are not being served. There are strong similarities between the governance arrangements and their scope across the main professional institutions.

In 'Architecture Depends', Professor Jeremy Till (2009) deconstructs the various elements of being an architect, and in the workings of the Architects Registration Board (ARB) and the RIBA, Till's analysis (2009, pp. 171–188) also serves for examining the characteristics of other built-environment professions:

> One of the most commonly made mistakes is to confuse professional propriety with an ethical position, as if acting in accordance with the codes of professional conduct will ensure ethical behaviour.

Till (2009) illustrates how the requirements of the ARB's and RIBA's codes of conduct, and similar professional bodies in North America, are about reasonable standards of competence and diligence, of keeping knowledge up to date and of prudent and honest business administration mainly in relation to the client's interests or those of other professionals; standards that 'even my hairdresser could meet', and so not intrinsically ethical or even professional. He argues that ARB's powers 'to protect the consumer' are for the benefit of the client and not the user of the building or others who may be affected by it.

Till (2009, Chapter 10, pp. 171–188) also asserts that simply meeting the requirements of a code or rules of conduct that serve only the client's interest 'may be unethical in my terms', as it may ignore the long term, the interests of the user or environmental responsibility; responsibilities which may be fulfilled by an enlightened client, but which may equally be subject to pressures from the 'short term, opportunist, and potentially exploitative' demands of the market.

He has an answer to the two obvious criticisms that the client pays, so is entitled to get what he or she wants, and that 'the whole idea of wider responsibilities smacks of idealism'. Till (2009, Chapter 10) maintains that social ethics are inherent in the design of any building or place: 'just to ignore them does not mean that they will go away. Better to face up to them, and in this deal with the tension between the values and priorities attached to the professional codes and implicit in social ethics […] not to engage with the dirty reality of short term demands is as much a form of escape as the positing of utopian proposals of a harmonious ethic.'

Research suggests that many valuers are influenced by clients and are willing to 'rationalise their position by claiming estimation error due to lack of market data, the notion of a range of defensible values, and issues of client satisfaction'. (Levy *et al.*, 2005, p. 188). Amidu and Aluko (2007) cite a range of research sources and set out further evidence to substantiate the view that clients influence valuers' opinions which suggests, inter alia, 'a reflection of the problem of non-compliance…with the professional code of conduct' (p. 85). This issue, despite a clear code of conduct, has not been effectively addressed, and there is a danger that value, to a greater or lesser extent, becomes a matter of the client's values as opposed to the real estate's value.

European Institutions

The apparent lack of teeth to ensure ethical behaviour is also seen in some German and European institutions. In Germany, architects are subject to architect laws and professional regulations, overseen by the 16 state architects' chambers (professional institutions). The laws regulate the business of the architects' chambers and the accreditation of its members, while regulations contain general principles regarding competency, the reputation of the profession, lifelong learning, cooperating with other architects and respecting intellectual property.

Although there is cooperation and coordination of laws and regulations between federal states, 16 different sets of architect laws and regulations exist in Germany. Therefore, the authors of this section have chosen to examine just the state of Baden-Württemberg in more detail. Here, the architect's primary duty is defined as the 'artistic, technical and economic planning of buildings' (AKBW, 2011, §1 (1)). Neither the architect law nor the regulations contain any professional duties in relation to (or, indeed, any mention of) the public interest or environmental concerns. By contrast, the main duty of the town planner is defined as 'the artistic, technical, economic, environmental and social planning of communities and cities' (AKBW, 2011, §1 (4)).

The authors' inquiry at the Baden-Württemberg architects' chamber confirmed that there is no explicit recognition of the public interest or environmental concerns and that any assumption of professional responsibility for them would require a very wide interpretation of the current laws and regulations. It would be difficult for an architect to rely on these in case of any conflict between the maximisation of the client's financial interests and acting responsibly in the public interest. In the authors' experience, however, fellow professionals in Baden-Württemberg usually take their public interest and environmental professional responsibilities seriously, despite there being little explicit encouragement or enforcement through their laws and professional regulations.

At supranational level, however, the Architects' Council of Europe's ethical code quite explicitly and comprehensively states that

> All providers of architectural services must respect and help to conserve and develop the system of values and the natural and cultural heritage of the community in which they are creating architecture. They shall strive not only to improve

the environment through the highest quality of design but also to improve the quality of the life and the habitat within such a community in a sustainable manner, particularly considering energy and water conservation and reducing carbon emissions in the context of world climate change, being fully mindful of the effect of their work on the widest interests of all those who may reasonably be expected to use or enjoy the product of their work.

(ACE, 2009, Principle 2.1)

Nevertheless, this code is only advisory and not binding on member institutions or individual professionals. On the authors' inquiry, staff at the ACE confirmed they had no information as to how it is used and whether it has been implemented at national level.

Architects, planners and surveyors may therefore often be left rather exposed in an ethical void in which the terms of their charters, whilst appearing to promise actions in the public interest, and codes which regulate professional behaviour cannot provide any moral guidance or framing for debate about the ethics of the project/assignment or the application of their knowledge and skill to it or to a wider societal understanding of what they should do.

Returning to the United Kingdom, engineers at the ICE are perhaps more fortunate, as their code of professional conduct is unequivocal: 'The duty upon members of the ICE to behave ethically is, in effect, the duty to behave honourably; in modern words, 'to do the right thing…Members of the ICE should always be aware of their overriding responsibility to the public good. A member's obligations to the client can never override this, and members of the ICE should not enter undertakings which compromise this responsibility…The "public good" includes care and respect for humanity's cultural, historical and archaeological heritage, (and) to protect the health and well being of present and future generations and to show due regard for the environment and for the sustainable management of natural resources'. (ICE, 2003, Introduction)

All this is in addition to the basic requirements of competency observed by Till (2009, Chapter 10) and a separate Charter for Sustainable Development based on the following principle: 'Sustainable Development is central to civil engineering and that ICE and the profession it serves must organise themselves accordingly. […] In fulfilling this role, civil engineers contribute to economic growth, to environmental protection and to improved quality of life […] equally recognising the need to protect and enhance the environment and to use resources in a way that does not disadvantage future generations' (ICE, 2008).

Other built-environment professionals, less constrained than civil engineers, may continue to maintain that their first responsibility is to their client's shareholder value, and indeed their own, as overriding fiduciary obligations: a view frequently heard by the authors, especially from surveyors. The charters or codes of conduct do not explicitly go as far as that and may, on the contrary, as in the 1881 Royal Charter of the RICS, describe one of the principal tasks of the surveyor as 'securing the optimal use of land and its associated resources to meet social and economic needs' (RICS, 2008, Clause 3). Note the inclusive and mandatory 'and'.

However, despite the moral ambivalence identified by Till (2009), taking refuge in the exigencies of company law to privilege shareholder value is no more of an escape from his 'dirty reality' than idealism. The UK Companies Act 2006 expanded the duties of directors to mirror objectives not unlike the ICE's. Section 172 of the Act (HMSO, 2006, Chapter 2) describes the duty to promote the success of the company, thus:

(1) A director of a company must act in the way he considers, in good faith, would be most likely to promote the success of the company for the benefit of its members as a whole and, in doing so, have regard (amongst other matters) to the following:

- The likely consequences of any decision in the long term
- The interests of the company's employees
- The need to foster the company's business relationships with suppliers, customers and others
- The impact of the company's operations on the community and the environment, […].

Historically, fiduciary obligation appears to have been interpreted by many investors as forcing them to disregard such matters in fulfilling their beneficiaries' interests. The 'long term' and 'community and environmental impact' were therefore new and intended to be 'defensive' and protective to ensure that directors were not regarded as being in breach of their fiduciary duty because they had had regard to those things. However, good parliamentary drafting enables many interpretations to be made of the same words, so it is clear that Section 172 of the Companies Act is also permissive and so 'provides a model for fiduciary investors to have the freedom to take a more enlightened approach to their responsibilities. The fact that fiduciary investors are themselves shareholders makes this case all the more compelling. At present, the Companies Act ethos of enlightened shareholder value is in direct conflict with the perception of these shareholders that their legal obligations actively prevent them from taking an enlightened approach' (Berry, 2011, p. 115). [Authors' emphasis]

The Deepwater Horizon oil rig disaster in the Gulf of Mexico is, perhaps, an extreme example of what happens when a perception of the pre-eminence of shareholder value overrides professional integrity and good practice. As Tim Bergin, former oil broker and usually a cheerleader for the oil industry, observed, 'Companies might have responsibilities to their employees, customers and the communities in which they operate, but these should only be met insofar as doing so facilitated the operation's primary role, which was maximising shareholders' returns' (Bergin, 2011, p. 28). One is left wondering what the directors of BP actually considered in relation to each of the four criteria in Section 172, if they did. The failures of governance within BP, in which managers came to institute negligence as corporate policy in the belief that they were serving the interests of shareholders, are still unexplained.

In France and Germany, mutual funds owe a statutory duty to act 'in the sole interest of investors and of the integrity of the market' (UNEP FI, 2005, p. 58). Similar regard could and should have been required, perhaps, under recent market conditions, to prevent some UK and other long-term fiduciary investors partaking in risky or short-term strategies which undoubtedly have compromised national and international financial stability, without serving the beneficiaries' long-term interests.

So, custodians and champions of shareholder value and fiduciary obligations are no more exempt from considering the tensions between the markets and moral and ethical issues, or taking responsibility for their choices and decisions, than professionals or, indeed, any other citizen. Indeed, the industry experts and engineers at Deepwater Horizon arguably had, by virtue of their special and unique knowledge and experience, especially onerous obligations to speak out and act in the public interest.

Whilst a company such as BP might commonly expect to be sued in the courts for damages resulting from its actions, a more interesting question is whether built-environment professionals could be sued for breach of their public interest obligations by citizens or an environmental NGO and whether that action might also join in the appropriate professional body 'responsible' for setting and safeguarding standards of professional behaviour and skill.

In the next section, we explore how societal obligations might apply more widely to professionals in relation to sustainable development.

Responsibility and Accountability for Outcomes: Future Professionals

The preceding discussion, particularly the example of the ICE, shows that the allocation of responsibility for acting in the public interest rests with both the individual professional and the institution and, in some cases, in supporting collaborative behaviour across the built-environment institutions. What is less clear is how changes occur where the public interest imperative needs to be strengthened. Are the institutions or individual professionals the most likely and effective agents for change?

In 2006, the main UK professional bodies concerned with planning, RICS and the RTPI commissioned, with others, the 'Future Planners' report in order to imagine the new roles and skills required of 'planners' to put into practice the disciplines of spatial planning, adopted as part of the UK procedural planning reforms of 2004 (see Bradwell *et al.*, 2007). Spatial planning was to be the new principal means of ordering and enabling sustainable development. There was a recognition that the professions would need to do different things, as well as doing existing things differently. According to one of the report's interviewees, head of planning for a London council, 'planners are implementing the same system they have always implemented, but it wasn't designed for a globalising world' (Bradwell *et al.*, 2007, p. 4).

Spatial planning was, therefore, understood to be a more dynamic and fluid process, needing to be constantly adaptive to the interactions between people, place and capital flows, which might now emanate from anywhere in the world. In this context, the challenge to the planner would be to mediate the tensions between local and extra-local priorities and imperatives. The report suggested new roles for planners, ranging from Enabler to Scenario Planner, to Provocateur and Judge. It gave the planner greater autonomy, but working within a framework of collective and collaborative effort from other professionals, people and politicians and managing knowledge flows and the content of planning debate: a world away from the traditional functions of policy writing and development control (Bradwell *et al.*, 2007).

To maintain credibility in this autonomous and highly responsible position, the planner would need a story about his or her role that would enable others to trust them as disinterested advocate of a better future. The authors of the 'Future Planners' report proposed the concept of 'Public Value', a term with some political currency for the decade around the turn of the century, to move the debate about public interest beyond the normal presumption of 'public investment good for all, private investment good for some'. The public interest should not be taken for granted but had to be proposed, debated and endorsed. 'We take "public value" to be the achievement of democratically legitimate sustainable development [...] integrating environmental sustainability and social justice with economic growth [...]. This requires all to take a long term view. It demands a reassertion of the idea [...] that the planning system aims to pursue the public interest' (Bradwell *et al.*, 2007, p. 5). The responsibility of the Future Planner was to manage this process of co-producing a sustainable future and to be held accountable by all the stakeholders in the co-production for the realisation of 'public value'.

Public value was, however, essentially a forward-looking construction of value, hard to reconcile with the pragmatism of development economics today. Whilst most forms of investment in new development have a relatively short-term investment horizon, often reliant more on sentiment-driven trading in speculative and inflationary land and asset values, both the costs of providing for the future and future accruals of value are routinely ignored. Planners would, therefore, have needed a revolution in practice, skills and status to put themselves and their profession into a position where this debate could reshape the operation of markets to deliver genuinely sustainable development, in any market.

The 'Future Planners' report was enthusiastically received by both professionals and their institutions in the United Kingdom; some individual professionals, not traditional planners, were inspired by the ambition of the report to develop new modes of practice and are operating effectively at the interesting margins of professional practice. It is not surprising, though, that none of the RICS, RTPI or mainstream professional firms or public offices have yet found a way to act on any of the ideas contained in the report, either individually or collectively. Assessing the future is regarded as being very difficult and uncertain. Taking responsibility for it seems an unnecessary distraction, when dealing with and mostly accommodating Till's 'dirty reality' of today is the best that can be managed.

Whereas planning does at least imply an interest in the future, the task is even harder for property professionals, especially for valuers whose principal responsibility is to assess the price at which a willing purchaser and vendor will agree to a transaction today. The valuer's dilemma is that the task of valuation, even if projecting future income flows, is essentially based on a backward look at the evidence of previous transactions and revenue performance. Valuing sustainable development is fundamentally different, not the least because it has to be based on a forward view of how to assess and manage an uncertain future and its potential risks and rewards.

There are also strong, almost moral prohibitions in their force that prevent valuers trying to 'shape' markets; they may only reflect it. As with the earlier observation about planners, however, that leaves valuers implementing the same system they have always implemented, but one that was not designed for a globalising world. However, sustainable development is now embedded fully in the global discourse about the future of the planet. Almost every aspect of national UK and EU public policy and an increasing body of regulatory requirements requires new development to carry the burden of environmental and social costs of sustainability, quite explicitly internalising to the cost of development, (and the holding of land for development), what was previously externalised or ignored as a 'harmless' or inconsequential by-product.

Valuation practice has not yet found a way to accommodate this view of the future, grounded as it is now in the neoclassical economic paradigm. But some leading economists understand the need for some aspects of this paradigm to change.

Reflecting the earlier concerns of the EU Environment Commissioner, Potočnik, Martin Wolf, Chief Economist at the Financial Times, explains what he sees as the faults of neoclassical economic theory:

> Something strange happened to economics about a century ago. In moving from classical to neo-classical economics, the dominant academic school today, economists expunged land or natural resources. Neo-classical value theory, based on marginalism and subjective valuation, still makes a great deal of sense. Expunging natural resources from the way economists think about the world does not. [...]
>
> All thinking about the world involves a degree of abstraction. Economics has taken this principle further than any other social science. This is a fruitful intellectual procedure. But it is also risky. The necessary process of abstraction may end up leaving essential aspects of the world out of the analysis. Thus, for both economic and political reasons, we should put natural resources into the heart of economics, thereby remedying a neoclassical mistake.
>
> (Wolf, 2010)

Therefore, in reaching an understanding of what the value of an asset should properly be, simply assuming a 'willing' buyer or seller may not be enough, as it does not necessarily also mean that they are wise, prudent, forward-looking, enlightened or any other virtuous quality that might be the necessary precondition for promoting sustainable development. In an imperfect system, therefore, it is hard to bring transparency to any understanding of value that does take account of the future expectations of sustainable development and accommodate future change and uncertainty.

At this stage, the constraints on shaping the market seem anachronistic and only capable of hindering the innovation, the development of new knowledge and the growth of an investment market for sustainable development. Whilst valuation, as a professional skill, may need to be as highly regulated as it currently is, the concept of value cannot ever be value-free, static or solely backward-looking. Even in 1871, Carl Menger could assert that 'the value of goods arises from their relationship to our needs, and is not inherent in the goods themselves. With changes in this relationship, value arises or disappears' (Menger, 1871, p. 120).

Other non-valuer property professionals, from land economics, construction cost estimating and management, building design and land-use management disciplines, as well as other built-environment professionals, all possess special knowledge and insight about many possible futures and, thus, many possible future values. They might be called 'Future Professionals' – a 'Built Environment Fellowship' (Ratcliffe, 2010, p. 90) – and be responsible for speaking out and sharing that knowledge and exploring and determining the limits of their knowledge, so that all parts of the market are better informed, about both future prospects and impacts and past performance, where that continues to be relevant.

Valuers and their clients may, therefore, be exposed to a wider base of evidence and public and professional discourse about the social, economic and environmental characteristics of a project or assignment and against which they may then be held more accountable than hitherto.

Taking Personal Responsibility for the Other

One key concern, within the context of challenges imposed by sustainable development to built-environment professionals, is that of 'non-responsibility'. It can be argued
that, in addition to the so-called vicious circle of blame (see: Hartenberger and Lorenz,
2008), there is another vicious circle operating at a more fundamental level within property and construction markets: the vicious circle of non-responsibility. The problem is
that many built-environment professionals give away responsibility and do not feel in
any way responsible for market outcomes. For example, valuation professionals do not
feel responsible, since responsibility is usually ascribed to the free market's 'invisible
hand'. Yet, surely, valuation professionals are inescapably bound into both the causes and
effects of the global financial crisis in which widely held professional and lay assumptions
about the value of property assets have been a material factor.

   In addition, designers and builders usually do not feel responsible for the actual performance of their buildings; responsibility is often ascribed to facility managers and users.
Although almost all designers and builders would agree that creating sustainable buildings is a key priority, very few go back, after the project has been completed, to check the
building's logbook (i.e. the actual performance) or have a role or stake in the actual performance of what they designed and built. So, whilst most professionals are interested
in compliance, usually with a hypothetical model, they have much less or no concern or
interest in the performance of the completed building. From a conceptual and methodological point of view, this is flawed (Lorch, 2011). Leaman *et al.* (2010, p. 575) thus argue
persuasively that 'the divisions of responsibility make it difficult to close the feedback
loop from building performance in use to briefing, design and construction'.

   It is not so much the 'invisible hand' of the market as the invisibility of ourselves and
our professional institutions when it comes to responsibility. This perpetuates the myth
that all is well, so that, 'most people live in stories made up by them and their societies,
and they call these stories "reality". We are the most dangerous force on Earth, to ourselves and the environment. It is the main aim of education to provide not information
or techniques, but a better set of perspectives for better seeing the invisible' (Kay, 2004).

   As a consequence, professional bodies and individual professionals are confronted
with the unequivocal challenge of becoming more responsible and accountable for
design and property market outcomes. Expressed in other words, the need for a 'new
professionalism' spans across the built-environment professions – they must find a new
role in proactive 'market shaping' and taking longer-term responsibilities for building
or place performance, and sharing learning, through the realisation of design objectives
in use (see: Hill and Lorenz, 2011). Otherwise, built-environment professionals could
find themselves operating in conflict with the stated goals and constitutions of their
professional bodies.

   One important key for solving this problem lies in fostering and providing conditions
under which built-environment professionals can take personal responsibility for
ethical behaviour. Favourable conditions for a change in behaviour are essential because
'the same combination of people, organizations, and physical structures can behave
completely different, if the system's actors can see a good reason for doing so, and
if they have the freedom, perhaps even the incentive, to change' (Meadows *et al.*,
2004, p. 237).

The assumption of personal responsibility is also Till's (2009) proposition. Rejecting a range of traditional definitions of ethics, he turns to Bauman (1993) and his inspiration, philosopher Emmanuel Levinas, 'Ethics is defined simply and directly as "being-for the Other". To assume an ethical stance means to "assume responsibility for the Other"' (Bauman, 1993, p. 13, cited in: Till, 2009, p. 173).

This sounds disarmingly simple. However, Bauman's explanation ensures that readers understand the complexity of what is being proposed: 'The ethical paradox of the post-modern condition is that it restores to agents the fullness of moral choice and responsibility, whilst simultaneously depriving them of the comfort of the universal guidance that modern self-confidence once promised' (Bauman, 1993, p. 13, cited in: Till, 2009, p. 173).

Till (2009) welcomes the fact that this means that professional bodies cannot police a brand of imperfect ethics. There cannot be a set of static ethical principles, based on 'absolute correctness. Instead, it works from within each situation, rather than imposing an abstract set of moral codes from without. These ethics have to work with the contingencies of each context, and not attempt to stifle them' (Till, 2009, p. 173). In Till's world, the professional bodies would have to articulate clear guiding principles for ethical and technical competence and behaviour, but few immovable rules, as these would have to be negotiated in the context of the actual situation in which the professional is engaged.

This proposition does not need to remain an abstract notion. An approach for taking personal responsibility was proposed in an earlier study in 2007 for the Royal Society of Arts, Professionals for a Sustainable World, and then developed further for RIBA Building Futures in 2009 (see Hill, 2009a). This study was based on over 60 interviews with practicing professionals, clients and policymakers in the United Kingdom, exploring the relationship between 'high-quality design' and the demands and disciplines of sustainable development. From the interviews, it was possible to identify three serious gaps in developing a workable concept of ethical professional practice, based on the responsible application of acquired specialist knowledge and skill. These are (Hill, 2009b) the following:

First gap: We, as built-environment professionals, are at the limit of what we know, but we do not have much honesty about what we know and what we do not yet know. We go into projects all the time pretending we know everything, even when we do not. We think it is professional to know everything. To admit that we do not know is seen as unprofessional in the eyes of peers and clients. That is dishonest, even for insurance purposes.

Second gap: There is no culture of explicitly learning on the job, recording what we do not know and using the project systematically to build up our knowledge in ways that embrace all the different professionals, as well as the client and any other stakeholders in the project.

Third gap: We need a more explicit set of ethical values that must be learned, tested and sustained in the social context of the project, within the team and in the way that team engages with the outside world. That is not to say that there can be a rigid set of ethical rules for sustainable development, as it would not be very useful if we did, as it would suggest that a 'sustainable development' was a finite and determinate phenomenon, whereas it is needs to be adaptive. However, it should always be legitimate to argue, debate and test the values that we need to embody in the profession and on specific projects.

Professional Sustainable Practices

Over 20 years ago, Lorch (1990, pp. 52–53) outlined a series of actions that the professional bodies should undertake in order to foster sustainable practices in the profession and in the construction industry. Some progress has been made on these actions, but it would also be fair to say that progress has been fragmented across the professions and still lacks a clear ethical context in which all the built-environment professions can work together to a set of common values. Why should a civil engineer have more onerous ethical obligations than an architect?

Implicit in all discussions and thinking at that time, in the 1990s and early 2000s, was the idea that the professional could deliver (what was then termed) environmentally sound buildings, provided there was the support of appropriate information and a motivated client. There was little questioning of whether the professional institutions or individual professionals themselves would be unwilling or unable to do this. The main barrier was seen as clients and the marketplace (Lorch, 2011). Therefore, based on and further developed from the Professionals for a Sustainable World study (Hill, 2009a,b), the authors of this chapter propose, amongst other things, that professional bodies should also consider the following:

- Whether and how they should make their public interest obligations more explicit to professional members, to clients, to government and the public at large, including the reform of charters and codes of conduct.
- How the professional's responsibilities should be extended from design through to in-use performance management and monitoring of places, buildings and plants.
- What should be the extent of professional responsibility when outcomes may be affected by user behaviour or choices that cannot be constrained by building designers or owners (e.g. taking energy efficiency gains in extra heat and comfort).
- How professional practice and contractual terms of engagement should be adapted to systematise action learning, knowledge capture and sharing and reflect new responsibilities.
- How professional institutions and individuals create the opportunity for debating openly ethical issues, both in live project situations and in the public life of the profession.
- How professional bodies could cooperate to create integrated communities of knowledge across traditional professional boundaries.
- How professional institutions should engage with academia and training providers to improve education and ensure both knowledge and personal skills are relevant to changing real-world conditions. (Ratcliffe (2011) makes the same point, and this is also dealt with in more detail in Hartenberger and colleagues (2013).)

Finally, the professional institutions, even if they cannot police ethics as comfortably as their current codes, will have to find a new and accessible way of representing, to society at large, the primary duty of the professional: responsibility for the Other.

Whilst a general duty of care to society is expressly or implicitly stated in most professional charters, it might often take some careful interpretation to read into many of the explicit ethical obligations that have been discussed here. It would be a brave professional body that puts 'Public first. Client second' on its annual membership cards. Even where that is stated, it is not always remembered, genuinely understood or observed. But the Other is sometimes also them or us, the professionals, so there also needs to be the idea that professionals should have to reconcile their ideas about the way they want to live personally and the way they should behave as a professional person. They should not expect more for themselves than they expect for the Other. That requires a social context, as the place where professional and personal values, ethical dilemmas and potential conflicts of interest can be openly discussed and tested and where professional behaviour may then be held up to account by both peers and the public. To do that, the roles of the traditional players may also need to be redefined and strengthened:

> Citizen clients: (as suggested in Mostafavi and Doherty, 2010), clients have a responsibility to be more informed, more robust, and more permissive, in the cause of enabling sustainable development to happen. They need to become co-producers with the professionals, accept they may not understand the question they are asking or that it is even the right question. Clients should expect to be challenged by the professionals.
>
> Citizen professionals: (a name suggested by Till, 2009), and a role advocated forty years earlier by Goodman (1972, p. 250): "By raising the possibilities of the humane way of producing places to live, by phasing out the elitist nature of environmental professionalism, we can move towards a time when we will no longer define ourselves by our profession but by our freedom as people."

Binding the two roles together is the late Tony Judt's injunction:

> Today, when the market and the free play of private interests so obviously do not come together to collective advantage, we need to know when to intervene [...]. As citizens of a free society, we have a duty to look critically at our world. But if we think we know what is wrong, we must act upon that knowledge
>
> (Judt, 2010, p. 206 & p. 237).

The ambition of these writers is both inspiring and difficult to live up to. However, there is no avoiding of the ethical and practical imperatives on built-environment professionals to act at global, national and local levels to meet the challenges of climate change, population growth and the depletion of natural resources or, in the words of the RICS Royal Charter, 'to promote the usefulness [authors' emphasis] of the profession for the public advantage in the United Kingdom and in any other part of the world' (RICS, 2008, Clause 3).

To the modern ear, 'usefulness' might seem too mundane an injunction to action in the public interest and lacking in urgency. But the nineteenth-century charter writers would have been thinking about professional tasks and responsibilities in the context of John Stuart Mill's great works Utilitarianism and On Liberty (Mill, 1859, 1863): both bestsellers in the late Victorian times. Mill described utilitarianism as the maximisation of utility as a moral criterion for the organisation of society that should aim to maximise the total utility of individuals, to achieve 'the greatest happiness for the greatest number of people' (Mill, 1863). This could be regarded as a legitimate proxy for the 'public advantage' in the RICS Charter and current terminology, such as 'the public interest' and 'community well-being', or even 'happiness' which is enjoying a twenty-first-century political revival. Mill makes it clear throughout On Liberty that he 'regard[s] utility as the ultimate appeal on all ethical questions' (Mill, 1859).

As Wolf (2011) observed, in the late nineteenth century, classical economic theory was the dominant paradigm and would have required the connection that is made in the charter, between 'land' and 'its associated resources' (i.e. minerals, water, air, the produce coming from the land, etc. which are all part of the classical definition of land) and their capacity to 'meet social and economic needs'.

So, twenty-first-century professionals and their professional bodies could usefully relearn what their Victorians predecessors well understood: the importance of being useful.

5.2

Professional Approach

Peter Dent and David Lorenz

Introduction

The world today is very different from that 50 years, 100 years, or 150 years ago. There are some overarching influences that form the backdrop to decision-making in many fields of real estate. These influences include, to a greater or lesser extent, financial deregulation, securitisation, environment and climate, international terrorism and North–South inequalities. Because of these influences, 'the kind of control that professionals have over their roles and bodies of knowledge is not what it once was, and is likely to continue to weaken' (Hughes *et al.*, 2011, p. 36). This does not mean that there is no role for professionals and professional institutions in the future. However, it does mean that, to remain relevant going forward, perhaps, there is a need to see the world differently, see themselves differently, upskill laterally: in other words, to challenge assumptions and mindsets established in the last century.

In the context of real-estate values and the valuation process, we would argued that bottom-line approaches need to be either understood and explained (both internally and externally) or mediated through a much more robust transformative process or developed as part of a qualitative assessment to include explicitly a meta-ethical dimension in line with professional guidelines. According to IVSC (2013), 'value is not a fact but an opinion' and, as such, requires the impartial judgement, objectivity and competence of the valuer. These are loaded terms which, in themselves, need further investigation. Impartial judgement implies that without bias, without prejudice, valuers will assess all aspects of the property in order to arrive at a value. In doing so, they will minimise 'the influence of any subjective factors on the process' (p. 12). They will also act with competence. This competence builds on a foundation of basic skills, technical knowledge and moral development and is 'developmental, impermanent and context-dependent' (Epstein and Hundert, 2002, p. 227).

These attributes of professionalism require not only ongoing development of technical knowledge and market intelligence but also an understanding of personal behaviours and an interpretation of, what might be called, societal zeitgeist.

In Ailon (2015), there is a case made that psychology is the main driver in the markets, so that objectivity becomes a negotiated ground as within financial markets, 'the calculative model itself assumes a spirit that is outside the "economic" and even contradicts it' (p. 594). This raises issues about the reliance on the accuracy of theoretical market models, their complexities and their diversities. If the real-estate market is inextricably linked to these financial markets, then the same would apply. So, therefore, the real-estate valuer requires 'strict discipline, reflexivity and resolve' (p. 608) in order, first, to understand the drivers of value, second, to unpick those drivers and incorporate them into a model and, finally, to calculate and interpret value.

It is not only the calculation that is important (although, of course, it does represent a signal) but, perhaps, equally important ' … is the ethos, the spirit, the imaginary through which the world of the screen, the floor, the office, and even the invisible collegial network is valued, assessed, and shaped. Markets may be about efficiency, but financial actors are not' … (Appadurai, 2011, p. 525). This is especially true when advice goes beyond the bottom line.

Bottom-Line Approaches

Financial markets are still attracted by approaches that seek only to find the bottom line. Miller (2008) highlights three of these. The first, shareholder value, is indicative of the finance and investment markets in terms of their one-dimensional measure of value. The second, best value, used extensively in the public sector is a key element in the privatisation of the public estate and again measures qualities in a quantitative way. Finally, what Miller terms the New-Age value. The principle here is encouraging, but the practical application is, too often, settled into a Newtonian business model, using ESG and CSR terminology alone to create competitive advantage.

1) *Shareholder value.* Using this measure, 'a company should judge itself not according to traditional criteria such as profit but upon its ability to create a rise in the value of its shares.' (p. 1124). In the context of property companies, investment funds, trusts and so on, there is a danger, as shown in the financial crisis, that value is created (or sustained) out of nothing. So, bottom-line thinking may create not a material value but an unsustainable virtual value. (p. 1125)

2) *Best value.* For the Government in the United Kingdom, this is more about financial than quality outcomes. It has been defined by the four 'C's. Challenge how and why a service is provided; compare with others; allow fair competition; consult with taxpayers and customers. 'But the ideal of value, was fatally weakened by the idea of best, which tried to retain a bottom-line logic of an ultimate benchmark against which everything could be measured, so that the appeal to the quantitiative undermined the potential of the qualitative.' (p. 1126). It often involves 'endless pages of fairly trite formulas, usually with no substantive content…' (p. 1126). Whilst related to 'public' value, it is promoted as an opportunity for consultants to privatise, outsource and 'rationalise' services. It extends the ground of this notion that anything can be valued in monetary terms as a commodity in the market. The aforementioned comments could equally be applied to the way that some valuers justify their assessments of 'investment' value

3) *New-Age value.* The New Age is associated with anti-rationalism, openness to new experiences, taking chances and emotionalism, and it is just those elements that encourage New-Age values to be 'promoted as a means to recapture the proper

harmony and holism of a functional corporation' (p. 1126). However, too often, they are diluted and misappropriated to promote concepts of 'leanness' and financial efficiency in organisations. This tends to eschew meaning or rather redefine meaning in quantitative terms alone, taking the ground back to shareholder value. On the other hand, holism (the abiding principle of New-Age value) should be seen principally as an expression of the relationship between things – that is, the reality and the ground from which both values and value could be derived. As such, it is concerning integral value relationships rather than simply the possible outcomes of those relationships expressed in the rather narrow parameters of money.

Alongside this gravitation to the bottom line, there is the widely held belief in the market as the source of certainty. These two ideas together provide 'the reward for disciplined focus on its messages and rhythms, and as the all-powerful power that rewards its own elect, so long as they obey its ethical demands' (Appadurai, 2011, p. 527). This, to Appadurai, is part of the magic of the market which has produced, inter alia, the following outcomes:

- Calculation techniques which produce certainties far beyond their capabilities. This, potentially, opens 'a new distance between expert and popular understandings of risk'.
- 'Probability and possibility have become dangerously confused in many popular understandings, thus opening the door to myriad schemes, scams, and distortions based on emergent forms of personal charisma.' (p. 528)
- 'The external or transcendent sources of ethics…have been replaced by various forms of immanent corporate ethics, indexed by terms like transparency, accountability, corporate social responsibility, good governance, and so forth, thus making the justification of calculative actions immune from broader ethical images and doctrines.' (p. 529)
- Finally, 'there has been a steady hybridization of the ideologies of calculative action, so that the casino, the racetrack, the lottery, and gambling in general have infused the world of financial calculation and vice versa, thus confusing the spheres of chance and risk as technical features of human life.' (p. 529).

What we find in these are techniques that suggest levels of certainty that do not exist; actions and statements that describe marketing values rather than ethical based values; risk analysis founded on charts which are as unscientific as astrological charts. However, it is suggested that these are the tools used to arrive at trading prices in the financial markets. If real estate is a subset of these markets, to what extent do these apply to the valuation of physical real estate, securitised or unitised real estate and/or other real-estate-backed investment vehicle?

A Way Forward

Returning now to the new value drivers, is there a way of resolving some of these shortcomings to ensure that clients and the public at large can have confidence that the advice that they are given is sustainable from an economic, a social and an environmental point of view?

'Responsibility is not just about the present, it is also about assuming responsibility now for future footprints … Above all, what is arguably needed is a mindset that can tackle complexity, uncertainty and change' (O'Brien *et al.*, 2009, p. 10). However, Curran argues that, because of the mismatch between those benefiting from the production of financial risk and the damage distribution of those risks, there is the level of irresponsibility that encourages the perpetuation of a boom/bust mentality or a cyclical crisis from exuberance to indifference (Curran, 2015). Theoretically, this should lead to change. However, without motivation, the behaviour that created the crisis is unlikely to provide a sustainable solution; 'future footprints' will remain outside of the calculative bottom line and beyond the risk parameters. This is partly because global impacts (social, environmental and financial) are very difficult to evaluate in financial terms alone; the level of uncertainty goes beyond the discounting formulas of traditional finance; and change is unsettling and potentially unprofitable for those in the market – the recent crisis suggests that governments will not allow systems to fail, thus reducing the downside risk and allowing individuals to take more extreme risks (or, perhaps, remain inert as in the case of real-estate values when all around is crumbling).

These complexities need to be built into valuation models, and the models themselves need to be more dynamic and both more responsive and more actively predictive.

The intention of this book has been not only to look beyond the price of real estate (i.e. in money terms) but also to ask the question, 'at what price are we willing to plan, develop and use real estate?': in other words, to consider the responsibilities of the valuer in using models of valuation. How far should these be purely commercially based on financial market models and how far purely professionally based on a set of ethics and a code of conduct provided by industry and governmental institutions?

Of course, the answer is not a compromise but a hybrid between the two. Client requirements are pivotal, but there has to be a view of the wider consequences. So, client influence will be a part of the valuation; it is inextricably linked to the calculated figure. However, a value based on specific criteria (to satisfy lenders, shareholders or the financial markets) cannot be disguised as a market value even if there are similarities.

Our proposition is that it is not appropriate for valuers to be ushered through unchallenged when times are good and then walk away from accountability when the market takes a downturn. Equally, it is not possible to turn a blind eye to the wider implications of decisions on value. These may spread across countries and financial markets, societies and environments, cultures and beliefs. The valuer, as a cog in the machine, has a responsibility for not only mitigating risks for clients but also ensuring not to create risks in the wider society (whether these risks are related to climate, social cohesion or fiduciary).

In valuing real estate, it is important to try to explain how things fit together and to complete the exercise within a specific culture/context. UNEP FI (2014) in the process of identifying best practice for real-estate management split the context under the headings of 'corporate', 'portfolio' and 'single building'. These should be interlinked and consistent, but each will have differing priorities. At the corporate level, there is interaction with shareholders; at the portfolio level, the interaction is with investors; and at the single-building level, the interaction is with the occupiers/users. In total, 24 recommendations of good practice are identified. It is important to see these as going beyond the bottom line, and where value determination is concerned, it is about adopting a more sustainable approach to the valuation of corporate assets.

However, underlying these best-practice recommendations is another layer of responsibility which should form a part of the valuer's toolkit. This is especially important in a global environment where different ways of working and ethical positions have evolved in different cultures. RICS (2015) draws attention to human rights, labour, environment and anti-corruption as crucial to the role to be played by those involved in the real-estate industry.

The second part of the title of this book is 'Value in a Changing Environment'. Sixty years ago, valuation was an art; 30 years ago, more scientific method was applied to the artist's craft. Today, it needs to have the qualities of transient art and quantum science. It is not a work of fiction or an oil painting; nor is it an engineer's equation or mathematical formula. It needs a dynamism and an uncertainty – a challenging edge.

At present, there are a lot of indices which tell us what has happened in the past, and there is a lot of confusion about what should be measured and how it should be measured (particularly when it comes to aspects that appear to have non-monetary worth such as the environment and social cohesion). Add to this the size and spread of the market, the complexity of the assets in that market and the financial structures around those assets, then it is hard to see how traditional approaches can do more than give a superficial impression of value. 'Technology, demographics and environmental issues are becoming new value drivers…real estate as an asset class is changing fast. Mega real estate managers are emerging, which are building and investing in real estate on an epic scale…the landscape is becoming more widespread and complex, with a wider range of risk and return than ever, plus new drivers of value' (PwC, 2014, p. 4).

Proposed Changes Regarding Current Valuation Practice and Standards

From this, it may be appropriate to review the approach to valuations. Any suggestion will add complexity to the traditional valuation service, and that service will need to address some mega issues. On the one hand, the approach should perform what Muldavin (2010) has termed financial 'sustainability sub-analyses' in order to determine single-valuation input parameters.

On the other hand, any approach competent to deal with the complexity of the asset and its environment will be required to perform or present what we term 'high level valuation analyses' which include a qualitative examination of the intangibles or, more precisely, 'not yet defined' monetary categories of value. This, in turn, results in consequences for the presentation of the valuation results as well as impacts upon the content and format of valuation reports.

Conclusion

A price is a comparative figure derived from incomplete information about a property, a client, a market sentiment and so on. As such, it is an interpretation of data, today, using sophisticated software but often relying on a less than sophisticated agent at the input and interpretative stage. It might be that in-house software provides an opportunity to weight different variables on a specific scale in a prescriptive manner based on 'extensive' analysis of past trends going back a number of years. This together with a range of indices and market intelligence enables a figure close to the client's requirements to be determined. There is a concern that this figure will tend to follow the current trend in the market; so, despite future income and yield projections, it is likely to be backward-looking. There is often a lack of awareness of the micro, macro and mega trends in the price determination even if there are clear noises in the marketplace about unsustainable trends upwards or downwards.

Unfortunately, often, fierce competition does not allow sufficient resource to be assigned to the valuation task, and there then is a danger that it becomes a straightforward number-crunching exercise without any real contextual intelligence being applied. Instinct is an important element, but that instinct should lead to greater mining of the variables across a range of areas using multidisciplinary tools. The development of these techniques should not be optional for professionals. Existing tools may need to be adapted for the changes that have taken place in the environment over the last two decades.

To summarise, the following points are relevant:

- Price alone has very little meaning. To give it meaning requires the valuer not only to explain assumptions and variables but also to set the overall context and to describe the whole as it derives from the parts.
- Techniques that encourage active interchange between valuer and software should be encouraged. Ceding all the power to the electronics is dangerous.
- Each asset is different; so, standard formulas, standard weightings, standard pro formas should constantly be questioned.
- Linear data is generally unrealistic, and non-linear data is hard to determine. However, professional advice relies on robust assumptions which often need to be sought out rather than waiting to be collected.
- There is no one model that suits all cases. The solution requires intelligent investigation and examination and the knowledge of what tools are available beyond in-house models.
- The exercise should not just be about the bottom line. It should be a process of bounded rationality and transparency contained within a broader value system that follows a stated code of conduct and embraces implications from non-monetary analysis.

If these points are not given due consideration then price, in itself, may lack meaning. It is the amount that is transacted for a real-estate asset, but it says very little beyond that. This then becomes comparable evidence for the next transaction. This creates a loop which drives the levels at which prices are pitched. This is why it is important to go beyond price to understand more about a value that the asset can sustain into the future.

Appendices

Appendix to Chapter 3.2

Guidelines for the Application of Regressed DCF

Valuation Guideline for Regressed DCF Application v.1

A. General Definitions

3.4.A.1	Regressed DCF may be used both for Property Valuation and for Assessing the Worth purposes.
3.4.A.2	The Application of Regressed DCF may involve previous valuation carried out by valuer in the area of the property to be valued. They may have been or have not been transformed into a real price.
3.4.A.3	The Application of Regressed DCF may involve the price found by valuer in the area of the property to be valued.
3.4.A.4	The Use of Value or Price or both must be clearly specified in the Valuation Counseling report.
3.4.A.5	The Final Output of a Regressed DCF for Property Valuation Purposes cannot be considered an opinion of value. It must be considered an estimated of value.
3.4.A.6	The Final Output of a Regressed DCF for Property Valuation Purposes can be considered a further method of mass appraisal/automated valuation methodology belonging to the direct comparison approach.
3.4.A.7	The Final Output of a Regressed DCF for Assessment of Worth cannot be considered having the same level of precision of a DCF
3.4.A.8	Regressed DCF is a family of three methods called A, B, and C. The formulas are different according to the different inputs considered.
3.4.A.9	All the data must be selected in the same geographic market segment.

B. Application of Regressed DCF as an AVM Methodology

3.4.B.1	Regressed DCF applications start with the collection of real-estate prices and DCF inputs of comparable commercial properties in the same area.
3.4.B.2	In the application of model A, direct capitalization together with DCF can also be collected even if the first application showed less precise results.
3.4.B.2	The data will be divided in two parts: the column of value or price collected. This will be the dependent variable.
3.4.B.3	The other columns will vary according to the specific model selected.

Value in a Changing Built Environment, First Edition.
Edited by David Lorenz, Peter Dent and Tom Kauko.
© 2018 John Wiley & Sons Ltd. Published 2018 by John Wiley & Sons Ltd.

| 3.4.B.4 | It will be necessary to adequate the price at the date of the valuation. |
| 3.4.B.5 | The logarithm will be calculated and then the data will be standardized. |

C. Application of Regressed DCF as a Discount Rate Methodology

| 3.4.C.1 | Inverting the formulas of models A, B, and C, the Discount Rate may become a dependent variable. |

D. Application of Regressed DCF as a Risk Premium Methodology

3.4.D.1	Inverting the formulas of models A, B, and C, the Discount Rate may become the dependent variable.
3.4.D.2	Assuming a risk-free rate, it is possible to define the risk premium as a difference between the discount rate and the risk-free.
3.4.D.3	Each single observation should have geographic coordinates.
3.4.D.4	Using the risk premium and the geographic coordinates, it is possible to develop a risk premium map.
3.4.D.5	The application of the model is conditioned to a positive spatial correlation among the observations.

Appendix to Chapter 4.2

Feature Maps (SOM Output) of Trondheim, 1993–2007

Each of the following map layers shows the variation in price per annual average income for the whole city area. The label denotes ward and is for identification only.

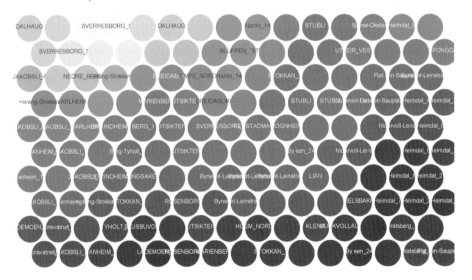

1993

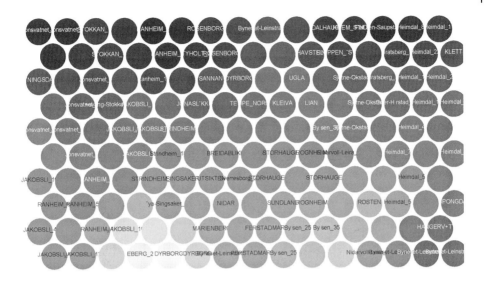

1994

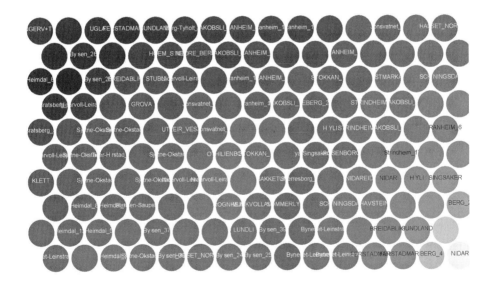

1995

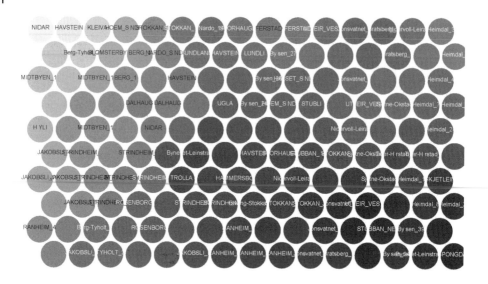

1996

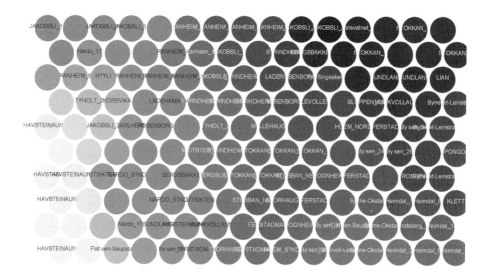

1997

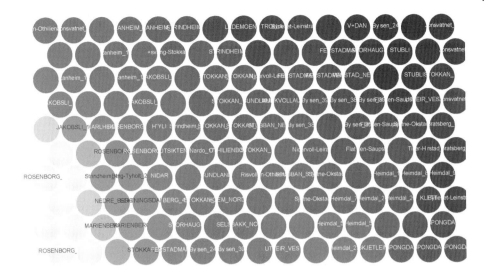

1998

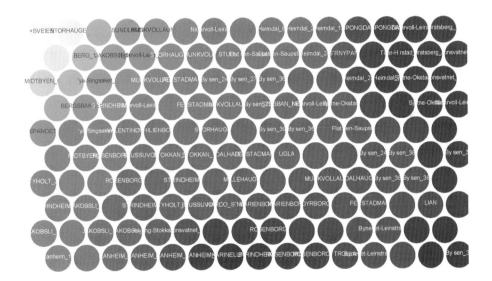

1999

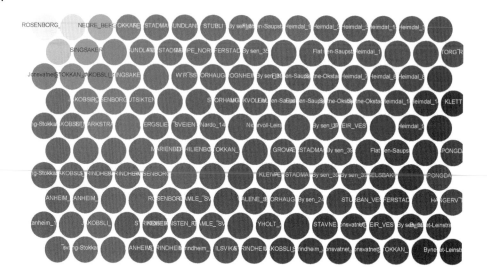

2000

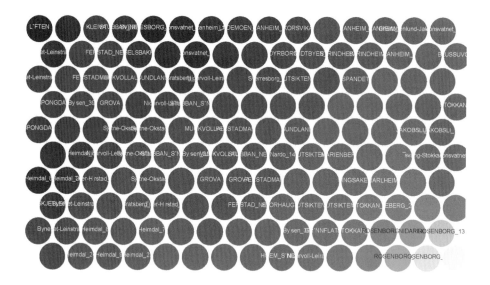

2001

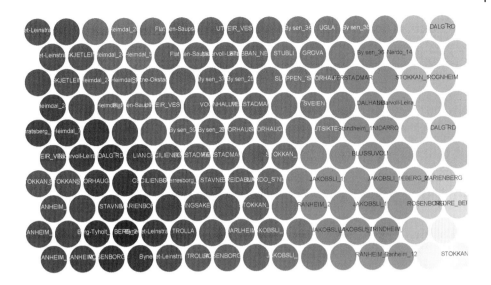

2002

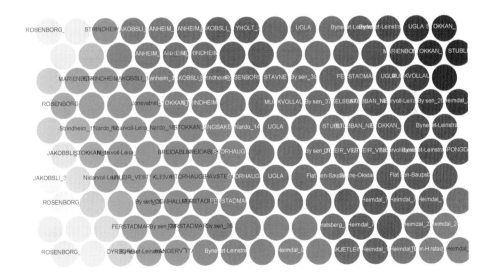

2003

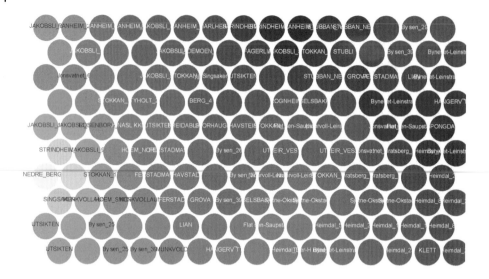

2004

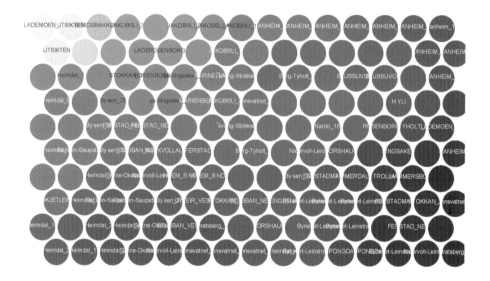

2005

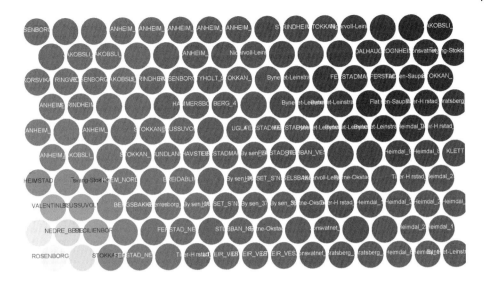

2006

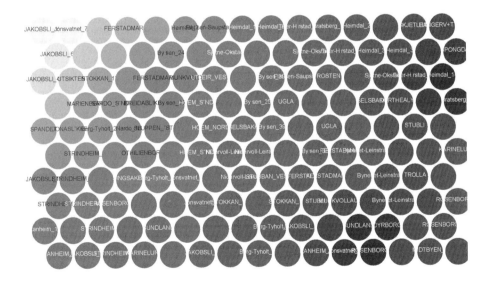

2007

Appendix 1 to Chapter 4.4

CB RICHARD ELLIS – MARKET INDEX – CEE OFFICES –

Prime Rent – Represents the top open-market tier of rent that could be expected for a unit of standard size commensurate with demand in each location, of highest quality and specification, and in the best location in a market at the survey date. Prime Rent should reflect the level at which relevant transactions are being completed in the market at the time but need not be exactly identical to any of them, particularly if deal flow is very limited or made up of unusual one-off deals. If there are no relevant transactions during the survey period, the quoted figure will be more hypothetical, based on expert opinion of market conditions, but the same criteria on building size and specification will still apply. For offices, the Prime Rent should represent the typical "achievable" open market headline rent that a blue-chip occupier would be expected to pay for:

- an office unit of standard size commensurate with demand in each location;
- typically 1,000 sq m (10,000 sq ft);
- an office unit of highest quality and specification;
- an office unit within the prime location (CBD, for example) of a market.

It is assumed that the occupier will also be agreeing to a package of incentives that is typical for the market at the time.

Prime Yield – Represents the yield that an investor would receive when acquiring a grade/class A building in a prime location (for offices in the CBD, for example), which is fully let at current market value rents. Prime Yield should reflect the level at which relevant transactions are being completed in the market at the time but need not be exactly identical to any of them, particularly if deal flow is very limited or made up of unusual one-off deals. If there are no relevant transactions during the survey period, a hypothetical yield should be quoted and is not a calculation based on particular transactions, but it is an expert opinion formed in the light of market conditions, but the same criteria on building location and specification still apply.

Appendix 2 to Chapter 4.4

Valuation Guideline for Cyclical Capitalization Application

A. General Definitions

4.5.A.1	Cyclical Capitalization is a family of income-oriented methodologies, which integrates the real-estate market cycle analysis with real-estate appraisal.
4.5.A.2	The final output of a Cyclical Capitalization is an opinion of value.
4.5.A.3	Cyclical Capitalization is a Methodology to estimate income-producing properties and in particular, those properties affected in particular way by market cycle.

B. Application of Cyclical Capitalization

4.5.B.1	The application of Cyclical Capitalization is conditioned by the availability of local time series, which may be implemented in order to integrate time series analysis with property valuation activity.
4.5.B.2	A reliable time series analysis is the necessary premises of the application of Cyclical capitalization modeling.
4.5.B.3	Time series analysis may be replaced by a Delphi method questionnaire or personal expertise of valuer supported by the evidence of the market.
4.5.B.4	The time series considered should be coherent with the market segment of the subject.

4.5.B.5	The time series should consider the rate of change of cap rate or the rate of change of local rent and prices.
4.5.B.6	Although the time series may have information on a longer interval of time, the valuer will consider the information temporally closer to the moment of valuation. Therefore, in a similar way to DCF, the valuer will select an appropriate backward-holding period.
4.5.B.7	An appropriate backward-holding period may be between 10 and 15 years.
4.5.B.8	The rate of change must be calculated on annual basis.

C. Choice of the Model

4.5.C.1	The choice of the right cyclical capitalization model is based on the nature of inputs, basis of value. As a rule of thumb, if there are similar temporal lengths of the phase of the cycles, the models pertaining to the primum group may be an interesting alternative.
4.5.C.2	The choice of the right cyclical capitalization model is based on the nature of inputs. As a rule of thumb, if there are similar temporal lengths available at overall cap rate, therefore, the models belonging to the secundum group may be an opportune alternative.
4.5.C.3	The choice of the right cyclical capitalization model is based on the nature of inputs. As a rule of thumb, if there are similar temporal lengths and there is explicit growth rent, therefore, the application of tertium group modeling may be required.

References

Aalbers, M.B. (2008) The financialization of home and the mortgage market crisis. *Competition & Change*, **12** (2), 148–166.

Abelson, A. (2007) After the Greenspan Put…, Barron's, August 13.

Abolafia, M.Y. (1998) Markets as cultures: an ethnographic approach, in *The Laws of the Market* (ed. M. Callon), Wiley-Blackwell, pp. 69–85.

Abraham, J.M. and Hendershot, P.H. (1996) Bubbles in Metropolitan Housing Markets. *Journal of Housing Research*, **7** (2), 191–208.

ACE (2009) European deontological code for providers of architectural services [online], Architects' Council of Europe, Brussels, Available at: http://www.ace-cae.eu/public/js/ tinymce/jscripts/tiny_mce/plugins/imagemanager/files/documents/Code_Final_EN_ September_2009.pdf (accessed 12 January 2012)

Adam, B., Beck, U. and Van Loon, J. (ed) (2000), *The Risk Society and Beyond. Critical Issues for Social Theory*. Polity, Cambridge, UK.

Ailon, G. (2015) Rethinking calculation: the popularization of financial trading outside the global centres of finance. *Economy and Society*, **44** (4), 592–615.

AKBW (2011) Architektengesetz in der Fassung vom 28. März 2011 [online], Architektenkammer Baden-Württemberg, Stuttgart, Available at: http://www.akbw.de/ fileadmin/download/dokumenten_datenbank/AKBW_Merkblaetter/Architektenrecht_ Berufsrecht/Merkblatt35-Architektengesetz2011.pdf (accessed 15 January 2012).

Aldred, J. (2009) *The Skeptical Economist*, Earthscan, London.

Amidu, A.-R. and Aluko, B.T. (2007) Client Influence on Valuation: aperceptual Analysis of the Driving Factors. *International Journal of Strategic Property Management*, **11** (2), 77–89.

Appadurai, A. (2011) The ghost in the financial machine. *Public Culture*, **23** (3), 517–539.

Appraisal Institute (2001) *The Appraisal of Real Estate*, 12th edn, Appraisal Institute.

AVM News (2008a) e-newsletter, issue July, August.

AVM News (2008b) e-newsletter, issue September, October.

AVM News (2008c) e-newsletter, issue November, December.

AVM News (2009) e-newsletter, issue January, February.

AVM News (2010) e-newsletter, issue September, October.

AVM News (2011) e-newsletter, issue January, February.

AVM News (2012) e-newsletter, issue January, February.

Value in a Changing Built Environment, First Edition.
Edited by David Lorenz, Peter Dent and Tom Kauko.
© 2018 John Wiley & Sons Ltd. Published 2018 by John Wiley & Sons Ltd.

Baker, D. (2008) The housing bubble and the financial crisis. *Real-World Economics Review*, (46), 73–81. http://www.paecon.net/PAEReview/issue46/Baker46.pdf (accessed 20 May 2008).

Ball, M.J. and Kirwan, R.M. (1977) Accessibility and Supply Constraints in the Urban Housing Market. *Urban Studies*, **14**, 11–32.

Barkham, R.J. and Geltner, D.M. (1995) Price discovery in the American and British property markets. *Real Estate Economics*, **23** (1), 21–44.

Barry, A. and Slate, D. (2002) Introduction: the technological society. *Economy and Society*, **31** (2), 175–193.

Baum, A., Crosby, N. and MacGregor, B.D. (1996) Price Formation, Mispricing and Investment Analysis in the Property Market. *Journal of Property Valuation and Investment*, **10**, 709–726.

Bauman, Z. (1993) *Postmodern Ethics*, Blackwell, Oxford.

Bergin, T. (2011) *Spills and Spin: the inside story of BP*, Random House, New York.

Berry, C. (2011) *Protecting Our Best Interests: Rediscovering Fiduciary Duty* [online], Published by: Fairshare Educational Foundation, London, Available at: http://www.fairpensions.org.uk/redisovering-fiduciary-duty (accessed 18 December 2011).

Bertalanffy, L. (1984) *Ogólna teoria systemów (in Polish)*, PWN, Warszawa.

Biłozor, A. and Jędrzejewska, K. (2012) Optymalizacja przestrzeni miejskiej – studium na przykładzie miasta Olsztyn (in Polish). *Studia i Materiały Towarzystwa Naukowego Nieruchomości*, **20** (2), 58–69.

Blake, J. (1999) Overcoming the 'value–action gap' in environmental policy: tensions between national policy and local experience. *Local Environment*, **4** (3), 257–278.

Bonta, M. and Protevi, J. (2004) *Deleuze and Geophilosophy: A Guide and Glossary*, Edinburgh University Press, Edinburgh.

Bordass, B. (2011) *Built Environment Professionals in the UK: 40 Years Back, 40 Years on?*, SB11 Keynote, Proceedings of the World Sustainable Building Conference (SB11), Helsinki, 18–21 October 2011.

Borio, C.e.V., Kennedy, N., and Prowse, S.D. (1994) Exploring Aggrefate Asset Price Fluctuations Across Countries, BIS Economic Papers, No. 40.

Bradwell, P. Johar, I., Maguire, C. and Mean, M. (2007) *Future Planners: Propositions for the Next Age of Planning* [online], Published by: Demos, London, Available at: http://www.demos.co.uk/publications/futureplannersreport (accessed 11 November 2011)

Bramley, G., Leishman, C. and Watkins, D. (2008) Understanding Neighbourhood Housing Markets: Regional Context, Disequilibrium, Sub-markets and Supply. *Housing Studies*, **23** (2), 179–212.

Bramley, G. and Power, S. (2009) Urban form and social sustainability: the role of density and housing type. *Environment and Planning B: Planning and Design*, **36** (9), 30–48.

Briand, R., Urwin, R. and Chia, C.P. (2011) *Integrating ESG into the Investment Process – From Aspiration to Effective Implementation*, MSCI ESG Research.

Brown, E. (2011) Lehman still loom large in commercial real estate, *Wall Street Journal*, September 12.

Bryson, J.R. and Lombardi, R. (2009) Balancing Product and Process Sustainability against Business Profitability: Sustainability as a Competitive Strategy in the Property Development Process. *Business Strategy and the Environment*, **18** (2), 97–107.

Bryx, M. (2006) *Rynek nieruchomości (in Polish)*, System i funkcjonowanie, Warszawa, Poltext.

Bulkeley, H. (2006) A Changing Climate for Spatial Planning. *Planning Theory & Practice*,
 7 (2), 201–230.

Byrne, P. (1995) Fuzzy analysis: A vague way of dealing with uncertainty in real estate
 analysis? *Journal of Property Valuation and Investment*, **13** (3), 22–41.

Callon, M. (1998) *The Laws of the Markets*, Blackwell, Oxford, UK.

Callon, M., Meadel, C. and Rabeharisoa, V. (2002) The Economy of Qualities. *Economy and
 Society*, **31** (2), 194–217.

Canonne, J. and Macdonald, R. (2003) Valuation without value theory: A North American
 "Appraisal". *Journal of Real Estate Practice and Education*, **6** (1), 113–162.

Carlson, E. (1998) Real estate investment appraisal of land properties using SOM, in *Visual
 Explorations in Finance with Self-Organizing Maps* (eds G. Deboeck and T. Kohonen),
 Springer, New York, pp. 117–127.

Case, B., Colwell, P.F., Leishman, C. and Watkins, C. (2006) The Impact of Environmental
 Contamination on Condo Prices: A Hybrid Repeat-Sale/Hedonic Approach. *Real Estate
 Economics*, **34** (1), 77–107.

Case, B., Goetzmann, W.N. and Watcher, S.M. (1997) *The Global Commercial Property
 Market Cycles: A Comparison Across Property Types*, Paper presented to the
 International AUREA Conference, Berkeley

Case, K.E. and Shiller, R.J. (1989) The Efficiency of the Market for Single-Family Homes.
 American Economic Review, **79**, 125–137.

Casebeer, W.D. (2008) The Stories Markets tell (chapter in *Moral Markets*, ed. Zak, P.K.),
 Princeton University Press, Princeton and Oxford.

Chen, F.Y. and Yu, S.M. (2009) Client Influence on Valuation: Does Language Matter?
 Journal of Property Investment and Finance, **27** (1), 25–41.

Clapp, J., Helleiner, E., Hester, A., Homer-Dixon, T., Rowlands, I.H., Swanston, L.,
 Thistlethwaite, J., VanNijnatten, D.L., Whalley, J. (2009) *Environmental Sustainability
 and the Financial Crisis: Linkages and Policy Recommendations*. CIGI Working Group
 on Environment and Resources. CIGI (The Centre for International Governance
 Innovation) Ontario, Canada.

Clark, M.E. (2002) *In Search of Human Nature*, Routledge, London.

Clayton, J. (1996) Market Fundamentals, Risk and the Canadian Property Cycle:
 Implications for Property Valuation and Investment Decisions. *Journal of Real Estate
 Research*, **12** (3), 347–367.

Cotgrave, P. (2003) *Science for Survival: Scientific Research and the Public Interest*, British
 Library, London.

Cox, J., Fell, D. and Thurstain-Goodwin, M. (2002) *Red Man, Green Man, Performance
 Indicators for Urban Sustainability*, RICS foundation.

Crain, W.C. (1985) *Theories of Development*. Prentice-Hall, New York.

Curran, D. (2015) Risk Illusion and organized irresponsibility in contemporary finance:
 rethinking class and risk society. *Economy and Society*, **44** (3), 392–417.

d'Amato, M. (2003) Cyclical dividend discount models: Linking property market cycles to
 property valuation. *International Journal of Strategic Property Management*, **7** (2), 55–69.

d'Amato, M. (2004) A comparison between MRA and Rough Set Theory for mass
 appraisal. A case in Bari. *International Journal of Strategic Property Management*, **8** (4),
 205–217.

d'Amato, M. (2006) *Rough Set Theory as Automated Valuation Methodology: The Whole
 Story*. Delft, International seminar on Advances in Mass Appraisal in Delft.

d'Amato, M. (2007) Comparing rough set theory with multiple regression analysis as automated valuation methodologies. *International Real Estate Review*, **10** (2), 42–65 (in corso di pubblicazione).

d'Amato, M. (2008) Rough Set Theory as Property Valuation Methodology: The whole story, in *Mass Appraisal Methods. An international perspective for property valuers* (eds T. Kauko and M. d'Amato), Blackwell Publishing, Oxford. RICS Research.

d'Amato, M. (2013) *Man Vs. Machine*. AVM News, 21, July-August, pp. 21–22.

d'Amato, M. (2015) Income Approach and Property Market Cycle. *International Journal of Strategic Property Management*, **19** (2), 207–219, in print.

d'Amato, M. and Anghel, I. (2012) *Regressed DCF, Real Estate Value, Discount Rate and Risk Premium Estimation*. A case in Bucharest, Aestimum.

d'Amato, M. and Kauko, T. (2008) Property market classification and mass appraisal methodology, in *Mass Appraisal Methods – An International Perspective for Property Valuers*. RICS Series (eds T. Kauko and M. d'Amato), Blackwell, Oxford, pp. 280–303.

d'Amato, M. and Kauko, T. (2012) Sustainability and risk premium estimation in property valuation and assessment of worth. *Building Research & Information*, **40** (2), 174–185.

d'Amato, M. and Siniak, N. (2003) An Application of Fuzzy Numbers for Property Investment and Valuation. *International Journal of Strategic Property Management*, 7 (3), 129–143.

d'Amato, M. and Siniak, N. (2008) Using Fuzzy Numbers in mass Appraisal: The Case of the Belarusian Property Market, in *Mass Appraisal Methods – An International Perspective for Property Valuers*. RICS Series (eds T. Kauko and M. d'Amato), Blackwell, Oxford, pp. 91–107.

Daly, J., Gronow, S., Jenkins, D. and Plimmer, F. (2003) Consumer behaviour in the valuation of residential property. A Comparative study in the UK, Ireland and Australia. *Property Management*, **21** (5), 295–314.

Daniels, P.L. (2003) Buddhist Economics and the Environment. *International Journal of Social Economics*, **30** (1–2), 8–33.

Daniels, P.L. (2005) Economic systems and the Buddhist world view: The 21st century nexus, *The Journal of Socio-Economics*, **34**, 245–268.

Davis, D. and Knell, J. (2003) The context and future of the professions, in *The Professionals' Choice - The Future of the Built Environment Professions, Building Futures* (ed. S. Foxell), Commission for Architecture and the Built Environment & Royal Institute of British Architects, London, pp. 19–36.

Deloitte LLP (2014) *Breakthrough for sustainability in commercial real estate*. Deloitte Center for Financial Services, USA.

Deng, Y., Li, Zh., and Quigley, J.M. (2010) *Economic Returns to Energy-Efficient Investments in the Housing Market: Evidence from Singapore*. IRES Working Paper Series, August (IRES2010-008).

Dent, P. and Dalton, G. (2010) Climate change and professional surveying programmes of study. *International Journal of Sustainability in Higher Education*, **11** (3), 274–291.

Dent, P., Patrick, M. and Xu, Y. (2012) *Real Estate: Property Markets and Sustainable Behaviour*, Routledge, Abingdon, UK.

Dent, P. and Temple, M. (1998) *Economic Value – A Methodological Dilemma?* 'The cutting Edge' conference proceedings 1998. Available at: http://www.rics.org/site/scripts/download_info.aspx?downloadID=1506 (Accessed at 28 June 2010).

Des Rosiers, F., Theriault, M., Villeneuve, P., and Kestens, Y. (1999) *House Price and Spatial Dependence: Towards an Integrated Procedure to Model Neoghborhood Dynamics*, Paper presented at 1999 AREUEA annual meeting.

Diaz, J. III (1998) *The First Decade of behavioral Research in the Discipline of Property.* 'The Cutting Edge 1998' -conference proceedings, ISBN 0-85406-922-4.

Diaz, J. III, and Hansz, J.A. (2010) A taxonomic field investigation into induced bias in residential real estate appraisals. *International Journal of Strategic Property Management*, **14**, 3–17.

Dilmore, G. (1971) *The New Approach to Real Estate Appraising*, Prentice Hall, Upper Saddle River, NJ.

Downie, M.L. and Robson, G. (2007) *Automated Valuation Models: An International Perspective*, The Council of Mortgage Lenders (CML), London.

Downs, A. (1996) Characteristics of various economic studies. *The Appraisal Journal*, **34**, 329–338.

Égert, B. and Mihaljek, D. (2008) *Determinants of House Prices in Central and Eastern Europe.* Czech National Bank working paper. Copy available at: http://www.eukn.org/eukn/themes/Urban_Policy/Housing/Housing_management/Housing_finance/House_prices/House-Prices-in-Central-and-Eastern-Europe_1011.html (accessed 25 May 2009)

Ehrenfeld, J.R. (2008) Sustainability needs to be attained, not managed. *Sustainability: Science, Practice and Policy*, **4** (2), 1–3.

Eichholz, P., Kok, N. and Quigley, J. (2009) *Why Do Companies Rent Green? Real Property and Corporate Social Responsibility*, RICS Research, London.

Eichholz, P., Kok, N. and Quigley, J. (2010) Doing Well by Doing Good? Green Office Buildings. *American Economic Review*, **100** (December), 2492–2509.

Ellison, L., Sayce, S. and Smith, J. (2007) Socially responsible property investment: Quantifying the relationship between sustainability and investment property worth. *Journal of Property Research*, **24** (3), 191–219.

Epstein, R.M. and Hundert, E.M. (2002) Defining and assessing professional competence. *Journal of the American Medical Association*, **287** (2), 226–235.

Escobar, A. (2005) Economics and the space of modernity. *Cultural Studies*, **19** (2), 139–175.

Evans, A.W. and Hartwich, O.M. (2005) *Bigger Better Faster More. Why Some Countries Plan Better than Others.* Policy Exchange, London. Copy available at: http://www.policyexchange.org.uk/images/publications/pdfs/pub_39_-_full_publication.pdf (accessed 25 May 2009).

Fama, E.F. (1965) The Behavior of Stock-Market Prices. *Journal of Business*, **38** (1), 34–105.

Fama, E.F. (1971) Efficient capital markets: A review of theory and empirical work. *Journal of Finance*, **25** (2), 383–417.

Fama, E.F. (1991) Efficient capital markets: II. *Journal of Finance*, **46** (5), 1575–1618.

Fotheringham, A.S., Brundson, C. and Charlto, M. (2000) *Quantitative Geography: Perspective on Spatial Data Analysis*, Sage, Los Angeles CA.

Fourcade, M. and Healy, K. (2007) Moral Views of Market Society. *Annual Review of Sociology*, **33**, 285–311.

French, N. and Cooper, R. (2000) Investment Valuation Models. *Journal of Property Investment and Finance*, **18** (2), 225–238.

Frew, J. and Jud, D. (2003) Estimating the value of apartment buildings. *Journal of Real Estate Research*, **25** (1), 77–86.

Fuerst, F. and McAllister, P. (2011) Green noise or green value? Measuring the effects of environmental certification on office values. *Real Estate Economics*, **39** (1), 45–69.

Fuerst, F., McAllister, P. and Murray, C.B. (2011) Designer buildings: Estimating the economic value of 'signature' architecture. *Environment and Planning A*, **43**, 166–184.

Fusco Girard, L. (2008) Democratic Concerns and Governance in Planning Evaluation, in *New Principles in Planning Evaluation* (eds D. Miller, A. Khakee, A. Hull and J. Woltjer), Ashgate, Aldershot, pp. 259–273.

Gaddy, W.E. and Hart, R.E. (2003) *Real Estate Fundamentals, 6th edn*. Dearborn Real Estate Education.

Galbraith, J.K. (1999) *The Affluent Society*, 2nd. (1st edn. 1958.) edn, Penguin, London.

Galuppo, L.A. and Tu, C. (2010) Capital markets and sustainable real estate: What are the perceived risks and barriers? *Journal of Sustainable Real Estate*, **2** (1), 143–159.

Gayer, G., Gilboa, I. and Lieberman, O. (2007) Rule-based and case-based reasoning in housing prices. *The B.E. Journal of Theoretical Economics*, **7** (1Article 10), 1–35. Available at: http://www.bepress.com/bejte/vol7/iss1/art10 (Accessed at 18 November, 2009).

Gelman, A. (2007) *Scaling Regression Inputs by Dividing by Two Standard Deviations*. Technical Report, Department of Statistics, Columbia University.

Gibbons, M., Limoges, C., Nowotny, H. *et al.* (1994) *The new production of knowledge: The dynamics of science and research in contemporary societies*, SAGE, London.

Gibler, K.M., and Nelson, S. L. (2003) Consumer behavior applications to real estate education. *Journal of Real Estate Practice and Education*, **6**(1), 63–89.

Goering, J. (2009) Sustainable real estate development: The dynamics of market penetration. *Journal of Sustainable Real Estate*, **1** (1), 167–201.

Goodman, R. (1972) *After the Planners*, Penguin, London.

Gordon, M. (1962) *The Investment, Financing and Valuation of the Corporation*, Irwin, Homewood.

Gordon, M. and Shapiro, E. (1956) Capital equipment analysis: The required rate of profit. *Management Science*, **3**, 102–110.

Gregory, R., Flynn, J., Johnson, S.M. *et al.* (1997) Decision-Pathway Surveys: A Tool for Resource Managers. *Land Economics*, **73** (2), 240–254.

Gren, M. and Zierhofer, W. (2003) The Unity of Difference: a critical appraisal of Niklas Luhmann's theory of social systems in the context of corporality and spatiality. *Environment and Planning A*, **35**, 615–630.

Grissom, T. and De Lisle, J.R. (1999) A multiple index analysis of real estate cycles on structural change. *Journal of Real Estate Research*, **18** (1), 97–130.

Grossman, S.J. and Stiglitz, J.E. (1980) On the impossibility of informationally efficient markets. *American Economic Review*, **70**, 393–408.

Guala, F. (2007) How to do things with experimental economics, in *Do Economists make Markets?* (eds D. MacKenzie *et al.*), Princeton University Press, Princeton and Oxford.

Guy, S. and Harris, R. (1997) Property in a Global-risk Society: Towards Marketing Research in the Office Sector. *Urban Studies*, **34** (1), 125–140.

Haldane, A. G. (2016) *The Great Divide*, speech given at Bank of England New City Agenda Annual Dinner.

Hartenberger, U. and Lorenz, D. (2008) *Breaking the Vicious Circle of Blame – Making the Business Case for Sustainable Buildings*, The Royal Institution of Chartered Surveyors, London, RICS FiBRE Series, June 2008.

Hartenberger, U., Lorenz, D. and Lützkendorf, T. (2013) A shared built environment professional identity through education and training. *Building Research & Information*, **41** (1), 60–76.

Harvey, J. (2000) *Urban Land Economics*. 5th Edition, Macmillan Press Ltd, Basingstoke and London, UK.

Hausman, D. (2003) Philosophy of Economics [online], Stanford Encyclopaedia of Philosophy. Available at http://plato.stanford.edu/entries/economics/ (accessed on 20 June, 2017).

HEA (2006) *Sustainable Development in Higher Education: Current Practice and Future Developments*, York, Higher Education Academy.

Hekman, J.S. (1985) Rental price adjustment and investment in office markets. *Journal of the American Real Estate and Urban Economics Association*, **13** (1), 32–47.

Hemphill, L., Berry, J. and McGreal, S. (2004a) An indicator-based approach to measuring sustainable urban regeneration performance: Part 1, conceptual foundations and methodological framework. *Urban Studies*, **41**, 725–755.

Hemphill, L., Berry, J. and McGreal, S. (2004b) An indicator-based approach to measuring sustainable urban regeneration performance: Part 2, empirical evaluation and case-study analysis. *Urban Studies*, **41**, 757–772.

Hendershott, P.H. and Hendershott, R.J. (2002) *On Measuring Real Estate Risk*, Real Estate Finance, Winter, pp. 35–40.

Hill, S. (2009a) The end of the Age of Audit – A time for justice for the professions? in *Practice Futures - Risk, Entrepreneurialism* (ed. D. Robinson), Practice and the Professional Institute, RIBA Building Futures, Available at: http://www.buildingfutures.org.uk/projects/building-futures/practice-futures (Accessed: 22 November 2011).

Hill, S. (2009b) *Justice for the Professions or a Moment of Destiny?*, In: RIBA Research Symposium Papers Changing Practice, RIBA Books, London, Available at: http://www.architecture.com/Files/RIBAProfessionalServices/ResearchAndDevelopment/Symposium/2009/StephenHill.pdf, (Accessed 08 November 2011).

Hill, S. and Lorenz, D. (2011) Rethinking professionalism: Guardianship of land and resources. *Building Research & Information*, **39** (3), 314–319.

Hill, S., Lorenz, D., Dent, P. and Lützkendorf, T. (2013) Professionalism and ethics in a changing economy, *Building Research & Information*, **41** (1), 8–27.

HMSO (2006) *Companies Act 2006*, Her Majesty's Stationery Office, London.

Hoesli, M. and MacGregor, B. (2000) *Property Investment: Principles and Practice of Portfolio Management*, Longman, Harlow, GB.

Hughes W. and Hughes C. (2013) Professionalism and professional institutions in times of change. *Building Research and Information*, **41** (1), 28–38.

Hunt, E.K. (2003) *Property and Prophets*, Seventh edn, ME Sharpe, Armonk, New York, London.

IAAO (2003) *Standard on Automated Valuation Models (AVM)*, International Association of Assessing Officers, Chicago, IL.

ICE (2003) *Charter for Sustainable Development*, Institution of Civil Engineers, London.

ICE (2008) *Royal Charter, By-Laws, Regulations and Rules*, Institution of Civil Engineers, London.

IVSC (2011a) *International Valuation Standards*, International Valuation Standards Council.

IVSC (2011b) *Technical Information Paper n.1, The Discounted Cash Flow (DCF) Method –Real Property and Business Valuations, Exposure Draft*, International Valuation Standards Council, www.ivsc.org (accessed 03 March 2017).

IVSC (2011c) *IVS 230, Real Property Interests*, International Valuation Standard Council, London.

IVSC (2013) *International Valuation Standards*. IVSC, London.

Jackson, T. (2005) *Motivating Sustainable Consumption: A Review of Evidence on Consumer behaviour and behavioural Change*, SDRN, Surrey, UK.

Jones, C., Leishman, C. and MacDonald, C. (2009) Sustainable urban form and residential development viability. *Environment and Planning A*, **41**, 1667–1690.

Joss, S. (2011) Eco-cities: The mainstreaming of urban sustainability – key characteristics and driving factors. *International Journal of Sustainable Development Planning*, **6** (3), 268.

Judt, T. (2010) *Ill Fares the Land*, The Penguin Press, New York.

Kaiser, R. (1997) The Long Cycle in Real Estate. *Journal of Real Estate Research*, **14** (3), 233–257.

Kauko, T. (2001) Combining theoretical approaches: The case of urban land value and housing market dynamics, review article, Housing. *Theory and Society*, **18** (3/4), 167–173.

Kauko, T. (2002) Modelling location in house prices - neural network and value tree approaches. PhD Thesis. Utrecht.

Kauko, T. (2004a) Sign value, topophilia and house prices. *Environment and Planning A*, **36** (5), 859–878.

Kauko, T. (2004b) Infusing 'institution' and 'agency' into house price analysis. *Urban Studies*, **41** (8), 1507–1519.

Kauko, T. (2004c) Towards the 4th generation – An essay on innovations in residential property value modelling expertise. *Journal of Property Research*, **21** (1), 75–97.

Kauko, T. (2006) *Urban housing patterns in a tide of change: Spatial structure and residential property values in Budapest in a comparative perspective*, DUP Science Publication, Delft.

Kauko, T. (2008a) From modelling tools towards the market itself – an opportunity for sustainability assessment? *International Journal of Strategic Property Management*, **12**, 95–107.

Kauko, T. (2008b) AVMs, Empirical Modelling of Value, and Systems for Market Analysis, in *Mass appraisal methods – an international perspective for property valuers* RICS Series (eds T. Kauko and M. d'Amato), Blackwell, Oxford, pp. 307–319.

Kauko, T. (2009a) Policy impact and house price development at the neighbourhood-level – a comparison of four urban regeneration areas using the concept of 'artificial' value creation. *European Planning Studies*, **17** (1), 85–107.

Kauko, T. (2009b) The housing market dynamics of two Budapest neighbourhoods. *Housing Studies*, **24** (5), 587–610.

Kauko, T. (2010) Value stability in local real estate markets. *International Journal of Strategic Property Management*, **14**, 191–199.

Kauko, T. (2012) Sustainable development of the built environment: The role of the residential/housing sector"open access" book, in *Sustainable Development* (ed. C. Ghenai), InTech, Rijeka, pp. 161–174, available at http://www.intechopen.com/books/sustainable-development-education-business-and-management-architecture-and-building-construction-agriculture-and-food-security/sustainable-development-of-the-built-environment-the-role-of-the-residential-housing-sector (Accessed 25 May, 2012).

Kauko, T. and d'Amato, M. (2008) Introduction: Suitability issues in mass appraisal methodology, in *Mass Appraisal Methods – An International Perspective for Property Valuers* RICS Series (eds T. Kauko and M. d'Amato), Blackwell, Oxford, pp. 1–19.

Kay, A. (2004) *The Center of Why, 2004 Kyoto Prize Commemorative Lecture*, Viewpoints Research Institute, Glendale, CA.

Keen, S. (2009) Mad, bad, and dangerous to know. *Real-World Economics Review*, (49), 2–7. http://www.paecon.net/PAEReview/issue49/Keen49.pdf.

Kersloot, J. and Kauko, T. (2004) Measurement of Housing Preferences – A Comparison of Research Activity in the Netherlands and Finland. *Nordic Journal of Surveying and Real Estate Research*, **1** (2), 144–163.

Kimmet, P. (2006) *Theoretical Foundations for Integrating Sustainability in Property Investment Appraisal*. Paper presented to the Pacific Rim Real Estate Society Conference, University of Auckland, New Zealand.

Kimmett, Ph. (2008) On Value: Towards Validation. World Sustainable Building Conference, Melbourne Convention and Exhibition Centre, 21–25 September, Special Forum: Valuing Sustainability.

Klamer, A. (2003) A pragmatic view on values in economics. *Journal of Economic Methodology*, **10** (2), 191–212.

Kohlberg, L. (1976) Moral Stages and Moralization: The cognitive-developmental approach. In *Moral Development and Behavior: Theory, research and social issues* (ed. T. Lickona). Holt, Rinehart and Winston, New York, pp. 31–53.

Kollmuss, A. and Agyeman, J. (2002) Mind the Gap: why do people act environmentally and what are the barriers to pro-environmental behaviour? *Environmental Education Research*, **8** (3), 239–260.

Komorowski, J., Pawlak, Z., Polkowski, L. and Skowron, A. (1999) Rough sets: A tutorial, in *Rough fuzzy hybridization: A new trend in decision making* (eds S.K. Pal and A. Skowron), Springer-Verlag, pp. 3–98.

Krishnamurti, J. (1983) *The Flame of Attention*, Harper & Row, New York.

Kryvobokov, M. (2006) Mass valuation of urban land in Ukraine: From normative to a market-based approach. Doctoral Thesis in Real Estate Planning, Stockholm, Sweden.

Kucharska-Stasiak, E. (2005) *Nieruchomość a rynek*, Wydawnictwo Naukowe PN, Warszawa.

Kuznets, S. (1930) *Secular Movement in Production and Prices*, Houghton Misslin, New York.

Lash, S. (1999) *Another Modernity, a Different Rationality*. Blackwell, Maldon, Massachusetts.

Leaman, A., Stevenson, F. and Bordass, B. (2010) Building evaluation: Practice and principles. *Building Research & Information*, **38** (5), 564–577.

Levy, D. and Schuck, E. (2005) The influence of clients on valuations: The clients' perspective. *Journal of Property Investment and Finance*, **23** (2), 182–201.

Leyston, A. and Thrift, N. (1997) *Money/Space – Geographies of Monetary Transformation.* Routledge, London.

Lin, Y.T. (2002) *My Country and My People.* Foreign Language Teaching and Research Press, Beijing.

Lorch, R. (1990) *Construction Materials and the Environment: Preparing for Stricter Building Product Standards*, Economist Intelligence Unit, London.

Lorch, R., 2011, Personal Communication, 21. April 2011

Lorenz, D., d'Amato, M., Des Rosiers, F. *et al.* (2008) *Sustainable Property Investment & Management – Key Issues & Major Challenges*, RICSCopy available at http://www.rics .org/Newsroom/Keyissues/Sustainabilty/SPIM_r_230908.html (accessed 25 May 2009).

Lorenz, D. and Lutzkendorf, T. (2008) Sustainability in property valuation: Theory and practice. *Journal of Property Investment & Finance*, **26** (6), 482–521.

Lorenz, D.P., Trück, S. and Lützkendorf, T. (2006) Addressing risk and uncertainty in property valuations – a viewpoint from Germany. *Journal of Property Investment & Finance*, **24** (5), 400–433.

Lorenz, D., Trück, S. and Lützkendorf, T. (2007) Exploring the relationship between the sustainability of construction and market value: Theoretical basics and initial empirical results from the residential property sector. *Property Management*, **25** (2), 119–149.

Lützkendorf, T. and Lorenz, D. (2005) Sustainable property investment: valuing sustainable buildings through property performance assessment. *Building Research & Information*, **33** (3), 212–234.

Lutzkendorf, T. and Lorenz, D. (2011) Capturing sustainability-related information for property valuation. *Building Research and Information*, **39** (3), 256–273.

MacDonald, H. (1996) The rise of mortgage-backed securities: Struggles to reshape access to credit in the USA. *Environment and Planning A*, **28** (7), 1179–1198.

Maclennan, D. (1977) Some thoughts on the nature and purpose of house price studies. *Urban Studies*, **14**, 59–71.

Maclennan, D. and Tu, Y. (1996) Economic perspectives on the structure of local housing systems. *Housing Studies*, **11** (3), 387–406.

Malpezzi, S. and Watcher, S.M. (2005) The Role of Speculation in Real Estate Cycles. *Journal of Real Estate Literature*, **13** (2), 141–164.

Mandelbrot, B.B. and Hudson, R.L. (2004) *The (Mis)behaviour of Markets*, Profile Books, London.

Mander, J. (1992) *In the Absence of the Sacred: The failure of technology and the survival of the Indian nations.* Sierra Club Books, San Francisco, California.

Mansfield, J.R. (2009) The valuation of sustainable freehold property: A CRE perspective. *Journal of Corporate Real Estate*, **11** (2), 91–105.

Martin, R. (2011) The local geographies of the financial crisis: From the housing bubble to economic recession and beyond. *Journal of Economic Geography*, **11**, 587–618.

Marwell, G. and Ames, R.E. (1981) Economists free ride, does anyone else?: Experiments on the provision of public goods, IV. *Journal of Public Economics*, **15** (3), 295–310.

Massey, D. and Catalano, A. (1978) *Capital and Land.* Edward Arnold, London.

McGough, T. and Tsolacos, S. (1995) Forecasting commercial rental values using ARIMA models. *Journal of Property Valuation and Investment*, **13**, 6–22.

McIntosh, A. (2002) *Soil and Soul: People versus Corporate Power.* Aurum Press, London.

McQueen, M.P. (2010) House appraisal under fire. *Wall Street Journal.*

Meadows, D.H., Randers, J. and Meadows, D.I. (2004) *Limits to Growth – The 30-Year Update*, Chelsea Green Publishing, White River Jct.

Meen, D. and Meen, G. (2003) Social behaviour as a basis for modelling the urban housing market: A review. *Urban Studies*, **40** (5-6), 917–935.

Menger, C. (1871, 2004) *Principles of Economics, Translation of, Grundsätze der Volkswirthschaftslehre'*, Ludwig von Mises Institute, Available at: http://www.mises.org/etexts/menger/Mengerprinciples.pdf, (Accessed: 10 April 2010).

Mill, J.S. (1859) *On Liberty*. J. W. Parker and Son, London.

Mill, J.S. (1863) *Utilitarianism*. Parker, Son and Bourn, London.

Miller, D. (2002) Turning Callon the right way up. *Economy and Society*, **31** (2), 218–233.

Miller, D. (2008) The Uses of Value. *Geoforum*, **39**, 1122–1132.

Minton, A. (2006) *What kind of world are we building – The privatisation of public space*, The Royal Institution of Chartered Surveyors, London.

Mitchell, T. (2007) The Properties of Markets, in *Do Economists Make Markets?* (eds D. MacKenzie *et al.*), Princeton University Press, Princeton and Oxford.

Mooya, M.M. (2009) Market value without a market: Perspectives from transaction cost theory. *Urban Studies*, **46** (3), 687–701.

Mooya, M. (2011) Of mice and men: Automated valuation models and the valuation profession. *Urban Studies*, **48** (11), 2265–2281.

Moran, P.A.P. (1948) The Interpretation of Statistical Maps. *Journal of the Royal Statistical Society B*, **10**, 243–251.

Moran, P.A.P. (1950) Notes on Continuous Stochastic Phenomena. *Biometrika*, **37**, 17–23.

Mostafavi, M. and Doherty, G. (eds) (2010) *Ecological Urbanism*, Lars Müller Publishers, Harvard University Graduate School of Design.

Mrózek, A. and Płonka, L. (1999) *Analiza danych metoda zbiorów przybliżonych*, Akademicka Oficyna Wydawnicza PLJ, Warszawa.

Mu, L.L., Ma, J.H. and Chen, L.W. (2009) A 3-dimensional discrete model of housing price and its inherent complexity analysis. *Journal of System Science and Complexity*, **22** (3), 415–421.

Mueller, G.R., Laposa S.P., Mueller, G.R., and Laposa, S.P. (1994) *Evaluating Real Estate Markets Using Cycles Analyses*, Paper presented at American Real Estate Society Annual Meeting, Santa Barbara, CA, April 15.

Mueller, G.R. and Pevnev, A. (1997) An analysis of rental growth rates during different points in the real estate market cycle. The American Real Estate Society Meetings. Sarasota, Florida.

Muldavin, S.R. (2010) *Value Beyond Cost Savings*, Green Building Finance, Consortium, California.

Najder, Z. (1975) *Values and Evaluations*. Clarendon Press, Oxford.

O'Brien, G., Brodowicz, D. and Ratcliffe, J. (2009) *Built Environment Foresight 2030: The Sustainable Development Imperative*, The Futures Academy DIT.

O'Neill, J. (2002) Socialist Calculation and Environmental Valuation: Money, Markets and Ecology. *Science and Society*, **66** (1), Spring, 137–151.

O'Neill, J. (2007) *Markets, Deliberation and Environment*, Routledge, Abingdon, UK.

O'Neill, J., Holland, A. and Light, A. (2008) *Environmental Values*, Routledge, Abingdon, UK.

Op't Veld, D., Bijlsma, E. and van de Hoef, P. (2008) Automated valuation in the Dutch housing market: The web-application 'MarktPositie' used by NVM-realtors, in *Advances in Mass Appraisal Methods* (eds T. Kauko and M. d'Amato), Blackwell, Oxford, pp. 70–90.

Partnoy, F. (2010) *Infectious Greed: How deceit and risk infected the financial markets.* Profile Books, London.

Pawlak, Z. (1982) Rough sets. *International Journal of Information and Computer Science*, **11**, 341.

Pawlak, Z. (1991) *Rough sets: Theoretical aspects of reasoning about data*, Kluwer Academic Press, Dordrecht.

Pawlak, Z. (1997) *Rough Sets and their Applications*, Seminar Department of Computing – Macquarie University.

Peters, E. (1997) *Teoria chaosu a rynki kapitałowe*, Wydawnictwo Wig-Press, Warszawa.

Plato (1980) *The Republic*, Penguin Classics, Aylesbury, Bucks, UK.

Polkowski, L. (2010) Reductive Reasoning Rough and Fuzzy Sets as Frameworks for Reductive Reasoning, in *Approximate Reasoning by Parts: An Introduction to Rough Mereology*, Book Series: Intelligent Systems Reference Library, Vol. 20, Springer, Berlin, Heidelberg, pp. 145–190.

Price, C. (1993) *Time, Discounting and Value*, Blackwell.

Pritchett, C.P. (1984) Forecasting the impact of real estate cycles on investment. *Real Estate Review*, **13** (4), 85–89.

PwC (2014) *Real Estate 2020: Building the future.* PwC.

Pryke, M. and Lee, R. (1995) Place Your Bets: Towards an Understanding of Globalisation, Socio-financial Engineering and Competition within a Financial Centre. *Urban Studies*, **32**, 329–344.

Pyhrr, S.A. and Born, W.L. (2006) Theory and practice of real estate cycleanalysis. ARES annual meeting. Key West, Florida, University of Florida.

Pyhrr, S.A., Born, W., Manning, C.A. and Roulac, S.E. (2003) Project and portfolio management decisions: A framework and body of knowledge model for cycle research. *Journal of Real Estate Portfolio Management*, **9** (1), 1–16.

Pyhrr, S.A., Webb, J.R. and Born, W.L. (1990) Analyzing real estate asset performance during periods of market disequilibrium under cyclical economic conditions: A framework for analysis, in *Research in Real Estate*, Vol. 3 (eds S.D. Kapplin and A.L. Schwartz Jr.,), JAI Press, pp. 75–106.

Rabianski, J.G. (2002) Vacancy in market analysis and valuation. *The Appraisal Journal*, **April**, 191–199.

Raine, P. (2003) *Who Guards the Guardians?* University Press of America, Lanham, Maryland, USA.

Ramsey, R. (2004) The urban economics tradition: How heterodox economic theory survives in the real estate appraisal profession. *History of Economic Thought and Methodology*, **22-C**, 347–378.

Rao, C.R. (1994) *Statystyka i prawda*, Wydawnictwo PWN, Warszawa.

Ratcliff, R.U. (1972) *Valuation for Real Estate Decisions*, Democrat Press, Santa Cruz.

Ratcliffe, J.S. (2011) *Just Imagine!* RICS Strategic Foresight 2030. Report May 2011

Reed, R. and Wu, H. (2010) Understand Property Cycles in a Residential Market. *Property Management*, **28** (1), 33–46, Emerald publishing, Bradford.

Renigier, M. (2008c) Residuals analysis for constructing 'more real' property value, in *Mass Appraisal Methods – An International Perspective for Property Valuers*. RICS Real Estate Series (eds T. Kauko and M. d'Amato), Blackwell, Oxford, pp. 148–163.

Renigier-Biłozor, M. (2006) Zastosowanie analizy danych metoda zbiorów przybliżonych do zarządzania zasobami nieruchomości, Elbląg. *Journal of the Polish Real Estate Scientific Society*, **14** (1), 219–232.

Renigier-Biłozor, M. (2008a) Problematyka teorii zbiorów przybliżonych w gospodarce nieruchomościami, Olsztyn. *Journal of the Polish Real Estate Scientific Society*, **16** (1), 79–86.

Renigier-Biłozor, M. (2008b) Zastosowanie teorii zbiorów przybliżonych do masowej wyceny nieruchomości na małych rynkach, Acta Scientiarum Polonorium. *Administratio Locorum*, **7** (3), 35–51.

Renigier-Biłozor, M. (2010) Supplementing incomplete databases on the real estate market with the use of the rough set theory. *Acta Scientarum Polonorum Locorum, Administratio Locorum*, **9** (4), 107–115.

Renigier-Biłozor, M. (2011) Analysis of real estate markets with the use of the rough set theory, wyd. *Journal of the Polish Real Estate Scientific Society*, **19** (3), 107–118.

Renigier-Biłozor, M. and Biłozor, A. (2007) *Application of the Rough Set Theory and the Fuzzy Set Theory in Land Management*, Londyn, Paper presented at the conference "The European Real Estate Society" – ERES.

Renigier-Biłozor, M. and Biłozor, A. (2008) Aspekty i możliwości zastosowań teorii zbiorów przybliżonych i teorii zbiorów rozmytych w gospodarce przestrzennej, Poznań, Monografia pt.: Nowe kierunki i metody w analizie regionalnej, pp. 49–59

Renigier-Biłozor, M. and Biłozor, A. (2009a) The significance of real estate attributes in the process of determining land function with the use of the rough set theory. *Journal of the Polish Real Estate Scientific Society*. Monography, 103–107 (Available at: http://tnn.org .pl/tnn/publik/17/Monografia%20TNN%202009.pdf, (Accessed: 10 July 2017)).

Renigier-Biłozor, M. and Biłozor, A. (2009b) Procedura określania istotności wpływu atrybutów nieruchomości z wykorzystaniem teorii zbiorów przybliżonych, Przegląd Geodezyjny 6/2009 str. str.3-7

Renigier-Biłozor, M. and Wiśniewski, R. (2011a) *The Impact of Macroeconomic Factors on Residential Property Prices Indices in Europe, Italy*, Conference "APPRAISALS – Evolving Proceedings in Global Change" organized by The *Centro Studi di Estimo e di Economia Territoriale* - Ce.S.E.T. in November 14th and 15th 2011 in Rome.

Renigier-Biłozor, M. and Wiśniewski, R. (2011b) The efficiency of selected real estate markets in Poland. *Acta Scientiarum Polonorum, Oeconomia*, **10** (1), 95–110.

Renigier-Biłozor, M. and Wiśniewski, R. (2012) The Effectiveness of Real Estate Market Participants. *European Spatial Research and Policy*, **19** (1/2012), 95–110.

RICS (2007) *Financing and Valuing Sustainable Property: We Need to Talk*, Findings in Built and Rural Environments (FiBRE), RICS Research, April, available at www.rics.org.

RICS, [1881] (2008) *RICS Royal Charter*, The Royal Institution of Chartered Surveyors, London.

RICS (2009) *Sustainability and Commercial Property Valuation: Valuation Information Paper 13*, RICS, London.

RICS (2010a) *Is Sustainability Reflected in Commercial Property Prices: An Analysis of the Evidence Base*, RICS Research, London.

RICS (2010b) *Energy Efficiency and Value Project*. Final report. RICS Communities, March.

RICS (2013) Sustainability and commercial property valuation. RICS guidance note, global, 2nd edition (1st ed. 2009).

Robbins, L. (1935) *An Essay on the Nature and Significance of Economic Science*, 2nd edn, Macmillan, London.

Rogers, P.A. (1998) The evolution of the high performance alternative workplace. *New Zealand Strategic Management Journal*, Spring, 52–57.

Rogers, W.H. and Winter, W. (2009) The Impact of foreclosures on Neighboring Housing Sales. *Journal of Real Estate Research*, **31** (4), 455–479.

Ross, S.A. (1976) The arbitrage theory of capital asset pricing. *Journal of Economic Theory*, **13** (3), 341–360.

Rottke, N. and Wernecke, M. (2002) *Real Estate Cycles in Germany – Causes, Empirical Analysis and Recommendations for the Management Decision Process*, Paper presented at 8th Conference Pacific RIM Real Estate Society 21–23 January Christchurch New Zealand.

Roulac, S.E. (1996) Real Estate Market Cycles, Transformation Forces and Structural Change. *Journal of Real Estate Portfolio Management*, **2** (1), 1–17.

Roulac, S.E., Pyhrr, S.A. and Born, W.L. (1999) Real Estate Market Cycles and Their Strategic Implications for Investors and Portfolio Managers in the Global Economy. *Journal of Real Estate Research*, **18** (1), 7–68.

RTPI (2003) *Royal Charter of the Royal Town Planning Institute*, The Royal Town Planning Institute, London.

Ruggles, R. (1954) The Value of Value Theory. *American Economic Review*, **44** (2), 140–151.

Runde, T. and Thoyre, S. (2010) Intergrating sustainability and green building into the appraisal process. *Journal of Sustainable Real Estate*, **2** (1), 221–248.

Sagalyn, L.B. (1990) Real estate risk and the business cycle: Evidence from security markets. *Journal of Real Estate Research*, **5** (2), 203–219.

Sandel, M. (2009) *The Reith Lectures, the New Citizenship: Lecture 1, Markets and Morals*, BBC, London, Available at: www.bbc.co.uk/programmes/b00kt7rg, (Accessed 12 November 2011)

Sapir, J. (2008) Global finance in crisis: A provisional account of the "subprime" crisis and how we got into it. *Real-World Economics Review*, (46), 82–101. http://www.paecon.net/PAEReview/issue46/Sapir46.pdf.

Sayce, S., Ellison, L. and Parnell, P. (2007) Understanding investment drivers for UK sustainable property. *Building Research & Information*, **35** (6), 629–643.

Sayce, S., Sundberg, A. and Clements, B. (2010) *Is Sustainability Reflected in Commercial Property Prices: An Analysis of the Evidence Base*, RICS Research, London.

Sennett, R. (2012) Putting the public interest back into the heart of public life, Speech held at the Citizens Assembly organised by the New Economics Foundation and others at the Royal Festival Hall, London, 31 January 2012.

Sharpe, W.F. (1964) Capital asset prices: A theory of market equilibrium under conditions of risk. *The Journal of Finance*, **19** (3), 425–442.

Shiller, R. J. (2008) *The subprime solution: How today's global financial crisis happened, and what to do about it?* Oxford: Princeton University Press.

Slater, D. (2002) From Calculation to Alienation: disentangling economic abstractions. *Economy and Society*, **31** (2), 234–249.

Słowiński, R. (1992) *Intelligent Decision Support. Handbook of Applications and Advances of the Rough Sets Theory*, Kluwer Academic Publishers, Dordrecht.

Smith, S. (1912) *Curtis on the Valuation of Land and Houses*, Estates Gazette, London.

Smith, R. (2011) *The New Vision for Planning [online]*, The Royal Town Planning Institute, London, Available at: http://www.rtpi.org.uk/item/296/23/5/3, (Accessed: 02 February 2012).

Smith, H.C., Corgel, J.B. and Ling, D.C. (1998) *Real Estate Perspective*, 3rd edn, Irwin McGraw Hill.

Smith Churchland, P. (1989) *Neurophilosophy: Towards a Unified Science of the Mind/Brain*. MIT Press, Cambridge.

Snelling, J., Sibley, D.T. and Watts, M. (eds) (1987) *The Early Writings of Alan Watts*, Celestial Arts.

Söderbaum, P. (2009) A financial crisis on top of the ecological crisis: Ending the monopoly of neoclassical economics. *Real-World Economics Review*, (49), 8–19. http://www.paecon.net/PAEReview/issue49/Soderbaum49.pdf.

Spielman, S.E. and Thiel, J.-C. (2007) Social area analysis, data mining, and GIS. *Computers, Environment and Urban Systems*, **32**, 110–122.

Stefanowski, J. (2001) Algorytmy indukcji reguł decyzyjnych w odkrywaniu wiedzy. Postdoctoral dissertation. Wydawnictwo Politechniki Poznańskiej.

Stefanowski, J. and Tsoukias, A. (2000a) *Valued Tolerance and Decision Rules* in: Ziarko, W. and Yao, Y (Eds.) Proceedings of the RSCTC 2000 Conference, Banff.

Stefanowski, J. and Tsoukias, A. (2000b) *Valued Tolerance and Decision Rules* in: Ziarko, W. and Yao, Y (Eds.) Proceedings of the RSCTC 2000 Conference, Banff.

Stevenson, S. and McGrath, O. (2000) *A Comparison of Alternative Rental Forecasting Models: Empirical Tests on the London Office Market*, paper presented at the 7th European Real Estate Society conference Bordeaux, France.

Stuhr, J.J. (2003) Pragmatism about values and the valuable: Commentary on 'A pragmatic view on values in economics'. *Journal of Economic Methodology*, **10** (2), 213–221.

Taltavull de la Paz, P. and d'Amato, M. (2002) An Application of CDD Model to Italian and Spanish Property Market, Paper Accepted at 18th American Real Estate Society Meeting, Neaples, FL.

Taylor, M.A. and Rubin, G. (2002) *Raising the Bar: Simulation as a tool for assessing risk for real estate properties and portfolios*, Real Estate Finance, Winter,, pp. 18–34.

Taylor Wessing (2009) *Behind the Green Façade: Is the UK Development Industry Really Embracing Sustainability?* Taylor Wessing sustainability report.

Thiet, V. (2011) *Head of Development, ICADE Germany*, (a real estate development and investment company): "Cognitive Buildings", CognitiveCities conference, Berlin 26 February, 2011, available at http://conference.cognitivecities.com/speakers/#vini-tiet) (accessed 4 July, 2011).

Till, J. (2009) *Architecture Depends*, MIT Press, Cambridge.

Tse, R.Y.C. (1997) An application of the ARIMA to real estate prices in Hong Kong. *Journal of Property Finance*, **8** (2), 152–163.

UN (2010) *Policy framework for sustainable real estate markets. Principles and guidance for the development of a county's real estate sector*, United Nations Economic Commission For Europe (UNECE), Working Party on Land Management (WPLA), Real Estate Market Advisory Group (REM), United Nations, Geneva.

UN and RICS (2015) Advancing Responsible Business Practices in Land, Construction and Real Estate Use and Investment.

UNEP (2014) *Sustainability Metrics: Translation and Impact on Property Investment and Management*, UNEP Financial Iniatiative, Switzerland.

UNEP FI (2005) *A Legal Framework for the Integration of Environmental, Social and Governance Issues into Institutional Investment [online]*, United Nations Environment Programme Finance Initiative, available at: http://www.unepfi.org/fileadmin/documents/freshfields_legal_resp_20051123.pdf, (Accessed: 24 March 2011).

Vatn, A. (2005) *Institutions and the Environment*, Edward Elgar, Cheltenham.

Velthius, O. (2005) *Talking Prices*, Princeton University Press, Princeton and Oxford.

Voith, R. and Crone, T. (1988) National Vacancy Rates and the Persistence of Shocks in the U.S. Office Markets. *Journal of the American Real Estate and Urban Economics Association*, **16** (4), 437–458.

Warren-Myers, G. (2011) Valuing sustainability: a new challenge for the profession. *Australia and New Zealand Property Journal*, **3** (3), 157–164.

Warren-Myers, G. (2012) The value of sustainability in real estate: A review from a valuation perspective. *Journal of Property Investment and Finance*, **30** (2), 115–144.

Warren-Myers, G. and Reed, R. (2010) The challenges of identifying and examining links between sustainability and value: Evidence from Australia and New Zealand. *Journal of Sustainable Real Estate*, **2** (1), 201–220.

Watkins, C.A. (2001) The definition and identification of housing submarkets. *Environment and Planning A*, **33**, 2235–2253.

Watkins, C. (2008) Microeconomic perspectives on the structure and operation of local housing markets. *Housing Studies*, **23** (2), 163–177.

Wheaton, W.C. (1987) The cyclical behaviour of the national office market. *Journal of the American Real Estate and Urban Economics Association*, **15** (4), 281–299.

Wheaton, W.C. (1999) Real estate "cycles": Some fundamentals. *Real Estate Economics*, **27** (2), 209–230.

Wheaton, W.C. and Torto, R.G. (1988) Vacancy Rates and the Future of Office Rents. *Journal of the American Real Estate and Urban Economics Association*, **16** (4), 430–455.

Wheaton, W.C., Torto, R.G., Sivitanides, P.S. *et al.* (2001) *Real Estate Risk: A forward-looking approach*, Real Estate Finance, Fall, pp. 20–28.

Willison, D.L. (1999) Towards a More Reliable Cash Flow Analysis. *The Appraisal Journal*, January, 75–82.

Wolf, M. (2010) *Why were resources expunged from neo-classical economics? [online]*, Martin Wolf's Exchange, Financial Times, London, Available at: http://blogs.ft.com/martin-wolf-exchange/2010/07/12/why-were-resources-expunged-from-neo-classical-economics/#axzz1kWatZS1n, (Accessed: 20 June 2017).

Worthing, D. and Bond, S. (2008) *Managing Built Heritage*, Blackwell Publishing.

Yu, Sh.-M. and Tu, Y. (2011) Are Green Buildings worth more because they cost more? IRES Working Paper Series, August (IRES2011-023).

Zhang, D. (2002) *Key Concepts in Chinese Philosophy*. Foreign Language Press, Beijing, China.

Zohar, D. and Marshall, I. (2004) *Spiritual Capital*, Bloomsbury, London, UK.

Internet

http://www.naukowy.pl/encyklopedia/Hipoteza_rynku_efektywnego,vstrona_2/- date of input 22.09.2010.

http://www.stat.gov.pl/cps/rde/xbcr/gus/PUBL_PBS_transakcje_kupna_sprzedazy_nieruch_2008.pdf date of input 22.09.2010.

http://www.mi.gov.pl/2-492414ae09dd9-1793287-p_1.htm data wejścia 22.09.2010.

www.money.pl date of input 27.09.2010.

www.egospodarka.pl date of input 27.09.2010.

www.gratka.pl date of input 28.09.2010.

www.oferty.net.pl date of input 28.09.2010.

http://www.stat.gov.pl/cps/rde/xbcr/gus/PUBL_ik_obrot_nieruchomosciami_2009.pdf
   date of input 28.09.2010.

Index

a

Appraisal of Real Estate   63
Architects Registration Board (ARB)   182
automatic valuation methods/models
        (AVMs)   57, 98, 99, 134–135
    house price analysis   121
    Lender Processing Services (LPS)   125
    price data accumulation   120
    Residential Mortgage-Backed Securities
        (RMBS) transactions   126
    UK residential mortgage markets   126

b

belief system   24–26
built environment
    behavioural characteristics   31
    cognitive economy   30–31
    moral values   31–32
    property ownership   30
    sustainable decision-making   33

c

capitalism   24, 35
Chinese philosophy   25
cognitive economy   30–31
Collatoralised Mortgage Obligations
        (CMOs)   174
Commercial Mortgage-Backed Securities
        (CMBSs)   174
Confucianism   24–25
cost–benefit analysis   18
cost minimisation   17
cyclical capitalization   210–211
    Cyclical Dividend Discount Models
        156

nonagency mortgage crisis   151
price and rent forecasts   152
primum group   157–162
quartum group   166–167
real-estate market cycle   152–153
secundum group   162–164
tertium group   164–166
time-series analysis   152, 167–171

d

Daoism   24, 25
data preparation   129–130
direct capitalisation   51
discounted cash-flow (DCF) analysis   40,
        63, 100, 153–154

e

Eastern investor   25
'Ecological Urbanism,'   180–181
ecological value   29
economic forces   43
economic sustainability   99
economic value   20
    attributive sense   37
    axiological sense   37
    decision-making process   35
    economic instability   35
    environmental aspect   35
    morality   34
    price   39–42
    principle of selfishness   35
    professional ethics and commercial client
        requirement   38
    property valuation   37
    quantitative sense   37

Value in a Changing Built Environment, First Edition.
Edited by David Lorenz, Peter Dent and Tom Kauko.
© 2018 John Wiley & Sons Ltd. Published 2018 by John Wiley & Sons Ltd.